I0810052

IMAGES
of America

BELEN

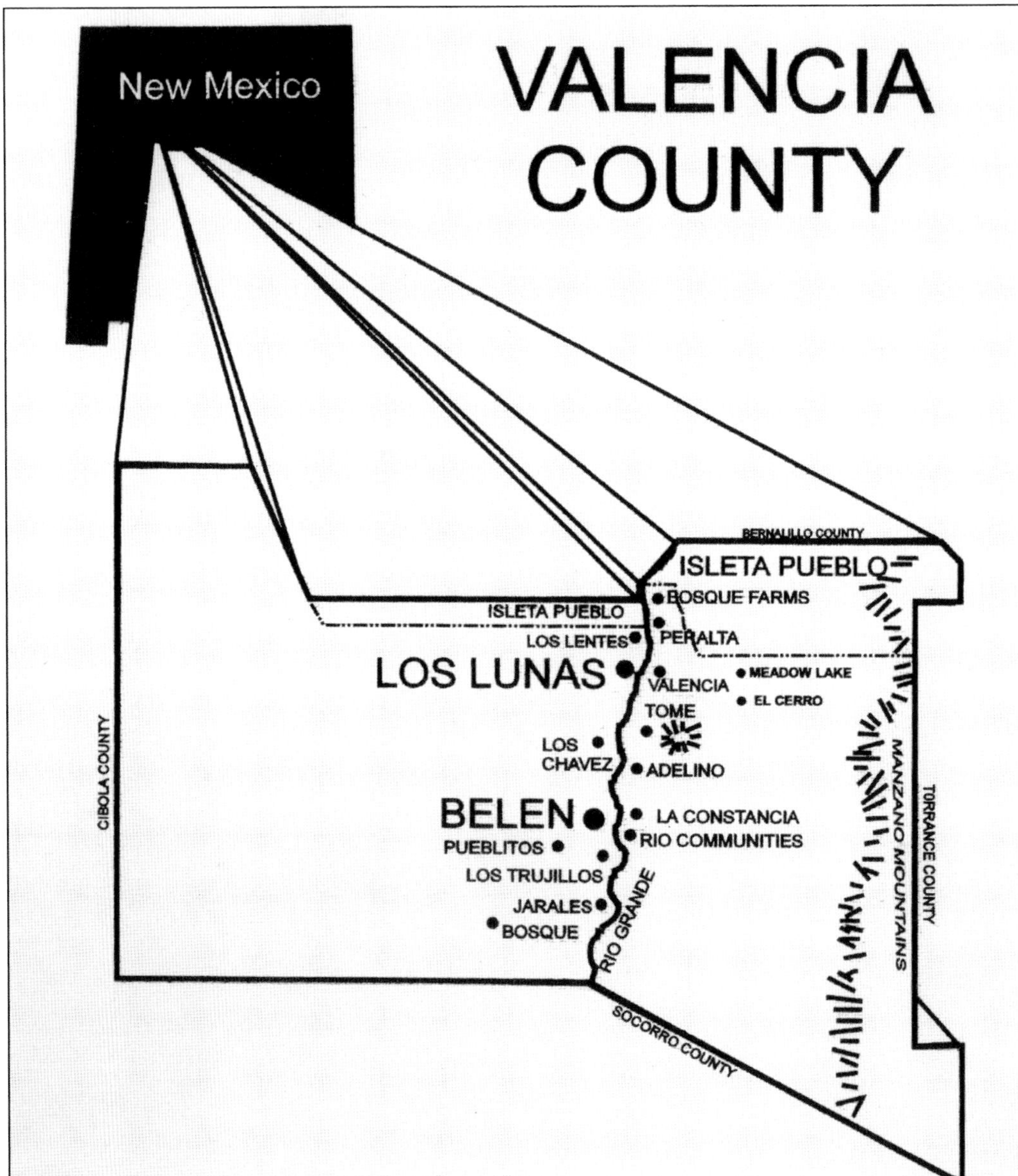

This map of Valencia County, New Mexico, drawn by Jill Chapman, shows the communities of Belen, Los Chaves, Pueblitos, Los Trujillos, Jarales, and Bosque that were the original plazas of the Belen Land Grant. Not shown is La Joya, which was located south of Bosque. (Courtesy of Valencia County Historical Society.)

On the Cover: Harry E. Byers operated a livery stable located near the intersection of the present Fifth Street and Baca Avenue in Belen. Town residents who owned horses could board them at the livery stable for a fee, and those without horses or carriages could rent them by the day or week from the stable as they were needed. Harry Byers is the tall man who is not holding the reins of a horse. The photograph was taken around 1900. (Courtesy of Valencia County Historical Society.)

IMAGES
of America

BELEN

Baldwin G. Burr

ARCADIA
PUBLISHING

Copyright © 2013 by Baldwin G. Burr
ISBN 978-1-4671-3053-0

Published by Arcadia Publishing
Charleston, South Carolina

Printed in the United States of America

Library of Congress Control Number: 2013948328

For all general information, please contact Arcadia Publishing:
Telephone 843-853-2070
Fax 843-853-0044
E-mail sales@arcadiapublishing.com
For customer service and orders:
Toll-Free 1-888-313-2665

Visit us on the Internet at www.arcadiapublishing.com

This book is dedicated to the memory of Tibo J. Chavez, Marion Herlihy, and Austin Lovett, founding members of the Valencia County Historical Society in 1969. They were not only an important part of Belen's history themselves, but they also valued and preserved that history so the town's story could be told and understood today.

Contents

ACKNOWLEDGMENTS

Many people helped make this book possible. My sincere thanks go to Dr. Richard Melzer, Francisco Sisneros, and John Taylor for their scholarly and critical reading of the text. Dr. Matt Baca, Maurine McMillan, Mike Moreno, Andrea Chavez, and Ricardo Gonzales all read and helpfully commented on portions of the text as well.

The photograph collections at the Valencia County Historical Society, the Belen Harvey House Museum, and the Los Lunas Museum of Heritage and Arts provided most of the images in this book. Maurine McMillan and Mike Moreno at the Belen Harvey House Museum and Cynthia Shetter, Andrea Chavez, and Ricardo Gonzales at the Los Lunas Museum of Heritage and Arts were especially helpful in gathering these materials.

I also want to thank Bill Hill, Michael Jaramillo, Theresa Torres Padilla, Dr. Richard Melzer, and Dr. Margaret Espinosa McDonald, who made photographs from their extensive personal collections available to me. Many of the images they provided have not been published before.

I would especially like to express my thanks to my wife, Laura Gilbert Burr. She graciously made the time to carefully read the text, offered insightful suggestions, and provided needed encouragement. She did this while pursuing her own extensive research and teaching activities.

Any errors or omissions that remain in the book are mine alone. I apologize in advance for any mistakes.

INTRODUCTION

Belen's nickname is "The Hub City." It is a hub for many reasons. The original settlement, founded on a Spanish land grant of nearly 200,000 acres in 1740, was named for the town of Bethlehem. The first settlers were Hispanic farmers from the Rio Arriba, or northern, part of the Spanish province of Nuevo Mexico. The settlement was configured like a wheel, with several separate compounds or plazas—Pueblitos, Los Trujillos, Jarales, Bosque, and La Joya—with the plaza of Belen as the hub.

These plazas were located along El Camino Real, the Royal Road to Mexico, and Belen became a hub for travelers and merchants who traveled this route from Chihuahua to Santa Fe. In Spanish New Mexico, the Royal Road was the only source of manufactured goods and the only market for local agricultural products. From the earliest days, the Belen community benefitted from its location.

In the 1880s, the railroad came to Belen, initially following the path of the Royal Road. The Atchison, Topeka, and Santa Fe Railway (AT&SF) tracks came into New Mexico from the north, from Colorado through Raton Pass, then through Belen on the way to El Paso, and then ultimately on to Galveston, Texas. When the AT&SF brought its main east-west rail line through Belen by way Abo Canyon, and established a major railroad service facility in town, Belen's reputation as a true "Hub City" was assured.

Belen's early economy was based on subsistence agriculture, and families struggled to produce enough food for themselves and their livestock. Both cattle and sheep were raised in the Belen area, but sheep were the most important animals raised in terms of income. The Rio Grande, which made agriculture possible in Belen, also threatened to destroy those efforts with frequent flooding. The only way early settlers of Belen could survive was to assist each other, and that sense of community exists to the present day.

Eventually, in the 1840s and 1850s, a few residents of Belen, most notably Jose Felipe Chavez and Antonio Gilbert, began to use the Camino Real trade route to establish merchant businesses. They traded agricultural products for goods that residents could not produce for themselves. In the 1860s, young German, French, and Swiss immigrants arrived in Belen and established stores of their own. One such immigrant in particular, John Becker, came to Belen in 1869 as an employee in one of these establishments. He opened his own business, was soon very successful, and expanded his interests to include a roller mill and a bank. In 1904, John Becker laid out the initial street grid for the town and formed the Belen Land and Improvement Company to provide homesites.

John Becker also provided land for the AT&SF rail facilities and donated the land for Anna Becker Park. He and his wife, Anna Vielstich Becker, also provided the land and the majority of funding for the building of the Zionist Lutheran Church, which still stands at the corner of Fourth Street and Reinken Avenue.

In the early 1900s, Jose Felipe Chaves and John Becker worked together to convince the AT&SF Railway to make Belen the junction of their north-south and east-west rail lines. The railroad required hundreds of employees, and those jobs and the salaries they provided created a cash economy that eventually replaced subsistence and barter agriculture. The railroad provided access to expanded markets for local agricultural products, and the prosperity it brought assured Belen's future.

In 1910, the Fred Harvey Company built the Belen Harvey House to provide consistent high-quality food and service to railroad passengers. In addition, several cafés and hotels were constructed to provide food and lodging for those same passengers, but the Harvey House established the standard. The Belen Harvey House survives today as a much-visited museum.

The economic potential of Belen in the early 1900s attracted more merchants, and the central part of the town was rapidly developed. Mercantile businesses were established by Frederick Becker, who was John's brother, Frederick Scholle, and Oscar Goebel, among others. Often, these men were initially employed at one local business before starting one of their own. Their successes attracted other merchants whose businesses prospered well into the 20th century.

Belen established a formal government structure in 1918 and began providing public services to residents of the town. Telephone service, natural gas and electric utilities and community water and sewer facilities were all soon established. These amenities attracted still more residents to the community. In return, residents served in various official capacities as officers of the town government.

Public education was provided in Belen with the building of the elementary school in 1907 and when Valencia County's first high school was built in Belen in 1916. School activities such as plays and dances, and especially sports, were extremely popular and furthered a strong sense of community.

The most important early influence on the life of Belen residents was the establishment, in 1798, of Our Lady of Belen Catholic Church. The support and guidance provided by the church was central to the lives of all who lived there. Protestant denominations also established churches in town. Lutheran, Methodist, Presbyterian, Baptist, and the multi-denominational Federated Church all served congregations in Belen and furthered a strong sense of community among residents.

The natural landscape surrounding Belen provided many recreational opportunities. Picnics and hiking in the cottonwood thick areas along the Rio Grande and hiking, hunting, and camping in the nearby Manzano Mountains were popular. Horses and carriages were replaced by automobiles, but residents of Belen enjoyed simply "traveling around."

One

The Hub City

Spanish Colonial New Mexico in the mid-18th century was characterized by small agricultural communities situated along the Camino Real, the "High Road to Mexico." Early colonists practiced subsistence agriculture and received little assistance or attention from colonial authorities located to the south in Mexico.

In 1740, the families of Diego de Torres and Antonio de Salazar, along with several other families, petitioned the governor and captain general of New Mexico, Don Gaspar Domingo de Mendoza, for a grant of land south of the village of Alburquerque (the original spelling of Albuquerque). The Belen Land Grant consisted of 200,000 acres bounded on the west by the Rio Puerco, on the east by the Manzano Mountains, on the north by the Tome and Los Chavez Land Grants, and on the south by the village of Bernardo.

Several compounds, or plazas, were formed on the grant, including Belen, Pueblitos, Los Trujillos, Jarales, Bosque, and La Joya. These communities worked together to prepare fields, establish irrigation ditches (or *acequias*), and provide protection from raids by Native American tribes.

The first "hub" represented by Belen was created by the proximity to the Camino Real, the major trade route between Chihuahua, Mexico, and Santa Fe. This road provided opportunities for traders, and later merchants, to provide goods and supplies colonists were not able to produce for themselves. Early merchants like Jose Felipe Chaves and Antonio Gilbert paved the way for immigrants such as John Becker, Oscar Goebel, and Frederick Scholle to establish their own businesses.

Belen benefitted as a community by the arrival of the Atchison, Topeka, and Santa Fe Railway's north-south line in 1880. The railroad opened new markets for local farmers' products and brought goods to the community that were not available before. When the AT&SF brought its east-west line to Belen via the Belen Cutoff, the town truly became The Hub City.

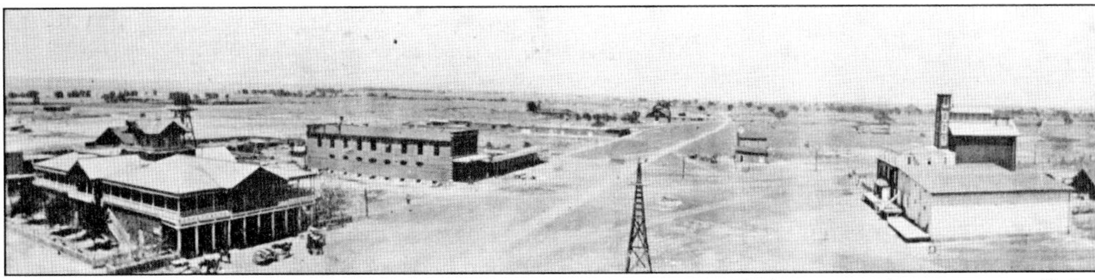

In 1740, several families from northern New Mexico petitioned the Spanish governor of New Mexico for a grant of land to the south. This 1900 scene shows the central part of Belen looking north. On the left is Fred Scholle's store, with John Becker's store to the right. Across Main Street from Becker's store is his flour mill. (Courtesy of the Bill Hill collection.)

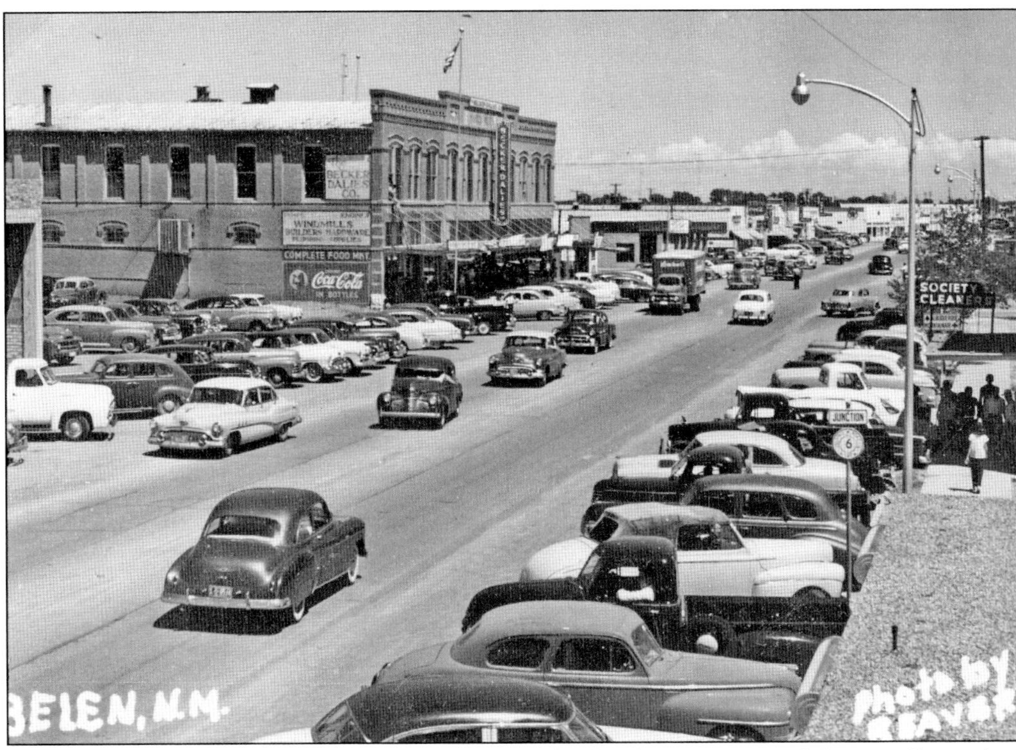

By the 1950s, Belen had become a thriving town with a bustling commercial district. Shown here in 1951 is Main Street looking north, near the intersection of Becker Avenue and Dalies Avenue. John Becker's store, seen in the previous photograph, is still the center of business activity in Belen. (Photograph by Beavers Studio, courtesy of the Bill Hill collection.)

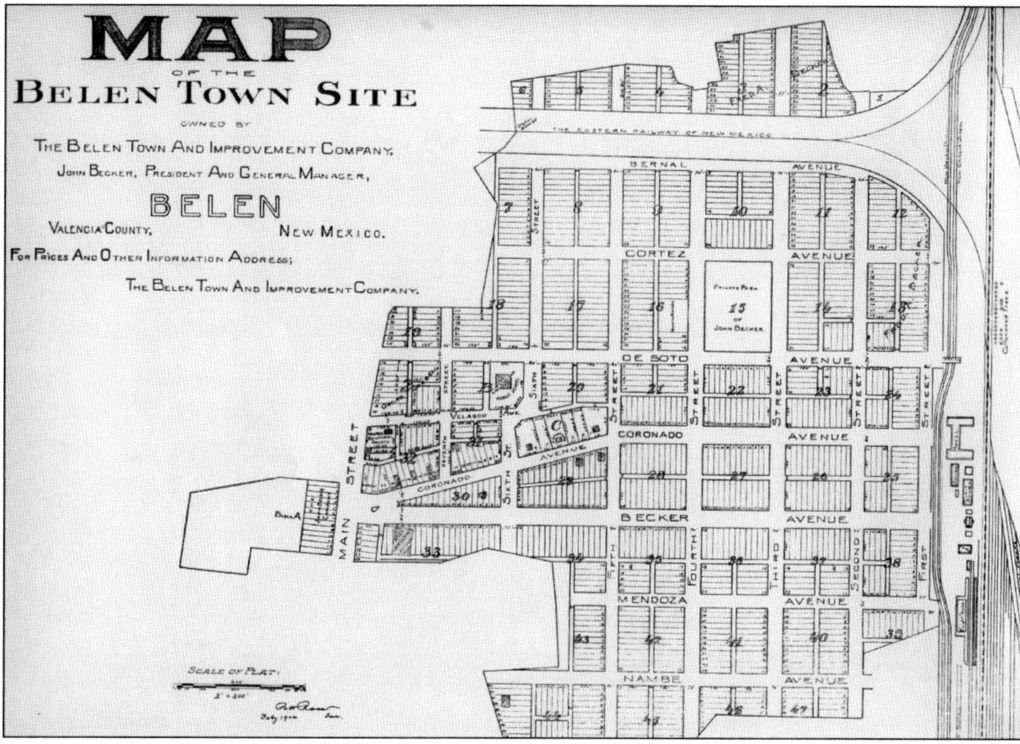

This is a map of the Belen Town Site, drawn in 1904. The plan for the town was laid out by John Becker. Note how the main streets (Becker and Coronado) converge on John Becker's Mercantile store. The map indicates that the town site was owned by the Belen Town and Improvement Company. (Courtesy of Belen Harvey House Museum.)

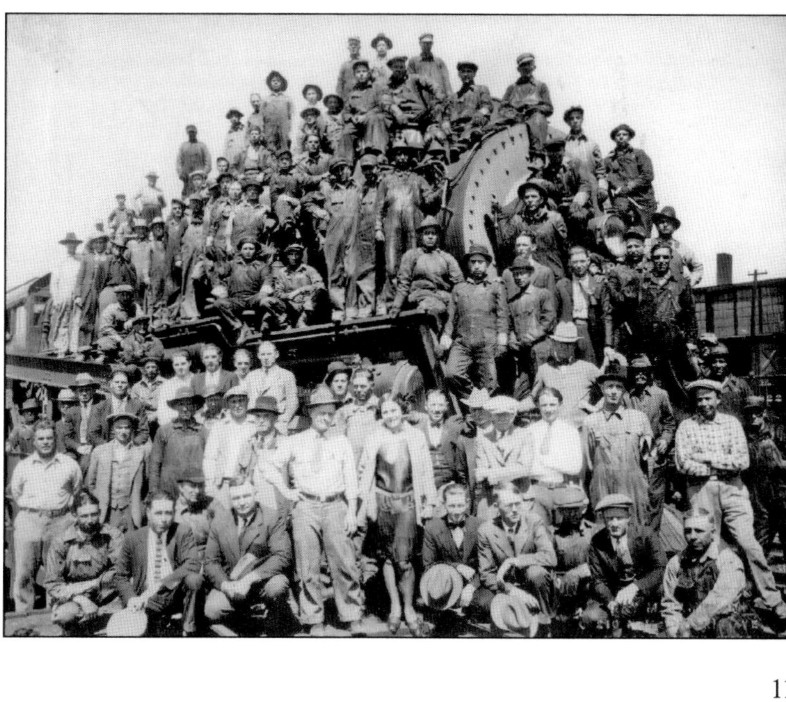

The Belen Cutoff, which ran through Abo Canyon to the east of Belen, joined the Atchison, Topeka, and Santa Fe Railway's north-south and east-west rail lines at the rail yard in Belen. The resulting increase in rail traffic brought hundreds of new residents to Belen to work for the railroad. (Courtesy of Patsy Stanford Nicholas.)

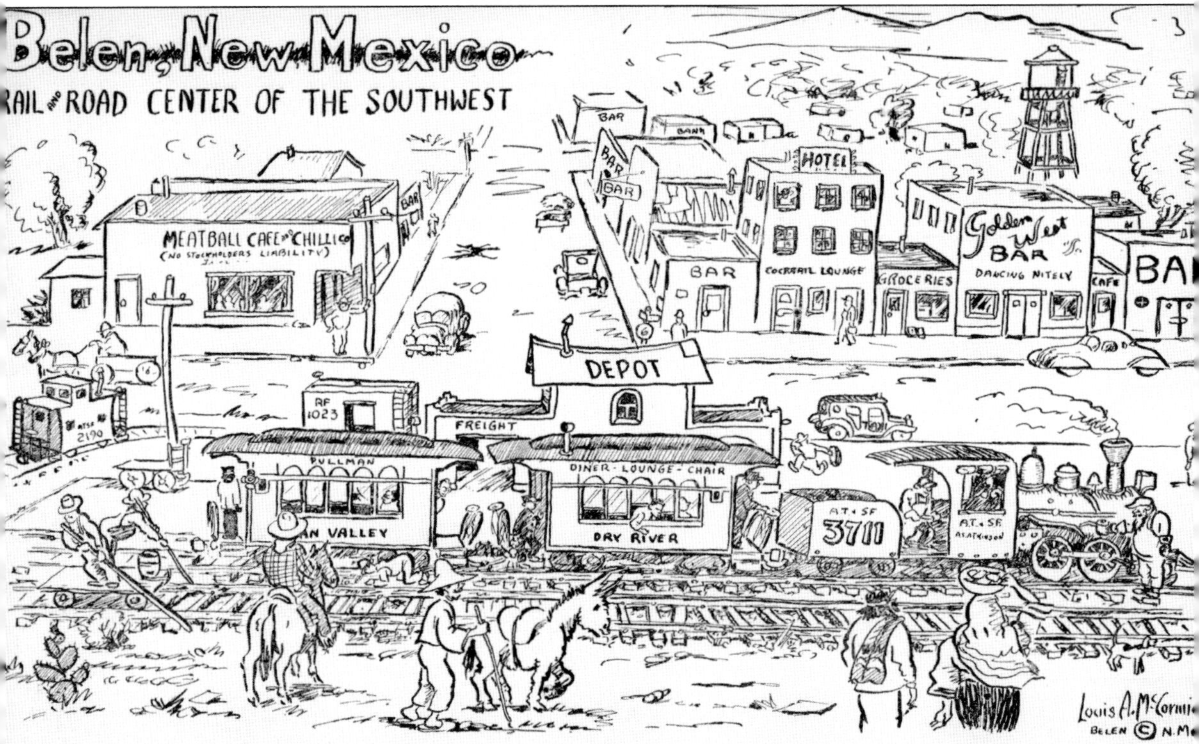

This cartoon of Belen was drawn by Louis A. "Hank" McCormick. He was a lifelong resident of Belen who worked for the AT&SF Railway and served on the Belen City Council. In Hank McCormick's cartoon, the most dominant features of the town appear to be the railroad and many bars. (Courtesy of Richard Melzer.)

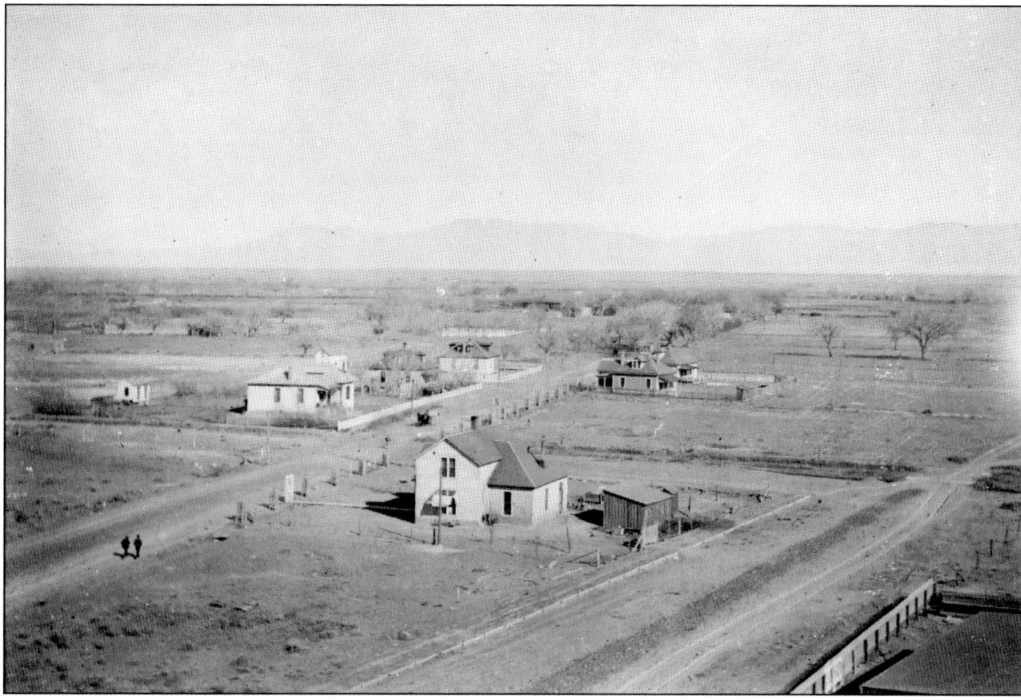

This photograph was taken from the top of the elevator tower of the Belen Roller Mill looking east toward the AT&SF railroad depot. The street where two men are walking is Becker Avenue. The photograph was taken in February 1904 by E.A. Ross. (Courtesy of Valencia County Historical Society.)

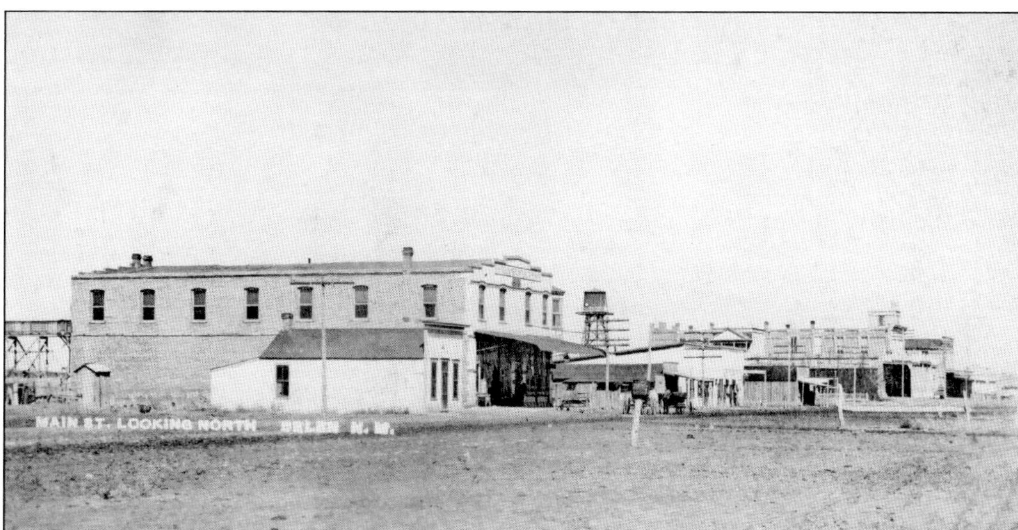

Pictured here is Main Street, looking north, in 1907. John Becker's mercantile store is seen in the foreground, and to the right of it is the mercantile owned by Oscar Goebel, later purchased by Paul J. Feil and William Ellermeyer. (Courtesy of the Bill Hill collection.)

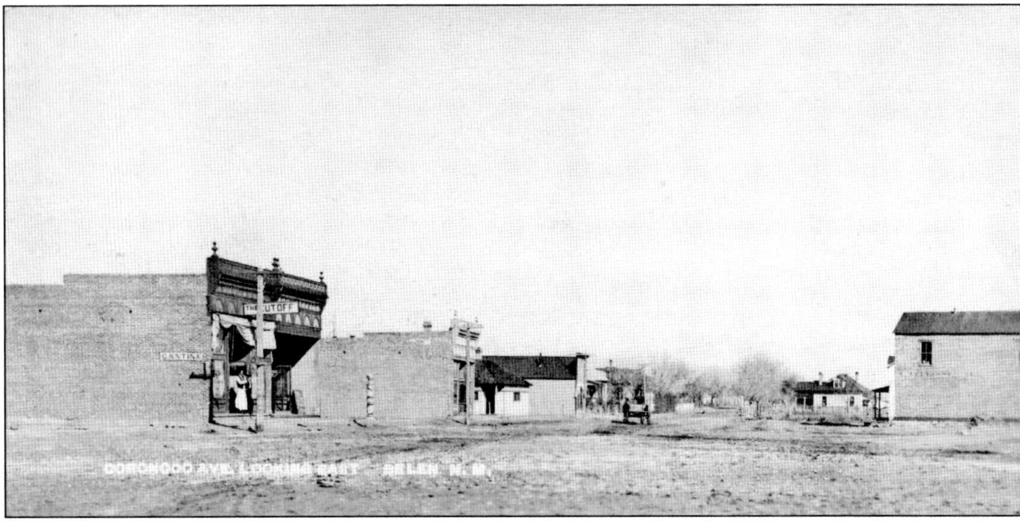

Pictured in 1908 is Coronado Avenue, before it was renamed Dalies Avenue, looking east. The building on the left is the Cutoff Cantina, named for the Belen Cutoff, which brought the east-west AT&SF rail line to Belen. A good meal at the cutoff cost 35¢, and one drink of whiskey cost 15¢ or two for 25¢. (Courtesy of the Bill Hill collection.)

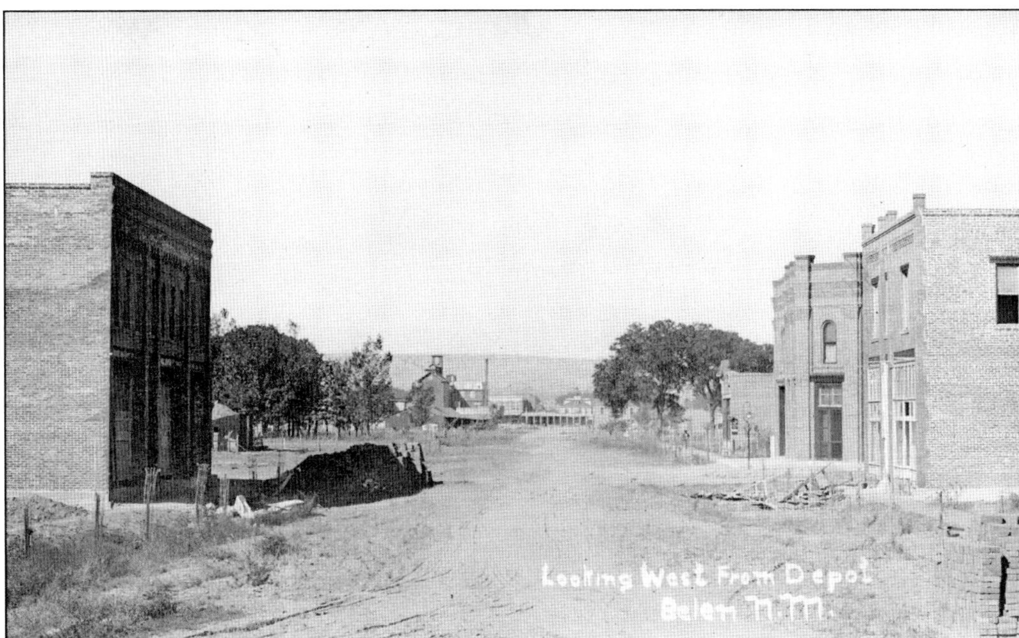

This photograph, taken in 1909 looking west on Becker Avenue from the Atchison, Topeka and Santa Fe Railway depot, shows Bertha Rutz's Belen Hotel, and next door, under construction, is the Central Hotel. Across the street is the Kuhn Hotel, which burned in 1924 and was rebuilt next to the present viaduct over Reinken Avenue. (Courtesy of the Bill Hill collection.)

John Becker outlined his business philosophy in this 1915 newspaper advertisement. The ad emphasized the company's willingness to listen to customer complaints and suggestions. Once a problem was recognized, the company and the customer could "thrash it out and set everything right." (Courtesy of the Bill Hill collection.)

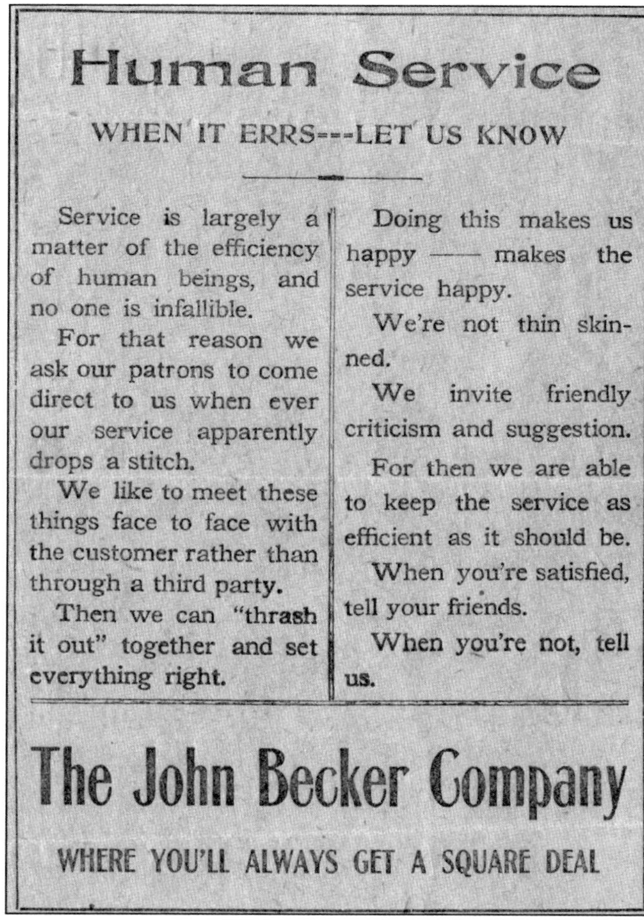

Human Service

WHEN IT ERRS---LET US KNOW

Service is largely a matter of the efficiency of human beings, and no one is infallible.

For that reason we ask our patrons to come direct to us when ever our service apparently drops a stitch.

We like to meet these things face to face with the customer rather than through a third party.

Then we can "thrash it out" together and set everything right.

Doing this makes us happy —— makes the service happy.

We're not thin skinned.

We invite friendly criticism and suggestion.

For then we are able to keep the service as efficient as it should be.

When you're satisfied, tell your friends.

When you're not, tell us.

The John Becker Company

WHERE YOU'LL ALWAYS GET A SQUARE DEAL

On the right is the Belen Hotel, built in 1907 by John Becker for Bertha Rutz. Rutz served for many years as the nanny for John Becker's children. This view is looking west up Becker Avenue toward Becker's store and the Belen Roller Mill. Looking to the future, the hotel was wired for electricity before electric service arrived in Belen. (Courtesy of Valencia County Historical Society.)

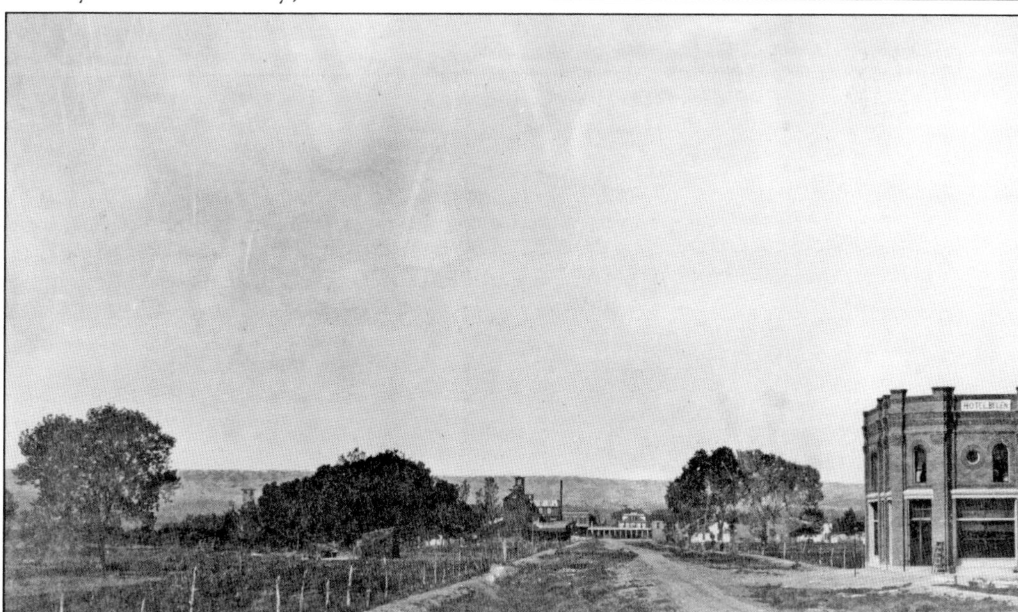

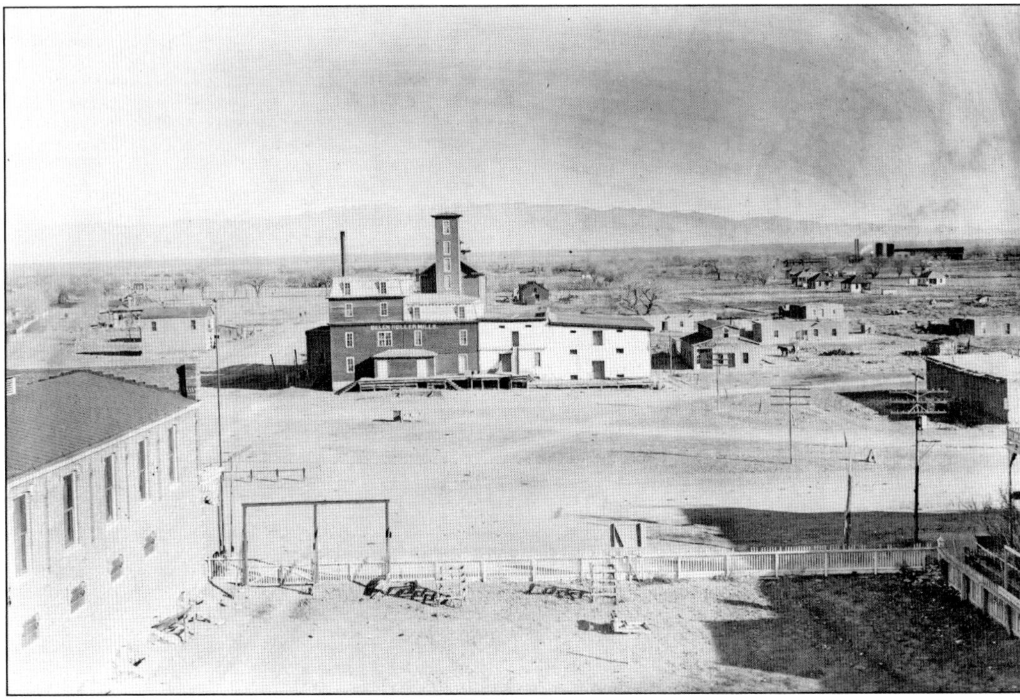

This photograph of the Belen Roller Mill, looking east, was taken around 1910 from the water tower behind John Becker's mercantile store. The mill was built by Becker in 1884. When it opened, it could produce 100 barrels of flour per day. By 1907, the milling rate had increased to 150 barrels per day. (Courtesy of Valencia County Historical Society.)

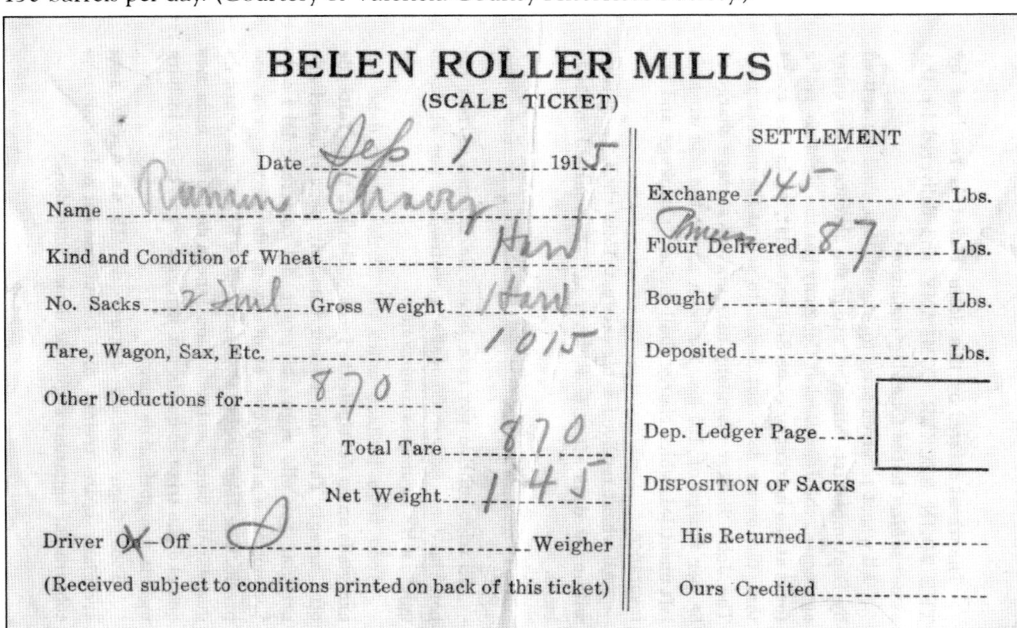

BELEN ROLLER MILLS

(SCALE TICKET)

Date Sep 1 1915

Name Roman Chavez

Kind and Condition of Wheat Hard

No. Sacks 2 ___ Gross Weight 1160

Tare, Wagon, Sax, Etc. 1015

Other Deductions for 870

Total Tare 870

Net Weight 145

Driver On—Off ___ Weigher

(Received subject to conditions printed on back of this ticket)

SETTLEMENT

Exchange 145 Lbs.

Flour Delivered 87 Lbs.

Bought ___ Lbs.

Deposited ___ Lbs.

Dep. Ledger Page ___

DISPOSITION OF SACKS

His Returned ___

Ours Credited ___

This September 1915 scale ticket from the Belen Roller Mill indicates that Roman Chavez delivered 145 pounds of wheat to the mill and received 87 pounds of flour in exchange. The mill retained 58 pounds of wheat as a fee for grinding the flour. (Courtesy of the Bill Hill collection.)

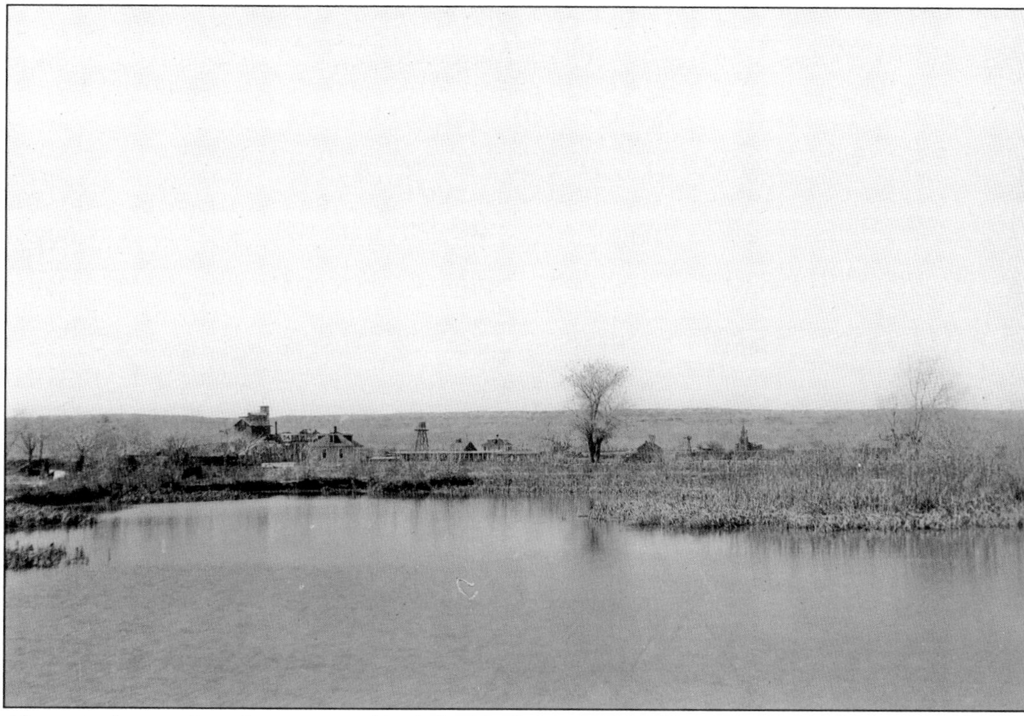

Above is the pond, or *desague*, used by John Becker to collect the irrigation water runoff from his alfalfa fields. The pond later became part of Anna Becker Park. John Becker deeded the land to the town for use as a park in 1927, which was named for John's wife, Anna Vielstich Becker. The labor to develop the park was provided by New Deal agencies, including the Civil Works Administration and the Federal Emergency Relief Administration, and additional funds were provided by Belen's Eastern Star Lodge, the Veteran's Council, and the Belen Chapter of the Women's Christian Temperance Union. (Both courtesy of Valencia County Historical Society.)

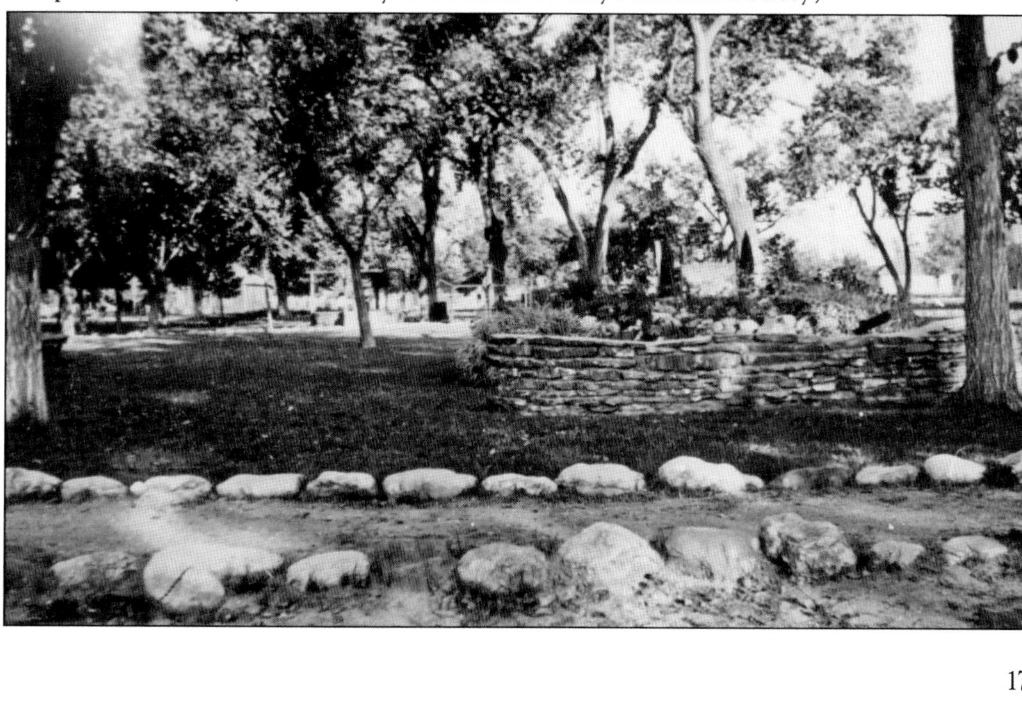

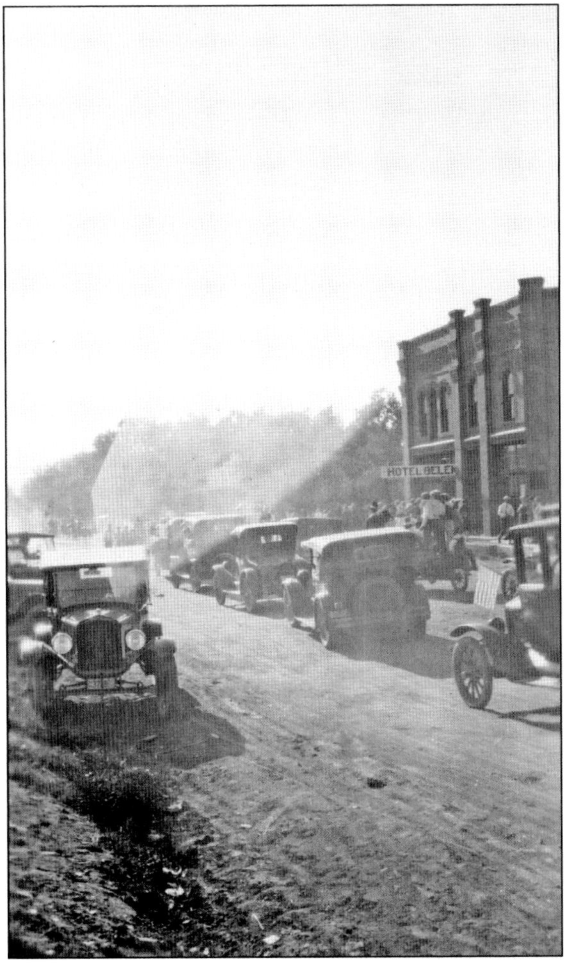

This photograph was taken in 1925 and shows Becker Avenue looking west, about a block from the Belen Harvey House. Onlookers are crowding the sidewalks as they watch a parade (probably for the Fourth of July) of automobiles, marchers, and people on horseback. The Hotel Belen is on the right. (Courtesy of the Bill Hill collection.)

On March 4, 1916, a spring blizzard struck Belen. Yards and streets were covered with more than a foot of snow, and activity around town came to a standstill. The heavy snow broke tree branches and downed power lines. This scene is of Dalies Avenue, west of the Atchison, Topeka and Santa Fe Railway depot. (Courtesy of Valencia County Historical Society.)

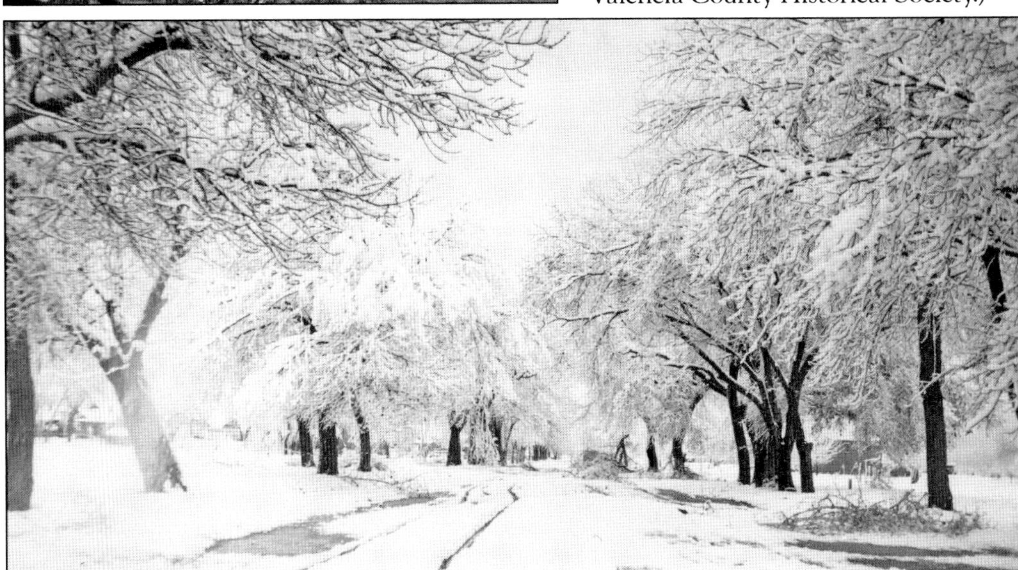

Before the creation of the Middle Rio Grande Conservancy District, the Rio Grande often flooded, changing the course of the river and causing considerable damage to Valencia County communities. The people in the image at right have piled their valuable possessions on a table in front of the house to protect them from the floodwaters. A flood in the last week of May 1937 inundated the downtown area of Belen. The image below of the flooded street depicts the front of Buckland Drugstore, south of the old elementary school. Many families were forced to abandon their *terrone*, or adobe homes, which were particularly vulnerable to floodwaters. Belen was flood-free for the next 32 years until three inches of rain fell in less than an hour in June 1969, causing the Belen Drainage Ditch to fail. (Both courtesy of Valencia County Historical Society.)

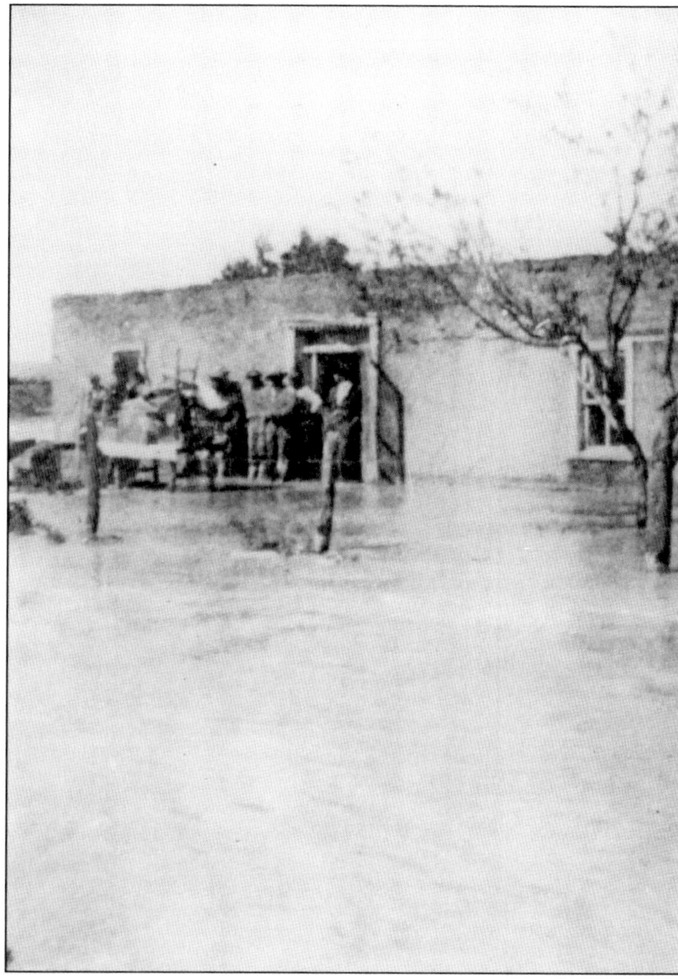

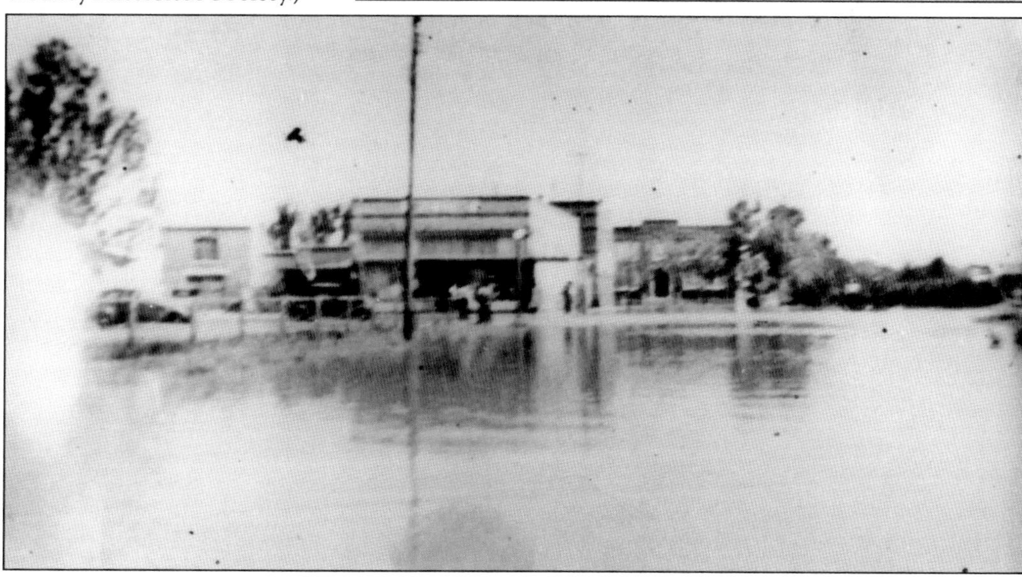

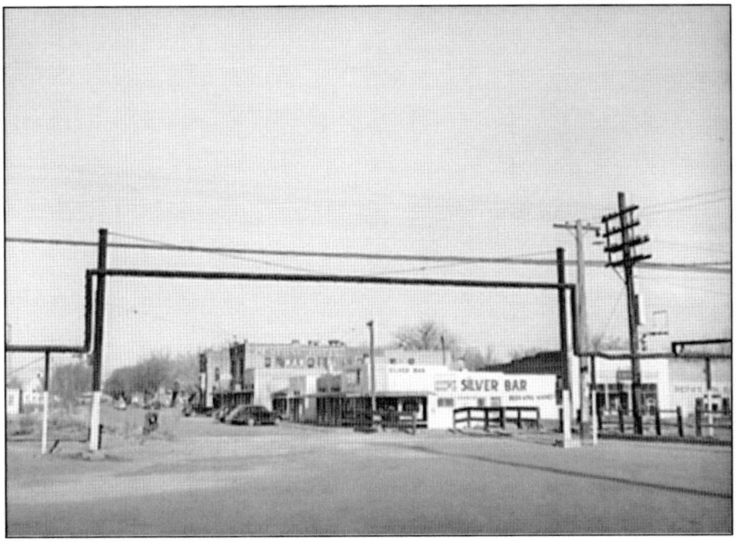

In March 1943, Farm Security Administration photographer Jack Delano came to Belen to photograph scenes related to the Atchison, Topeka, and Santa Fe Railway. This is a view of the town taken from the railroad yard looking northwest. (Courtesy of the Library of Congress, LC-USW3-022169-D.)

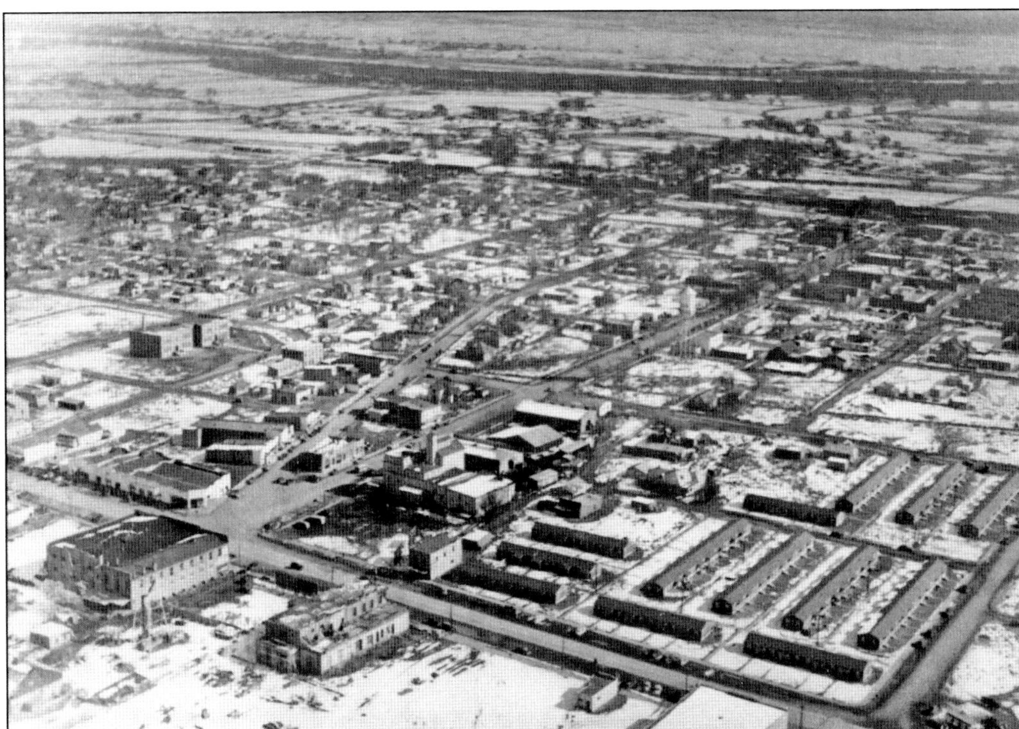

This 1947 aerial photograph, looking east, shows Becker Avenue and Dalies Avenue converging on the John Becker Company on Main Street. To the south of the Becker store is the Fred Scholle building, and one block south is the mercantile of John Becker's brother Frederick Becker. The photograph was taken by Weigun. (Courtesy of Valencia County Historical Society.)

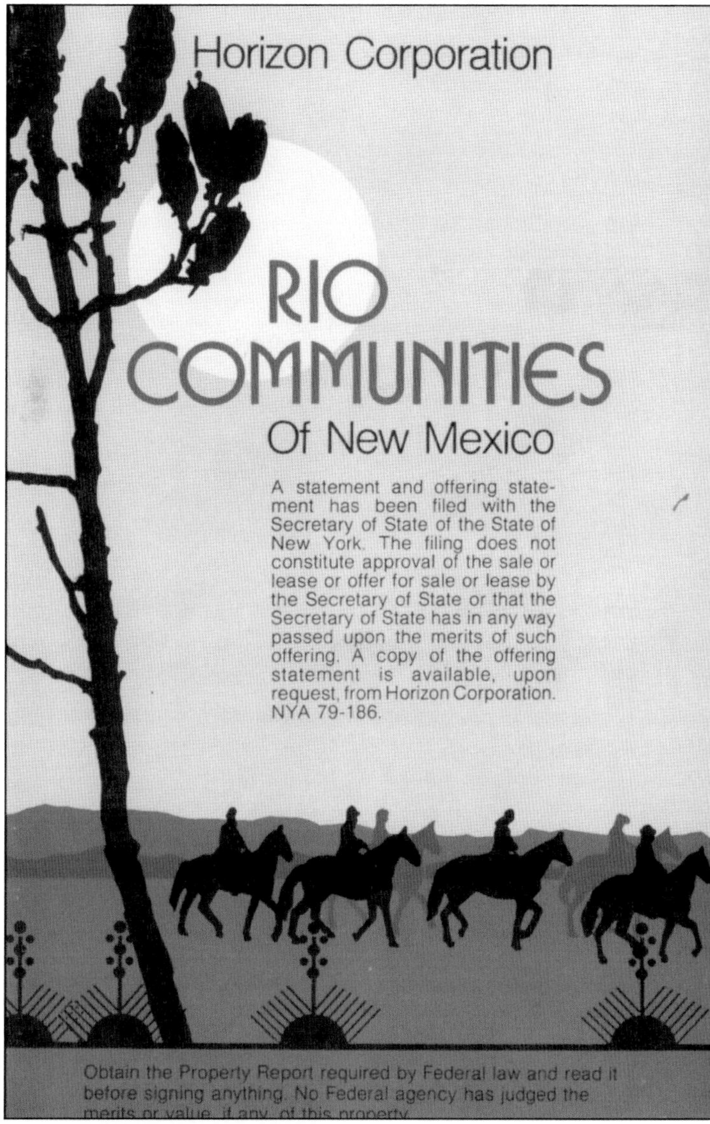

This is one of the brochures that promoted the Rio Grande Estates development of the Horizon Corporation. Horizon advertised land for sale east of Belen in publications throughout the United States. Horizon even maintained a sales office in the early 1970s at the US Overseas Mission Club in Seoul, South Korea. (Courtesy of Richard Melzer.)

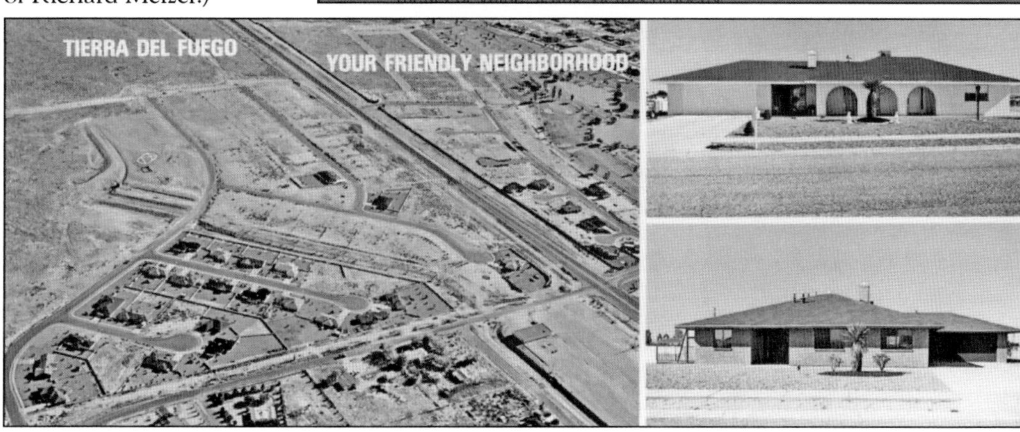

The Tierra del Fuego subdivision of the Rio Grande Estates (later Rio Communities) land development to the east and south of Belen was created in the late 1960s by the New York–based Horizon Corporation. The development initially contained more than 30,000 acres, and lots were sold to approximately 90,000 individuals, most living outside of New Mexico. (Courtesy of Richard Melzer.)

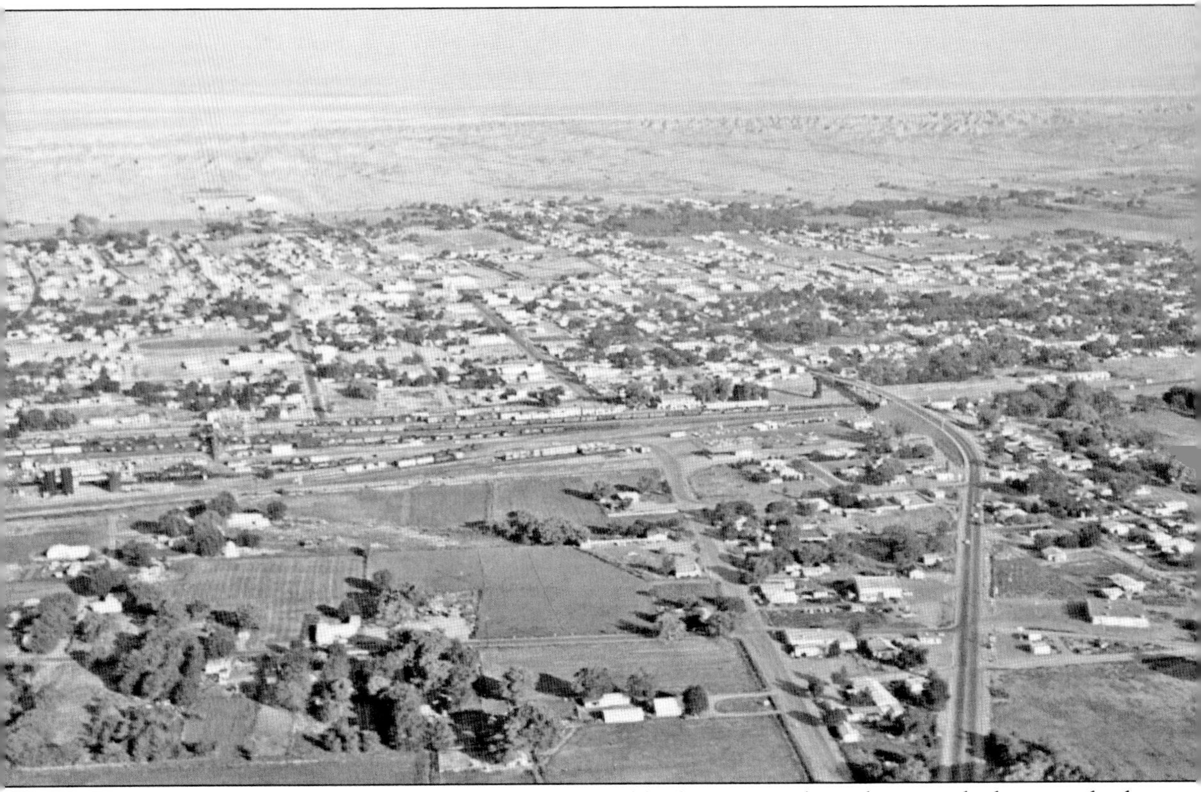

This aerial view of Belen, taken around 1960 and looking west, shows how much the town had grown since its beginnings. Dominating the center of the photograph is the Belen Rail Yard. River Road and the rail yard overpass can be seen on the right. (Courtesy of Richard Melzer.)

Two

An Agricultural Community

Farming has been an important activity in Belen since the earliest days of the Belen Land Grant. Prior to the Spanish colonists' arrival, Native Americans had grown corn, beans, and squash using primitive irrigation methods. The Spaniards added such Old World crops as wheat, peaches, grapes, tomatoes, and melons. Raising livestock was added as an activity and included horses, cattle, sheep, goats, and pigs.

Land grants were generally communal, and everyone pitched in to level fields, plow and plant, and tend the crops. Water for irrigation was provided by a main ditch, or *acequia madre*, drawing water from the Rio Grande. Everyone assisted in maintaining the acequia madre, as well as the smaller feeder ditches, or laterals, which brought water to individual fields.

As farmers became more successful, they were able to produce crops and livestock beyond the needs of mere subsistence. They could trade surplus agricultural goods for other needed or desired manufactured goods provided by traders and merchants. For example, they were able to replace wooden plows with more efficient metal plowshares and other farm machinery brought to Belen by the railroad.

There were always hardships for farmers. Some years, there was little or no water for the crops. Other years would bring devastating floods, as the Rio Grande raged with spring snowmelt from the northern mountains. Indian raids destroyed crops and drove off livestock. Insect plagues destroyed entire crops in a matter of days. In spite of these hardships, farmers in the Belen area had many successful harvests and were able to produce enough food for the winter and still have some surplus for barter.

The creation of the Middle Rio Grande Conservancy District (MRGC) in 1925 was intended to control the flooding of the Rio Grande, but the MRGC also brought other changes to agriculture in Belen. It imposed taxes on the land being irrigated, and this led to the ultimate demise of the Belen Land Grant. The grant was incorporated in 1918, and by 1938 the corporation had to borrow money to pay its assessment. When the loan could not be repaid, what remained of the grant passed into private hands.

Eventually, full-time farmers became a rarity in Belen, replaced by "weekend" farmers, who worked traditional jobs during the week to pay their bills and farmed on the weekends or at night.

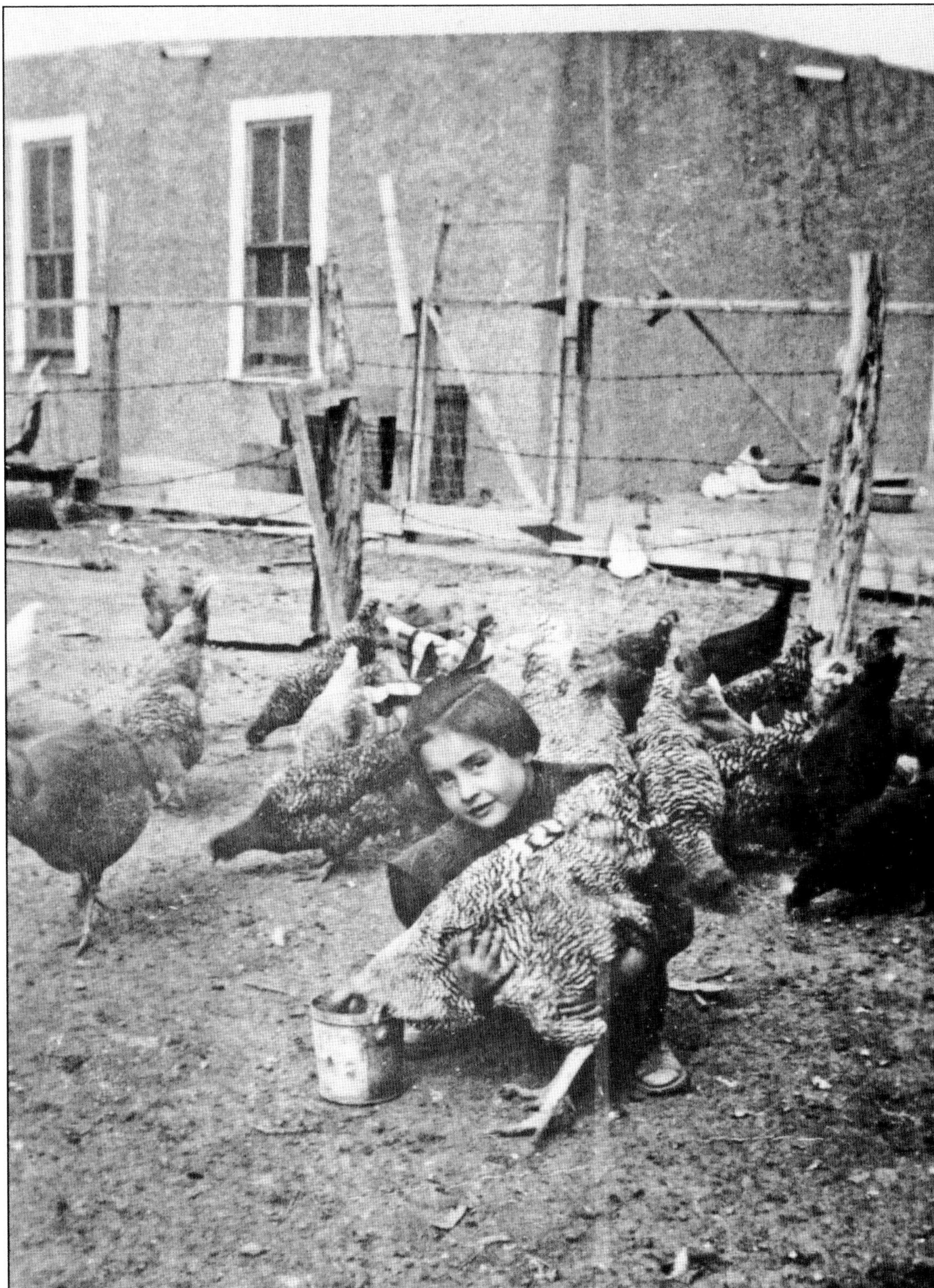
On the farms around Belen, everyone had to pitch in and help with the farmwork. Often, the first chore for young children was feeding the chickens. Pictured here is Catherine Delgado, daughter of Fidel A. Delgado and Gertrude Lacey Delgado, who first came to Belen in 1910. (Courtesy of Margaret Espinosa McDonald.)

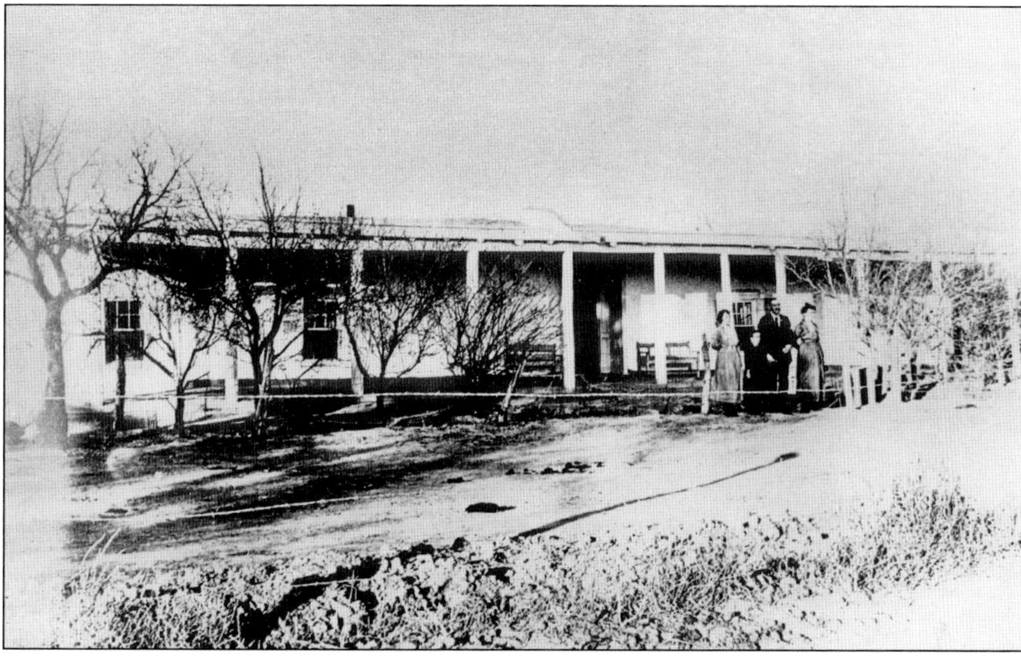

Felipe Castillo was the blacksmith in Pueblitos, a small village south of Belen, from 1901 until 1960. He also worked on his own farm, shown here around 1910. It is said that if he needed a piece of farm equipment, he would draw it on a piece of paper and then make it in his blacksmith shop. (Courtesy of Valencia County Historical Society.)

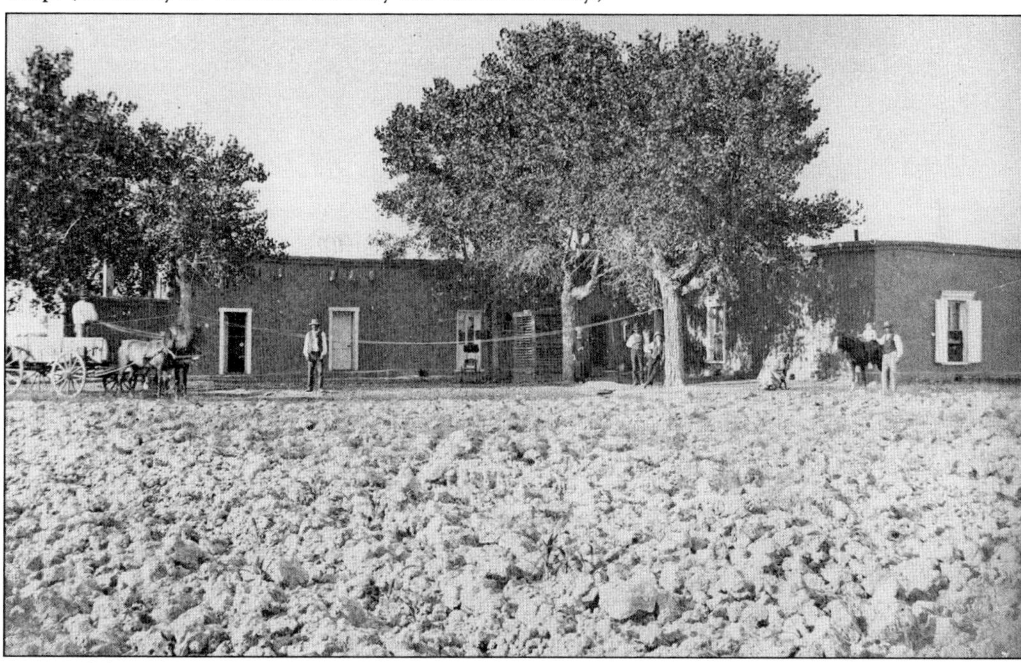

Many of the merchants in Belen also were active farmers. This freshly plowed field, seen around 1900, is on the farm of John Becker's brother Fred Becker. The farm was located near the present intersection of Second Street and Reinken Avenue. The single-story adobe farmhouse was built in the traditional Territorial style of architecture. (Courtesy of Valencia County Historical Society.)

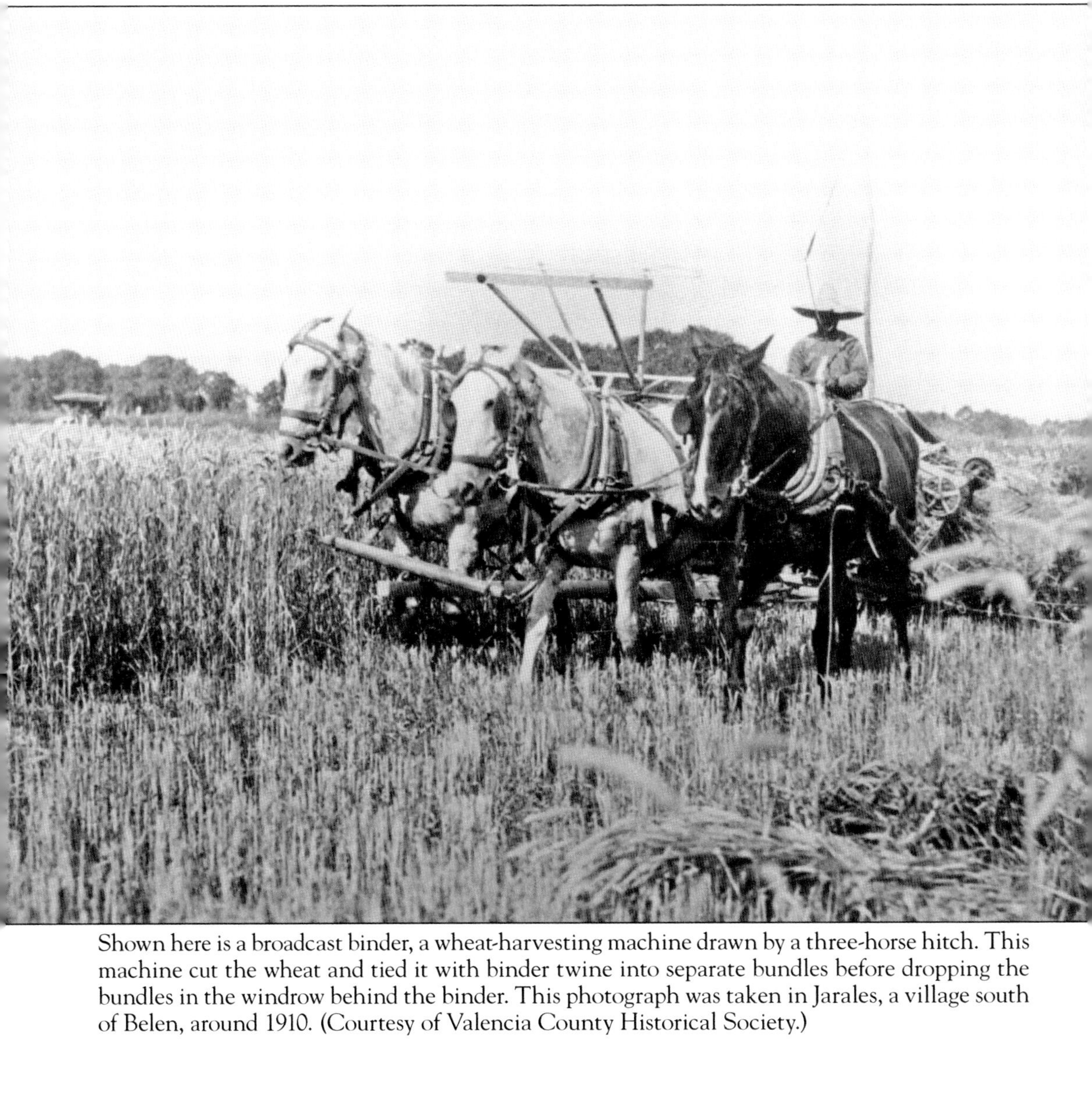

Shown here is a broadcast binder, a wheat-harvesting machine drawn by a three-horse hitch. This machine cut the wheat and tied it with binder twine into separate bundles before dropping the bundles in the windrow behind the binder. This photograph was taken in Jarales, a village south of Belen, around 1910. (Courtesy of Valencia County Historical Society.)

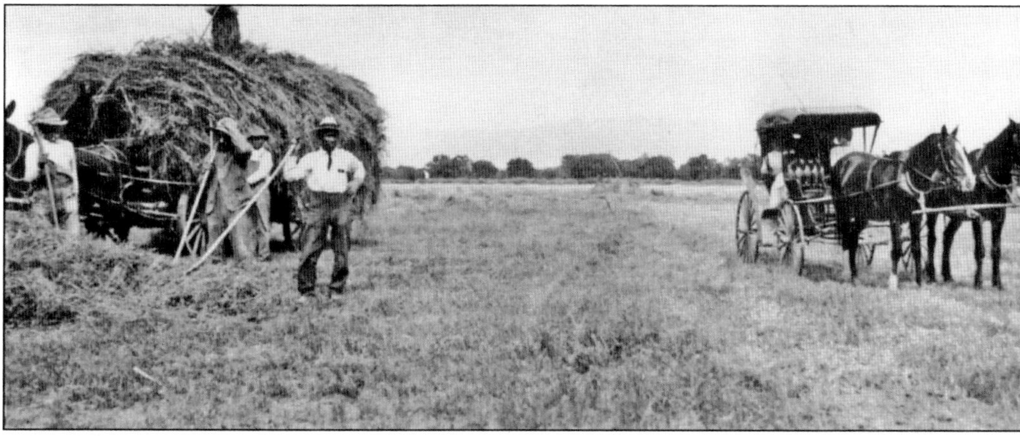

After alfalfa was mowed, it was left in the field for three days to dry. The cured alfalfa was picked up using a flat wagon, called a guanana, and transported to a stack near the livestock barn. It could be stored for feeding the farmer's own livestock or sold as a cash crop. This alfalfa field was in Jarales. (Courtesy of Valencia County Historical Society.)

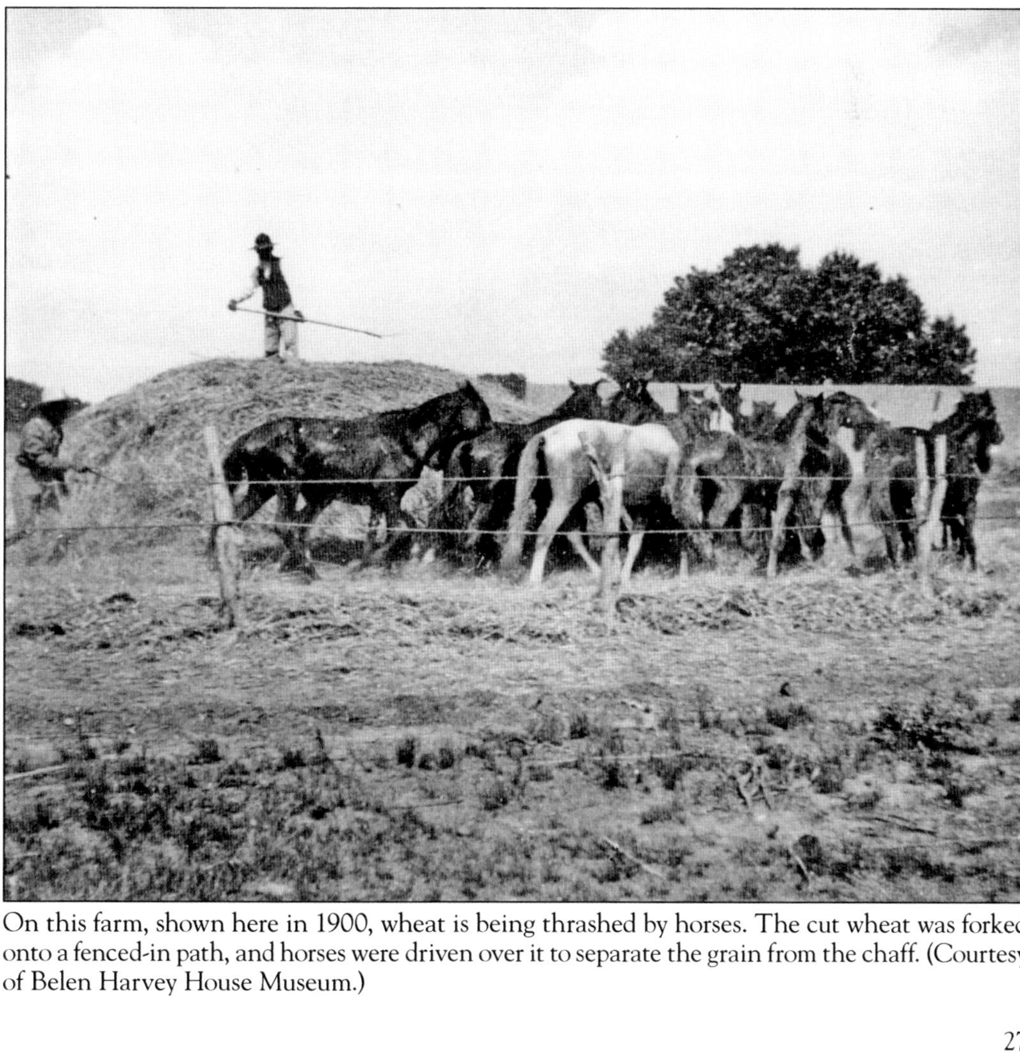

On this farm, shown here in 1900, wheat is being thrashed by horses. The cut wheat was forked onto a fenced-in path, and horses were driven over it to separate the grain from the chaff. (Courtesy of Belen Harvey House Museum.)

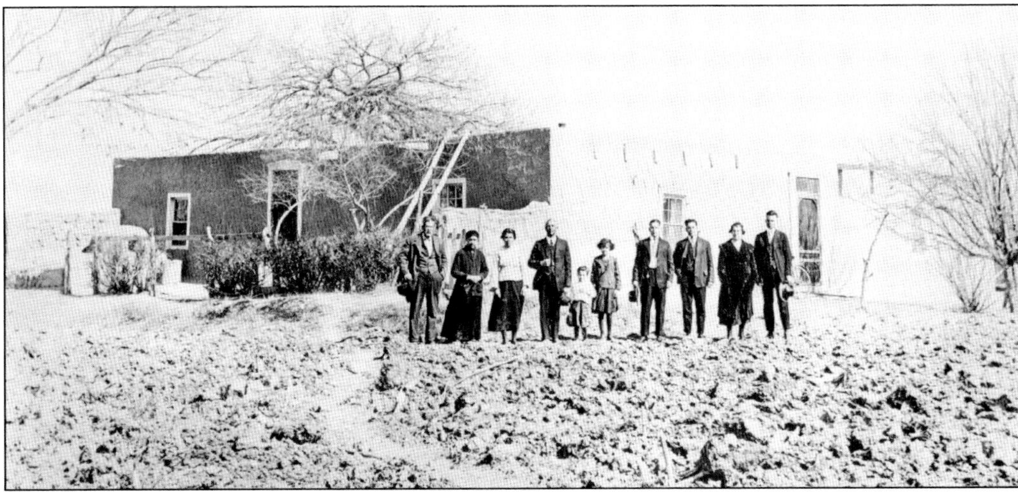

Pictured around 1900, this farm family poses in their best clothes outside their single-story adobe farmhouse for an itinerant photographer. Terrone walls, 18 to 24 inches thick, made the house warm in the winter and cool in the summer. The ladder was for access to the flat dirt roof and allowed for maintenance when the roof invariably leaked. (Courtesy of Valencia County Historical Society.)

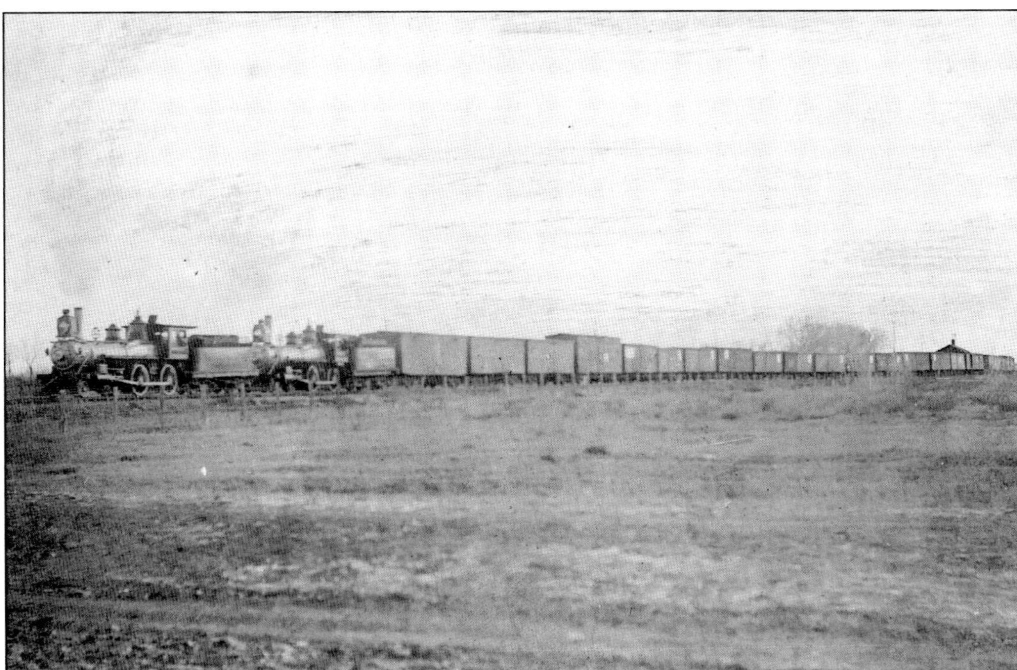

Raising sheep was an important agricultural activity in Belen. This train, pulled by tandem AT&SF engines, is composed of boxcars filled with wool from John Becker's warehouse in Belen. The wool was transported by train to Galveston, Texas, and from there by ship to Boston and the New England woolen mills. This photograph was taken in 1896. (Courtesy of Valencia County Historical Society.)

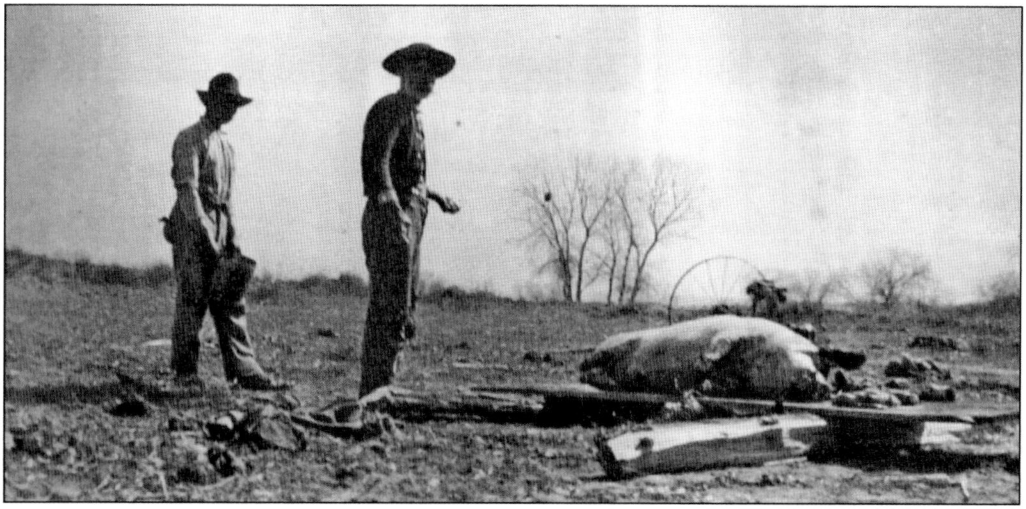

These men are butchering a hog for a *matanza* around 1900. A matanza was a late-fall celebration, where pigs were killed to obtain food for the Christmas season. Pork was used to make tamales and posole. Pork rind was boiled to make *chicharones*. Strips of pork were dried and soaked in red chile to make chile enchiladas. (Courtesy of the Los Lunas Museum of Heritage and Arts.)

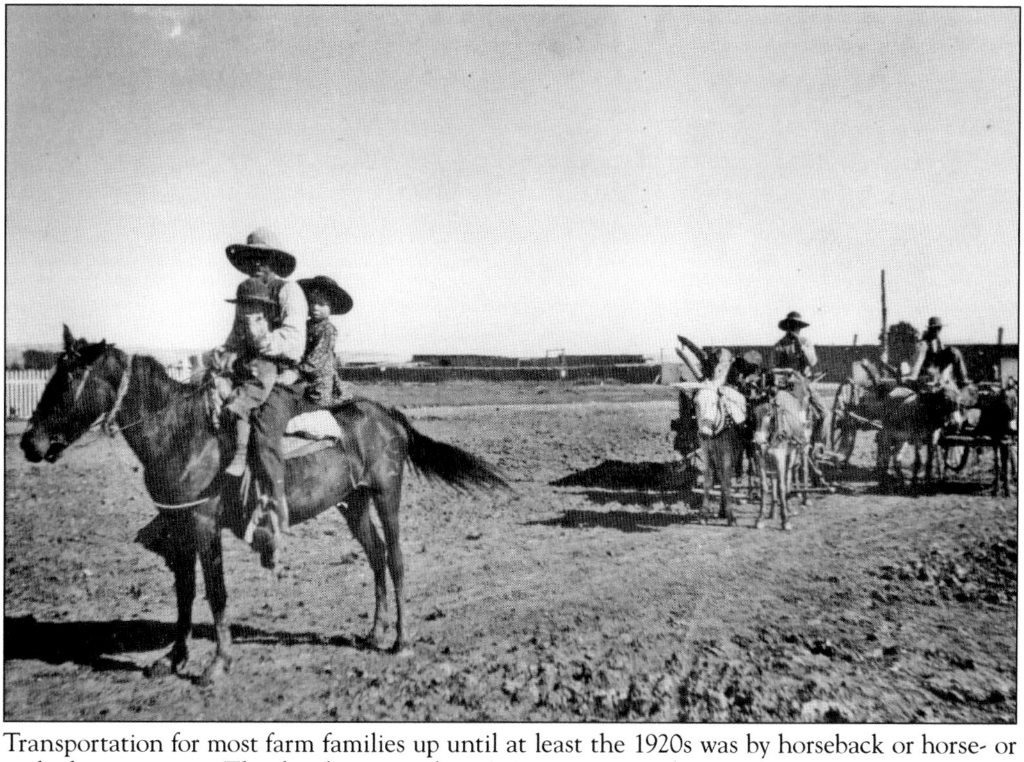

Transportation for most farm families up until at least the 1920s was by horseback or horse- or mule-driven wagons. This family, pictured in 1910, is getting ready to go to town to market surplus produce to obtain manufactured goods the family could not provide on their own. (Courtesy of Valencia County Historical Society.)

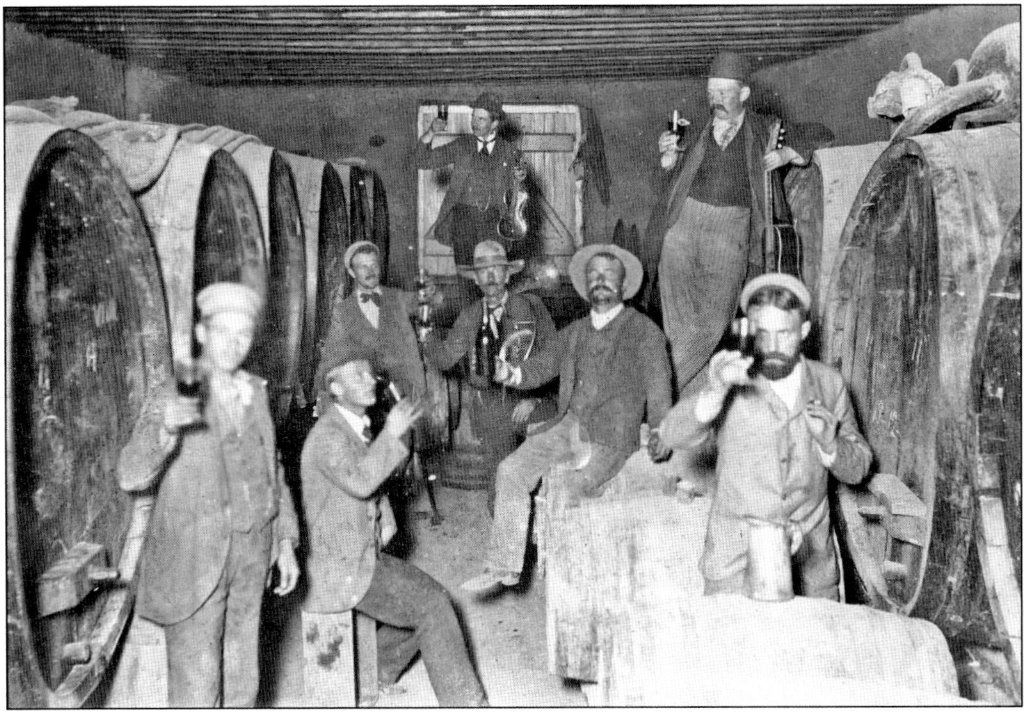

Winemaking was popular in Belen and an important part of German and Hispanic culture. Both John Becker and Adolph Didier had extensive and popular winemaking operations, and they sold their wines in New Mexico, Colorado, and northern Mexico. John Becker's winery was particularly noted for its green chile wine. With the coming of Prohibition, winemaking declined rapidly in the area. Shown above is the Adolph Didier Winery. Below is the John Becker Winery around 1890. (Both courtesy of Valencia County Historical Society.)

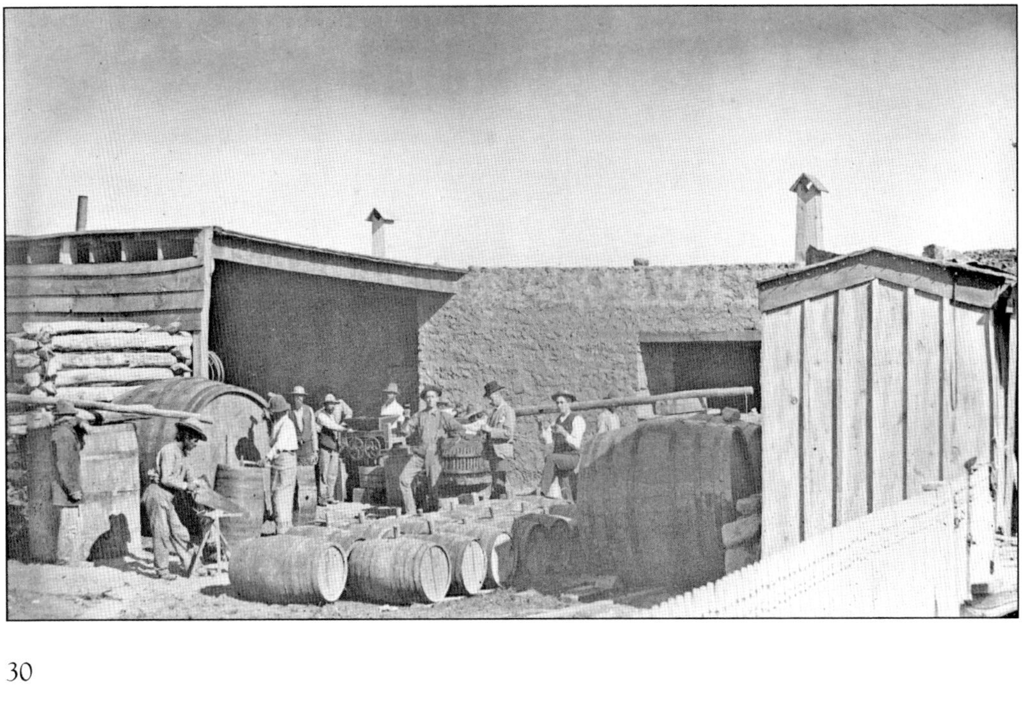

Three

The Railroad Comes to Belen

There is no question that the most significant event in the history of Belen was the establishment of a rail route east of town through Abo Canyon. This rail line, called the Belen Cutoff, joined the Santa Fe's north-south routes with its east-west routes. Belen was the hub of these rail routes, and this gave the town the nickname "The Hub City," by which it is known to this day. At one time, the railroad employed more than 600 people in Belen.

The railroad brought about dramatic changes in the lives of many Belen residents. In 1900, before the creation of the Belen Cutoff, the population of Belen was 633. In 1910, just two years after the opening of the cutoff, the population was 1,733. By 1920, the population of Belen had risen to 2,253. To illustrate the shift from agricultural to urban jobs, 77 percent of Belen's population was engaged in agriculture in 1900; by 1920, the number of farmers and ranchers had declined to 19 percent.

The railroad brought new people with new ideas and new energies to Belen. It also expanded the market for commercial goods and agricultural products, adding to the cash economy and overall prosperity of Belen. One symbol of that prosperity was the Belen Harvey House. The Fred Harvey Company created an unequaled standard of quality and service for railroad passengers throughout the western United States—the Belen Harvey House was no exception. Many of the Harvey Girls working at the Harvey House in Belen treasured the experience.

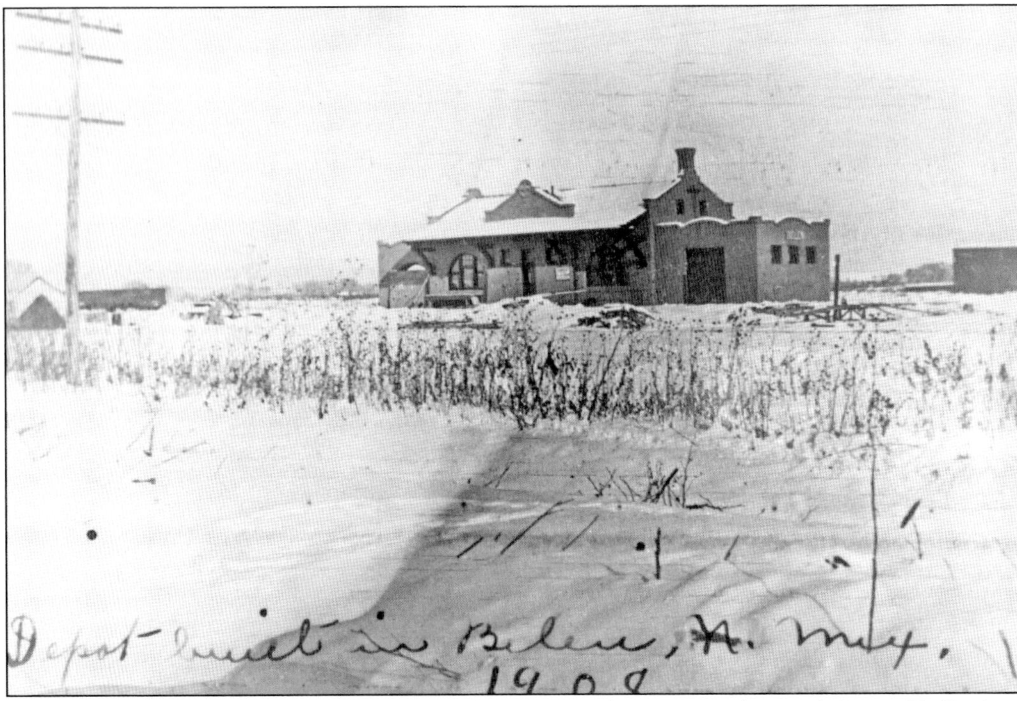

This depot, photographed in 1908, served as the Atchison, Topeka, and Santa Fe Railway headquarters in Belen before the creation of the Belen Cutoff dramatically increased rail traffic through town. When this depot was constructed, there was only a single north-south rail line through Belen. (Courtesy of Valencia County Historical Society.)

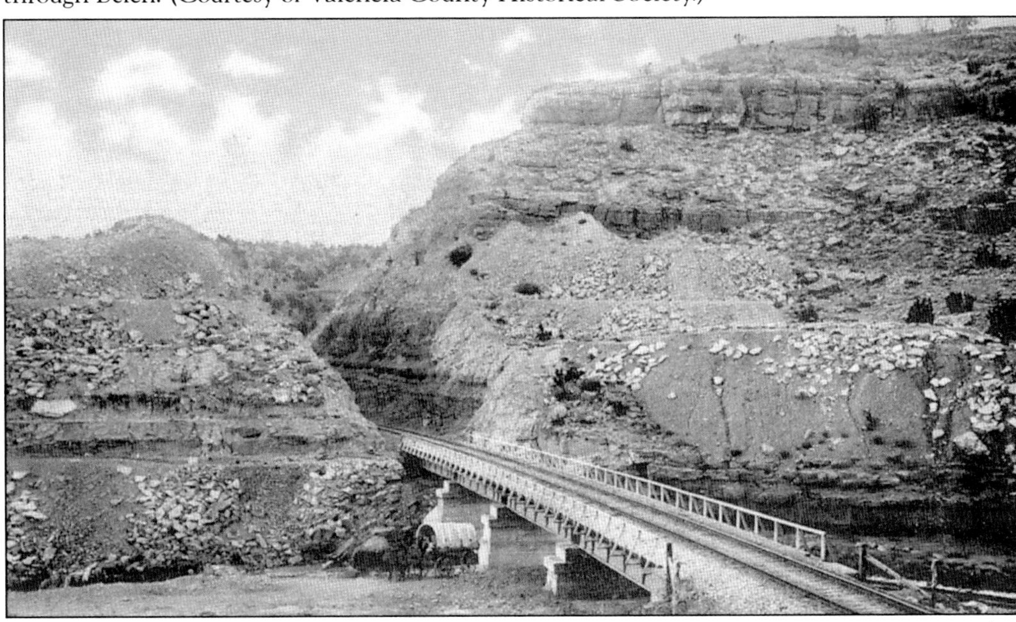

In 1880, the AT&SF Railway had established a north-south route through New Mexico, traveling over Raton Pass to the north, through Belen to Deming, and then on to El Paso to the south. When constructing the Belen Cutoff, Abo Canyon was crossed by bridges ranging from 200 to 500 feet in length. (Courtesy of Randy Dunson.)

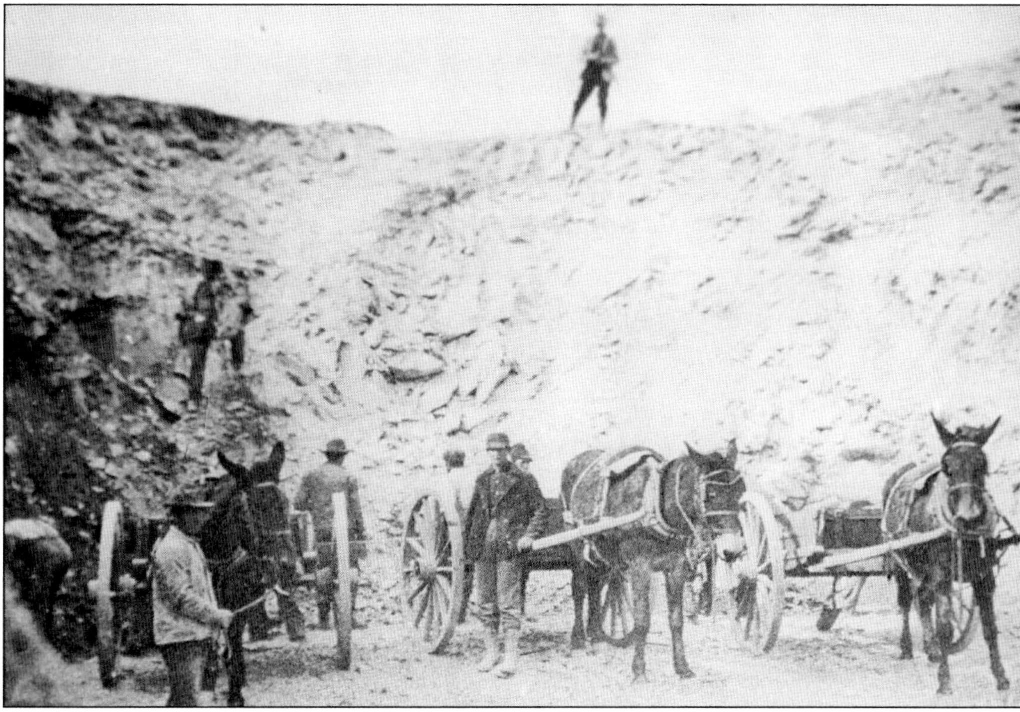

This image shows rock work at Sais Quarry in Abo Canyon in 1905. Steep grades and harsh winter weather conditions made the AT&SF route through Raton Pass in northern New Mexico slow and dangerous. In the early 1900s, the railroad began to plan for a low-grade, all-weather route as an alternative. Work began on the new route, to run from Amarillo to Belen via Abo Canyon, in 1905. (Courtesy of Randy Dunson.)

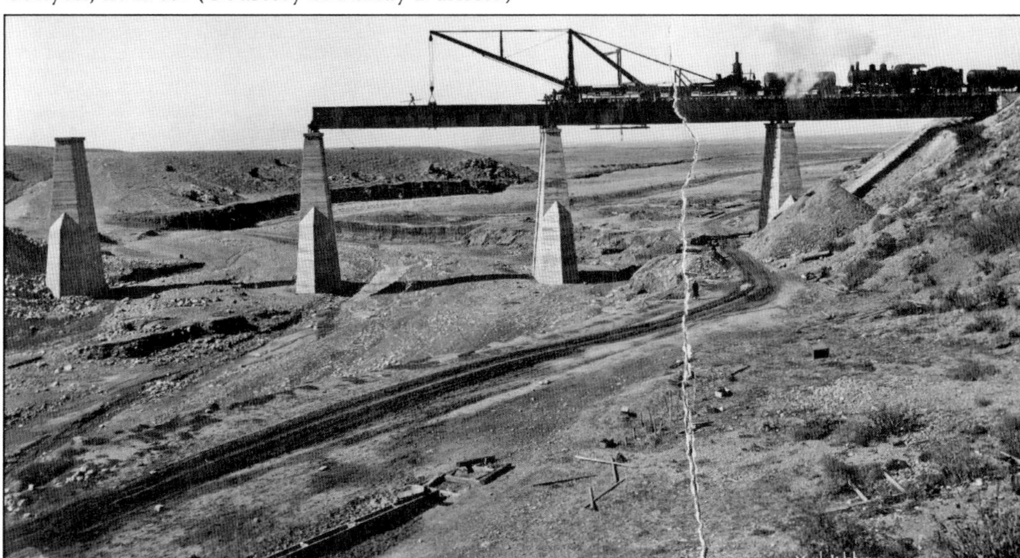

When construction began in 1905, seven bridges across Abo Canyon were built for the Belen Cutoff. Five pairs of 100-foot, 30-ton girders were used, each at a height of 70 feet, with a total cost of $250,000 per bridge. This photograph was taken by Moon and Keleher. (Courtesy of Valencia County Historical Society.)

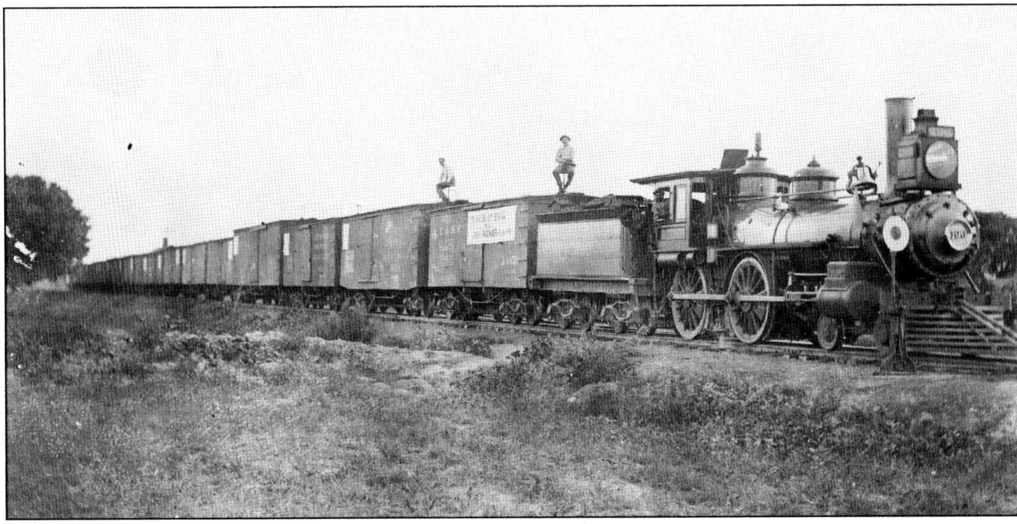

Engine No. 196, shown here in 1896, started life as No. 194, but that locomotive had a reputation as a "hoodoo" or "jinxed" engine, having killed seven engineers in its lifetime. When the original No. 196 was lost in a Rio Grande flood in June 1885, No. 194 was renamed No. 196 in an effort to erase its bad reputation. (Courtesy of Valencia County Historical Society.)

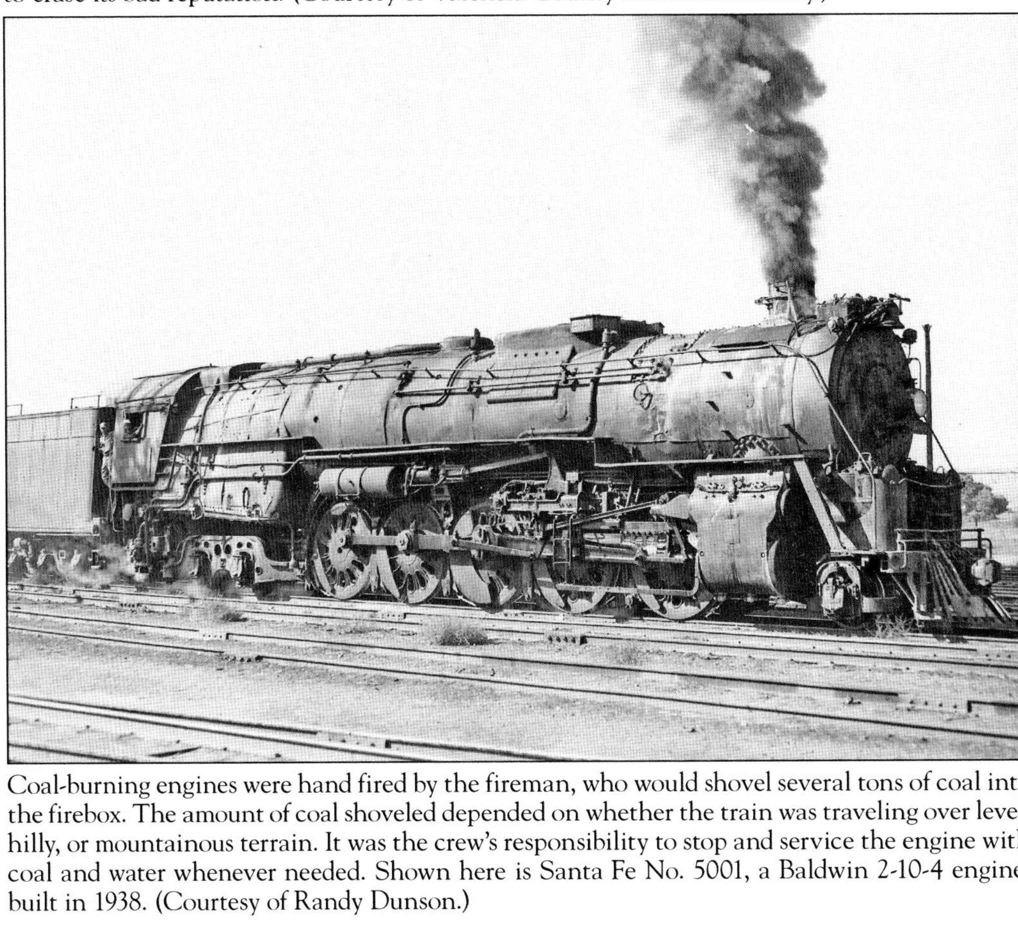

Coal-burning engines were hand fired by the fireman, who would shovel several tons of coal into the firebox. The amount of coal shoveled depended on whether the train was traveling over level, hilly, or mountainous terrain. It was the crew's responsibility to stop and service the engine with coal and water whenever needed. Shown here is Santa Fe No. 5001, a Baldwin 2-10-4 engine, built in 1938. (Courtesy of Randy Dunson.)

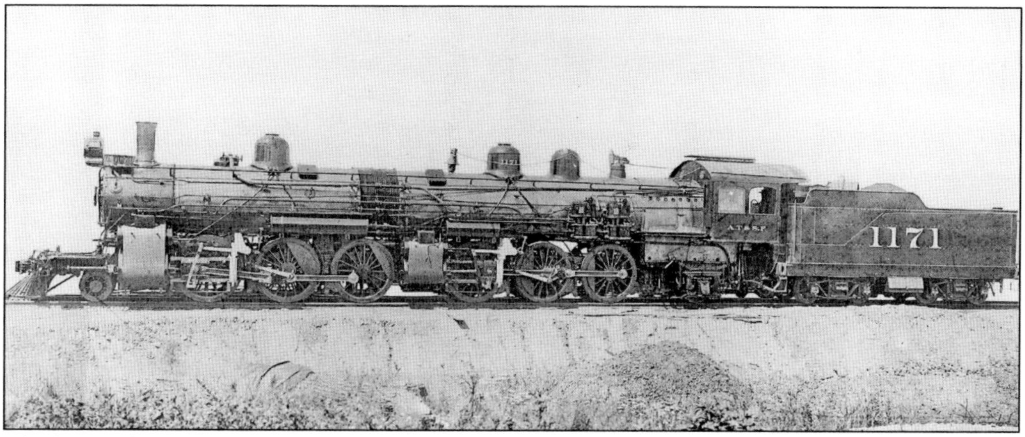

The largest locomotives on the Santa Fe at one time were designed especially for the steep Belen Cutoff. Shown here is AT&SF's No. 1171, a Prairie Mallet 2-6-6-2, built by Baldwin in 1910. Together, engine and tender weighed 533,800 pounds, with a water capacity of 9,000 gallons and a fuel capacity of 12 tons. The boiler operated at a pressure of 220 pounds per square inch. (Courtesy of Randy Dunson.)

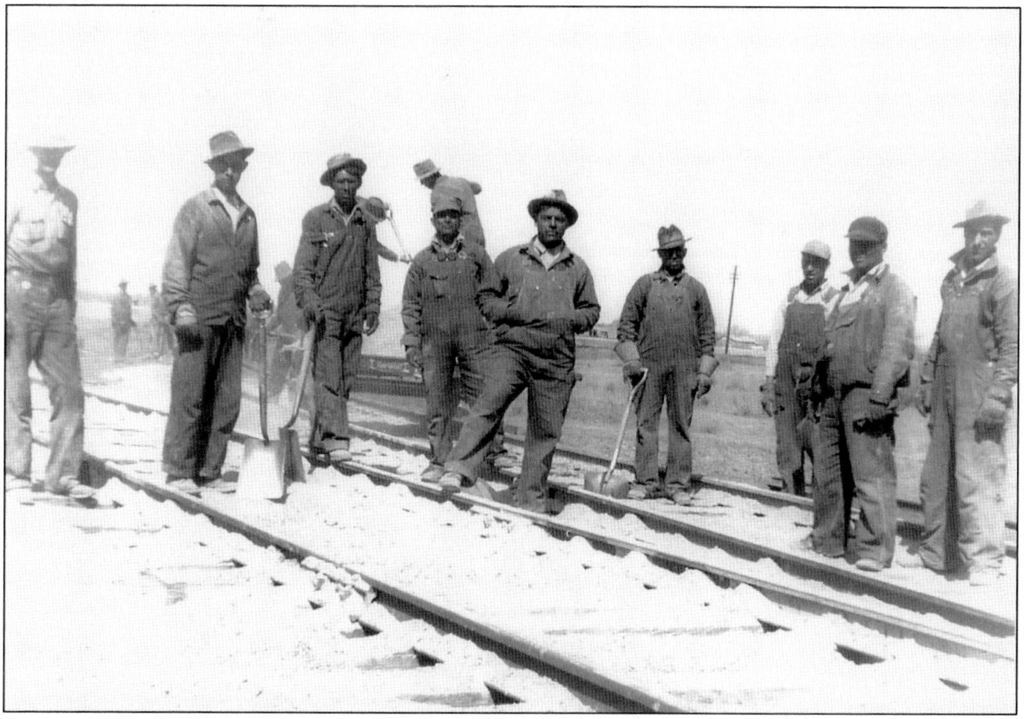

In steam-engine days, section crews consisting of 50 to 60 men were stationed every 30 miles to maintain a specific portion of track. Crew members who can be identified in this 1935 image include, from left to right (starting second from the left), Alejandro Salas, David Biviano, Herman Sisneros, and Leonardo Sisneros. (Courtesy of Randy Dunson.)

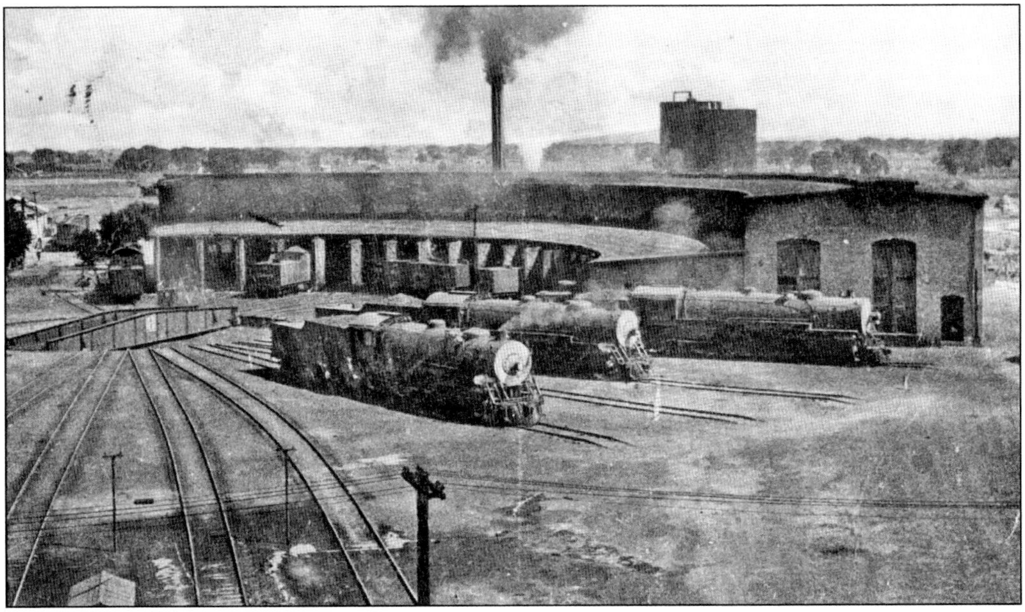

The railroad roundhouse in Belen had 30 stalls for locomotives to be serviced and repaired. The bridge-like device to the left rotated to line up with track sections leading into individual stalls. Crew members, called hostlers, moved the engines and their tenders in and out of the roundhouse. (Courtesy of Valencia County Historical Society.)

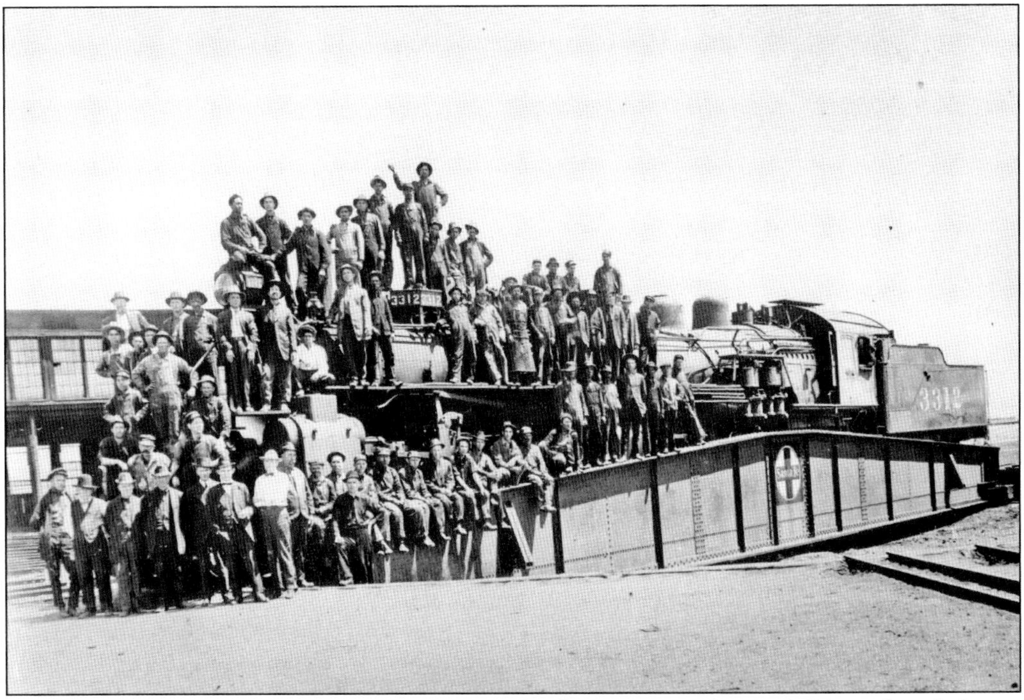

This is the Belen roundhouse crew. At the peak of its activity, the AT&SF employed almost 600 people in Belen, consisting mainly of train-operating, mechanical, and freight office personnel. The railroad became the town's number-one employer. (Courtesy of Valencia County Historical Society.)

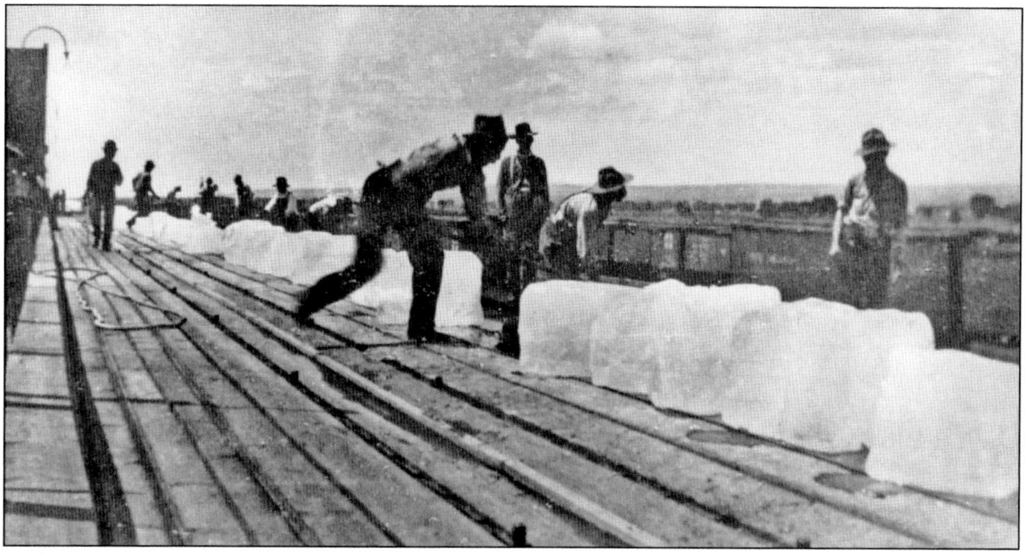

Before automatic refrigeration, perishable produce was transported in specially insulated railroad cars cooled with ice. The job of "icing" a car could require as many as 100 men working on the ice dock. The dock was as high as the top of the refrigerator cars. Three-hundred-pound blocks of ice were broken up and put inside the cars. (Courtesy of Valencia County Historical Society.)

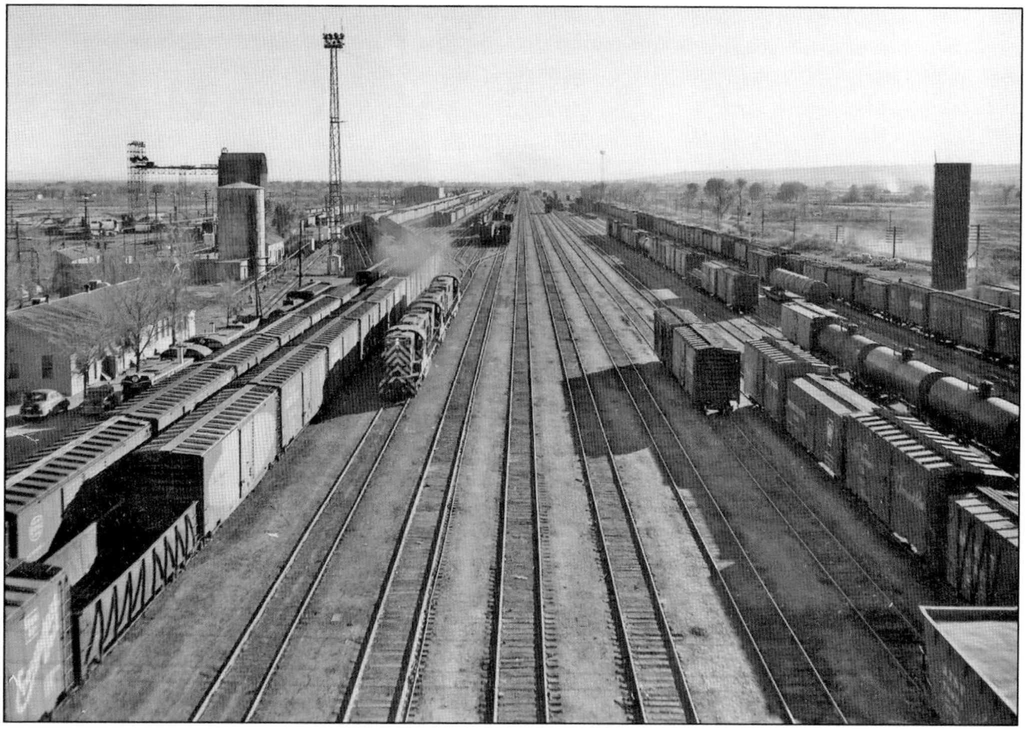

This photograph of the Belen train yard was taken from the Reinken Avenue Viaduct in 1953. Many of the freight trains coming into Belen are destined for the Gulf of Mexico and the East and West Coasts. Santa Fe Railway personnel in Belen classify and organize the cars into trains. Today, more than 100 trains per 24-hour period move through the Belen train yard. (Courtesy of Randy Dunson.)

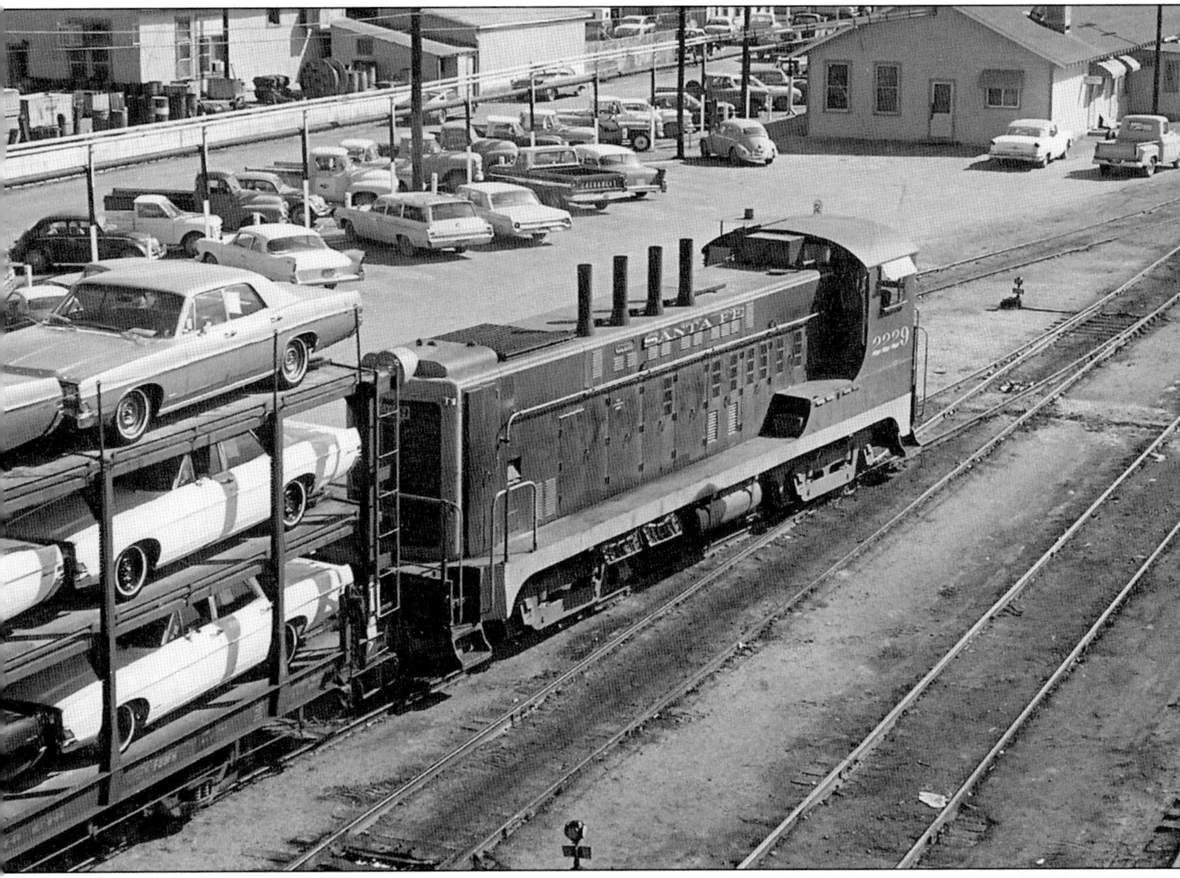

The Belen train yard is shown here in 1968. By this time, diesel-engine locomotives had replaced coal- or oil-fired steam locomotives. The last steam engine–powered freight train operated out of Belen on August 1, 1955. The engine was Santa Fe No. 2920, a Baldwin 4-8-4 locomotive. (Courtesy of Randy Dunson.)

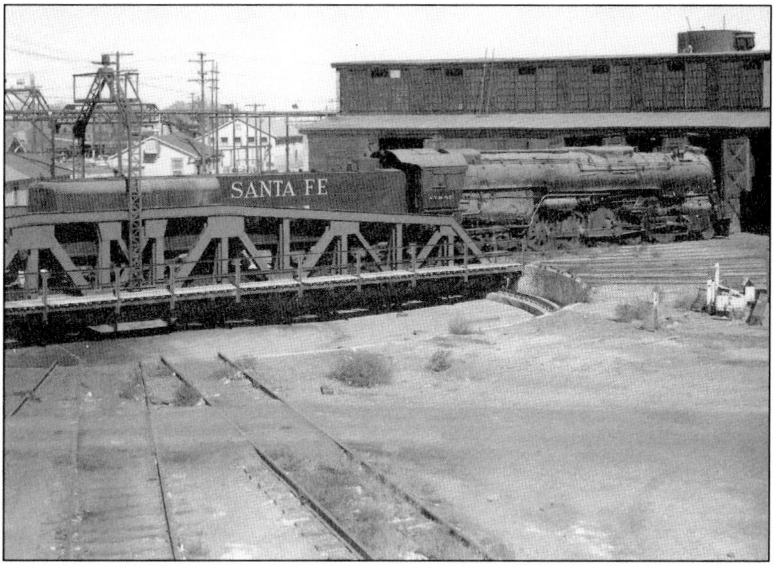

AT&SF engine No. 5021 is pictured at Belen around 1975. This locomotive is now at the California State Railroad Museum in Sacramento, California. A Baldwin 2-10-4, No. 5021 was built in 1944 and the engine with tender weighed 1,000,700 pounds. The boiler operated at 310 pounds per square inch pressure. (Courtesy of Randy Dunson.)

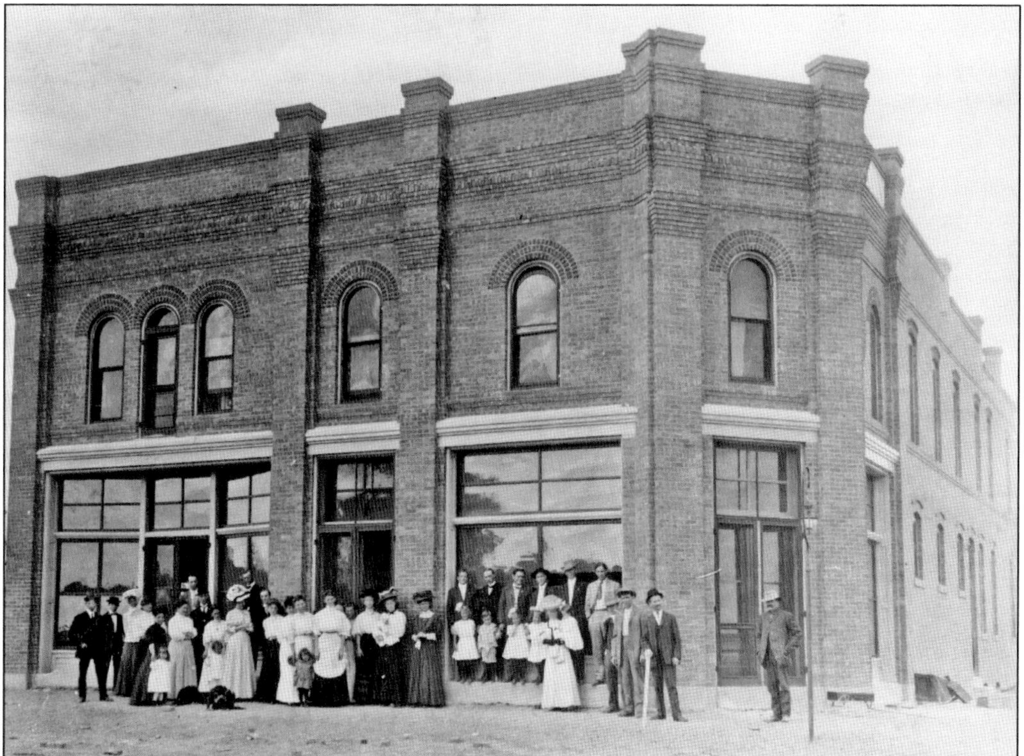

The Belen Hotel, located at the corner of Becker Avenue and Second Street, is seen here in 1907. The Bertha Rutz family and Belen residents lined up in front of the hotel for this photograph taken by an itinerant photographer. The presence of the railroad in Belen created the necessity for full-service hotels. (Courtesy of Valencia County Historical Society.)

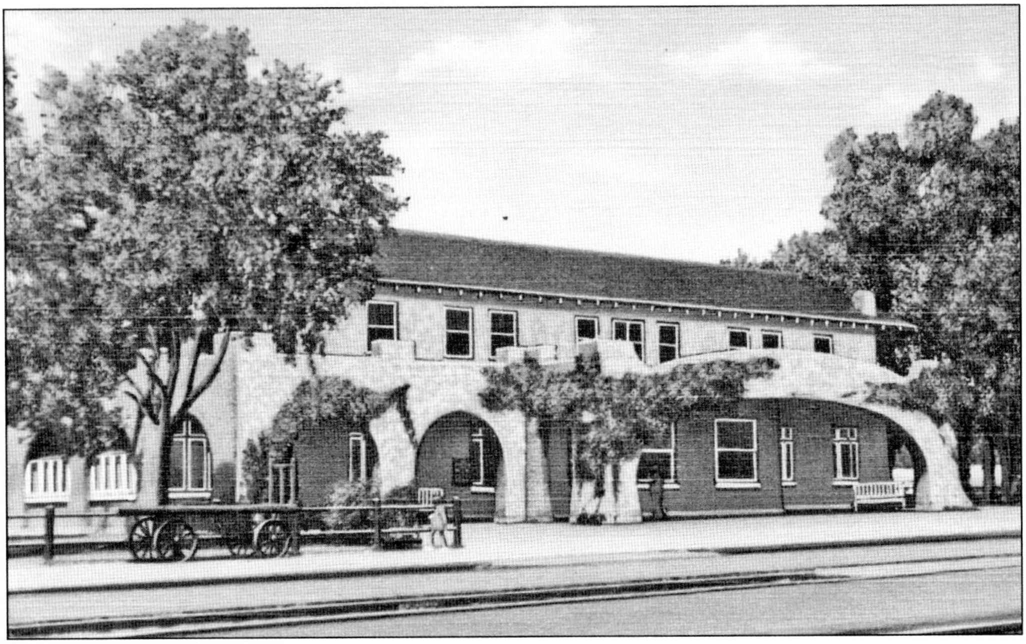

The Belen Harvey House was designed by Santa Fe Railway architect Myron Church in the California Mission Revival style. Construction was completed in December 1910 at a cost of $28,500 (or almost $700,000 in today's dollars). Joseph E. Nelson and Sons of Chicago constructed the building, and many of the workers were brought to Belen by the railroad for the job. Nearly all of the building materials were also shipped to Belen from other locations. In 1983, as a result of efforts by local citizens, the Santa Fe Railway transferred ownership of the Belen Harvey House building to the City of Belen. It is now a successful museum, featuring exhibits of AT&SF and Fred Harvey Company artifacts. It hosts nearly 1,000 visitors per month. (Above, courtesy of Richard Melzer; below, Michael Jaramillo.)

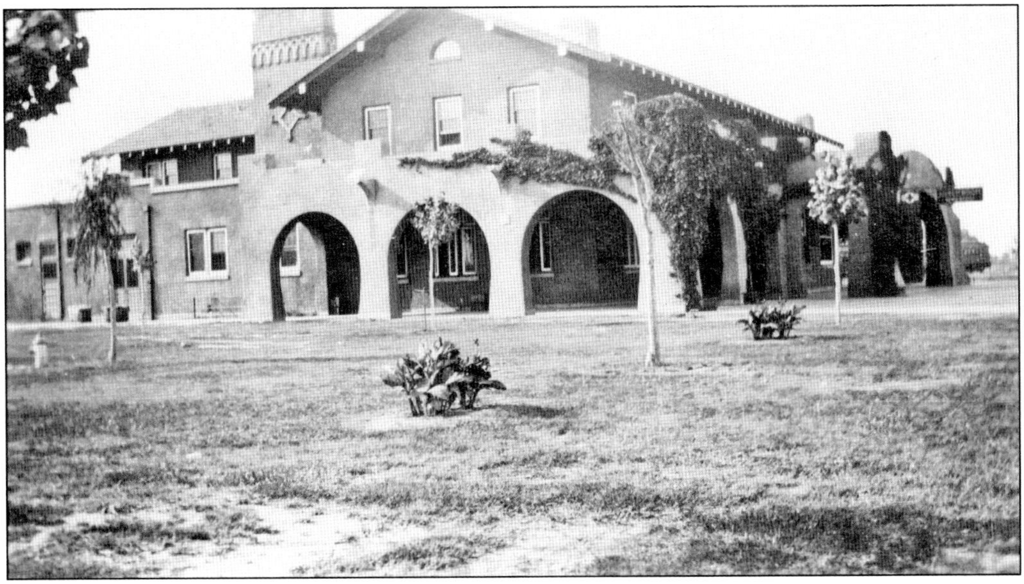

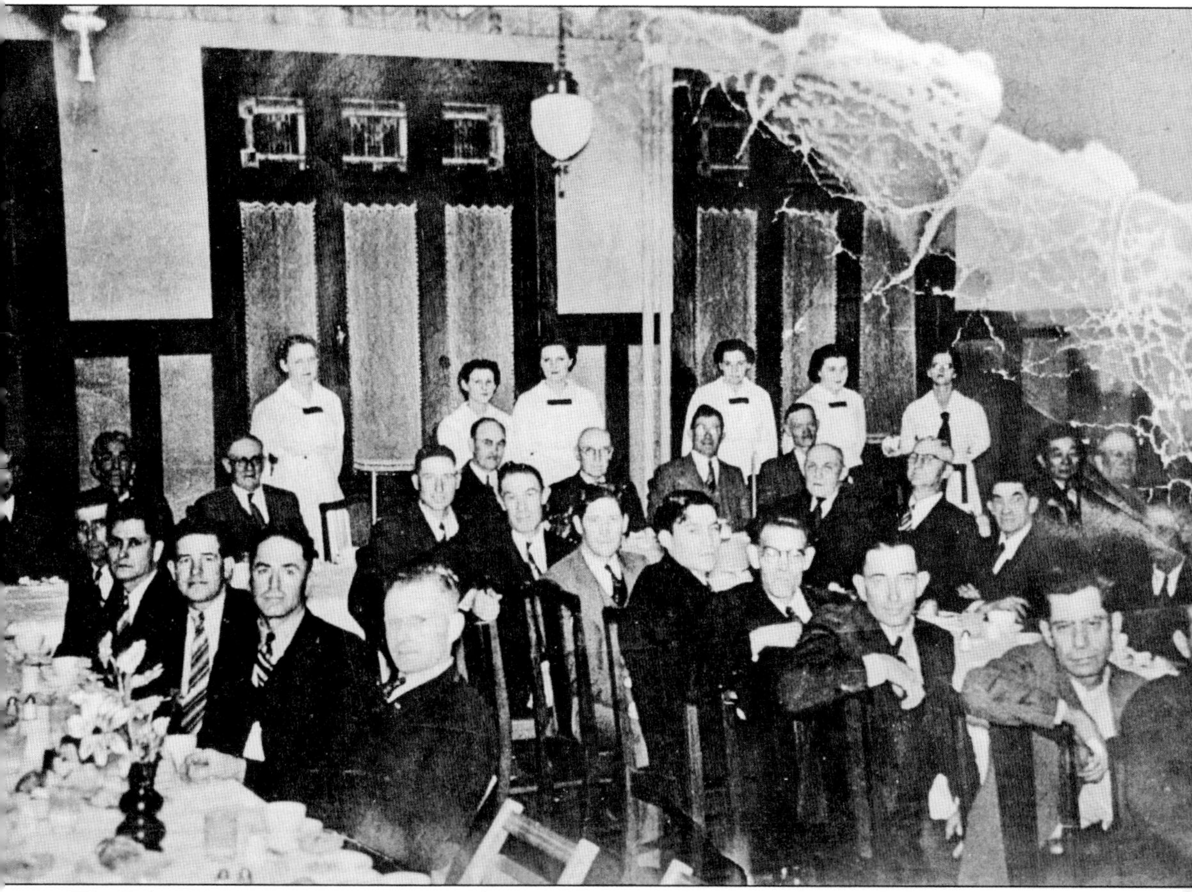

The Belen Harvey House was a center for social activities for the residents of Belen. It was popular among teens as the place to go for that "special" date, even though a Coca-Cola cost 10¢ there and 5¢ at other Belen locations. Civic groups, like the one pictured here in 1930, held many banquets at the building. Six Harvey Girls served this well-dressed crowd. (Courtesy of Valencia County Historical Society.)

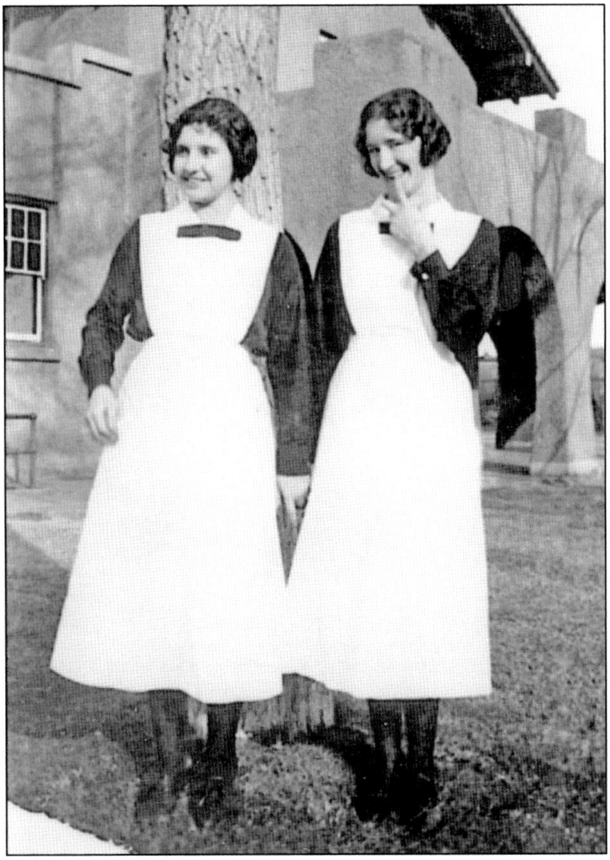

Harvey Girls, specially trained Harvey House servers, all wore a company prescribed uniform consisting of a black dress with a heavily starched white apron, black shoes, and a black bow tie. The girls had to pass daily inspections, and if uniforms became soiled in any way, they had to be changed. (Courtesy of Belen Harvey House Museum.)

Spotless and sparkling dining facilities, professional kitchen personnel, and well-trained and disciplined Harvey Girl servers were all hallmarks of the Fred Harvey operations throughout the West. Pictured here from left to right are Clara Raymond, Louise Pinkerton, Madge Pinkerton, Wilma Tinker, Rose Sanders, and Gena Powell. (Courtesy of Belen Harvey House Museum.)

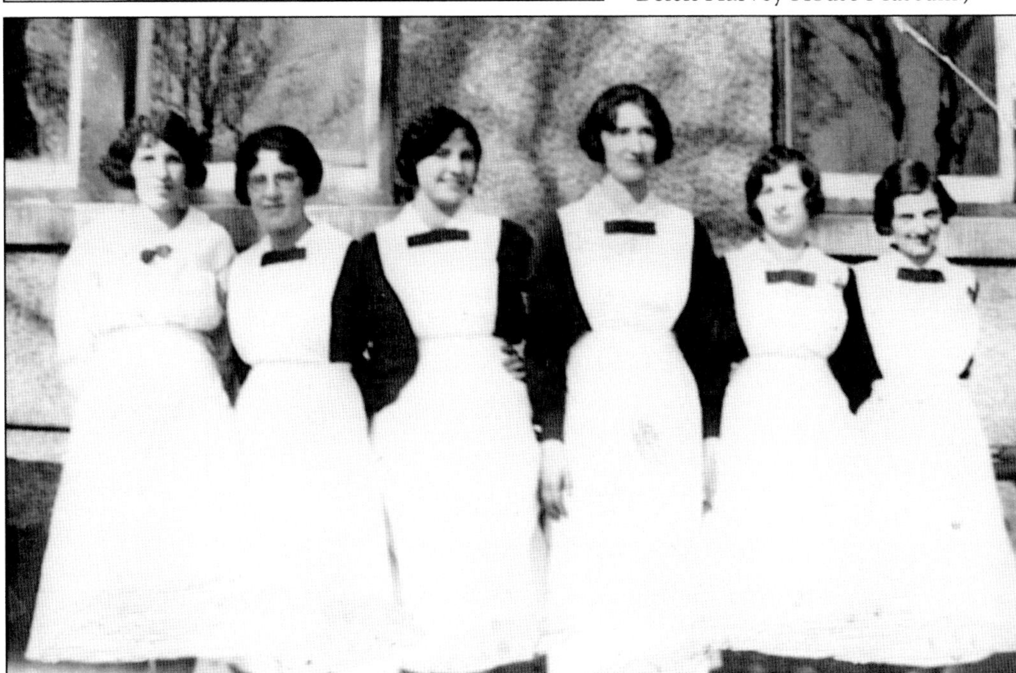

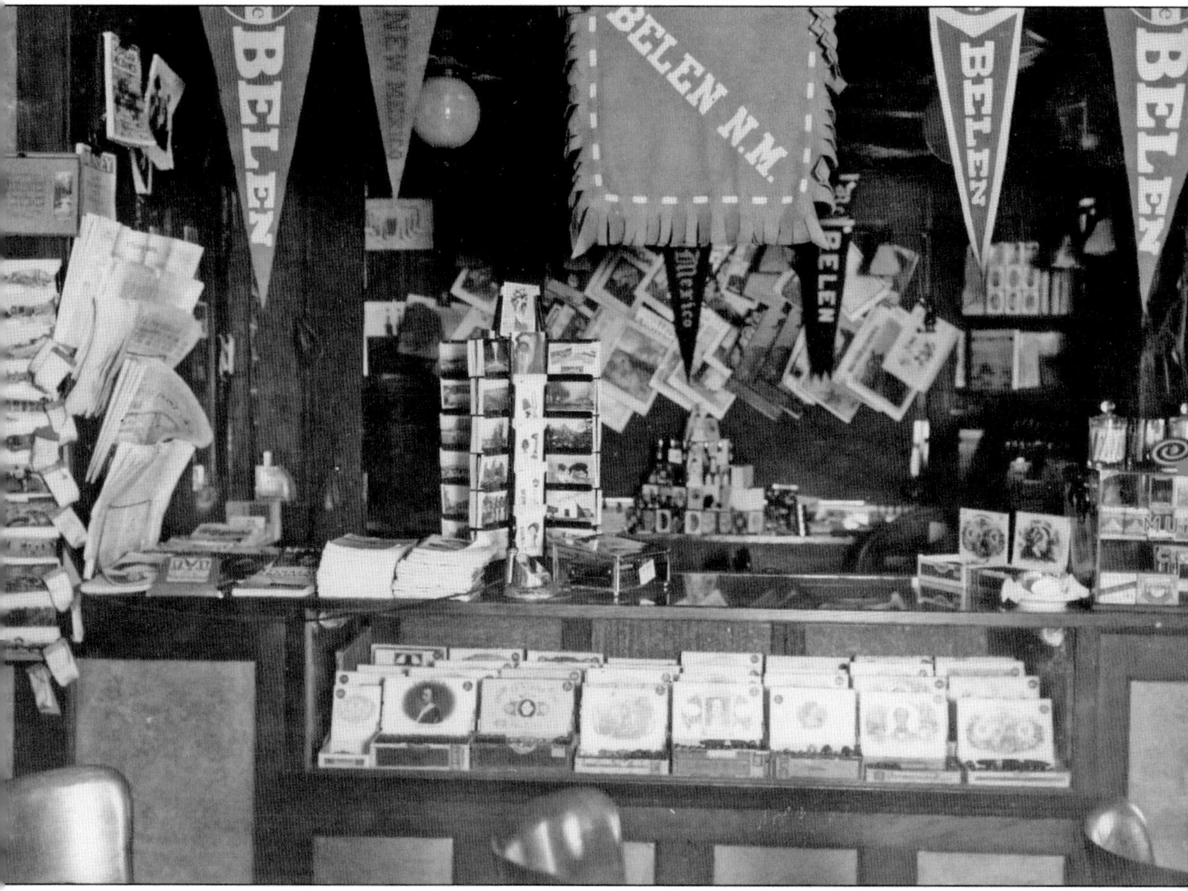

In order to insure high quality and fair pricing in supplying the needs of railroad passengers, the Fred Harvey Company operated newsstands at Harvey Houses. This photograph, taken by Bullock's Photography Studio, shows the large variety of items sold at the newsstand in the Belen Harvey House. (Courtesy of Belen Harvey House Museum.)

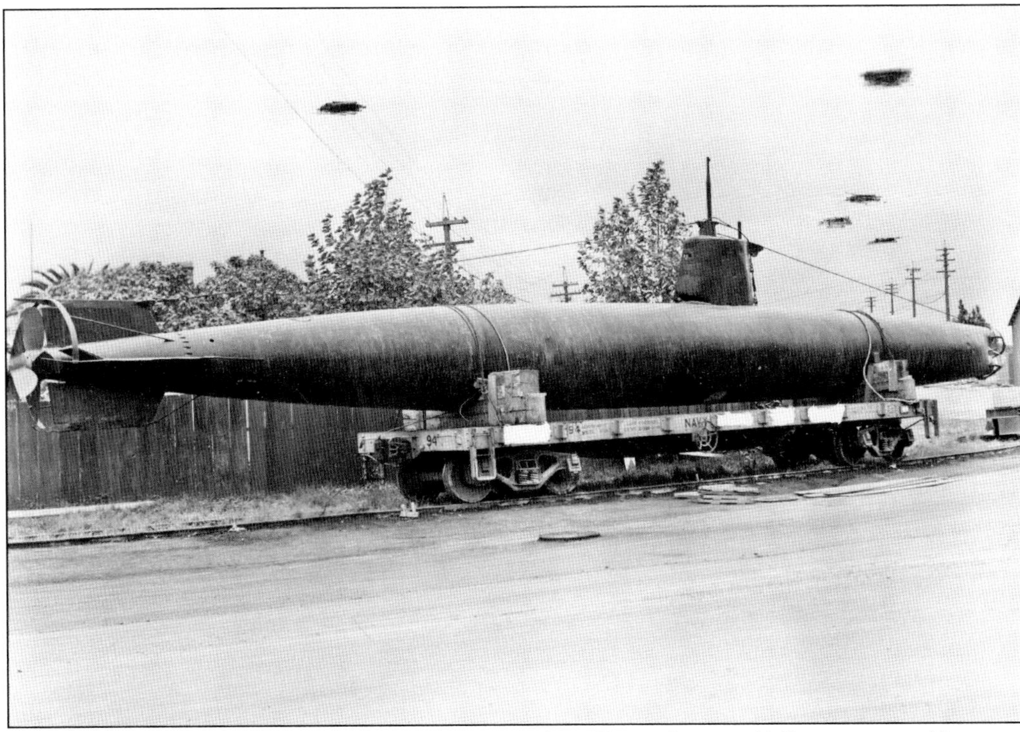

The railroad brought many unique attractions to Belen. Shown here in 1943 is a captured Japanese World War II mini-submarine. It is similar to the submarines that entered Pearl Harbor during the Japanese attack in 1941. This sub toured around the country, and local schoolchildren got time off from classes to see it and help sell war bonds. (Courtesy of Valencia County Historical Society.)

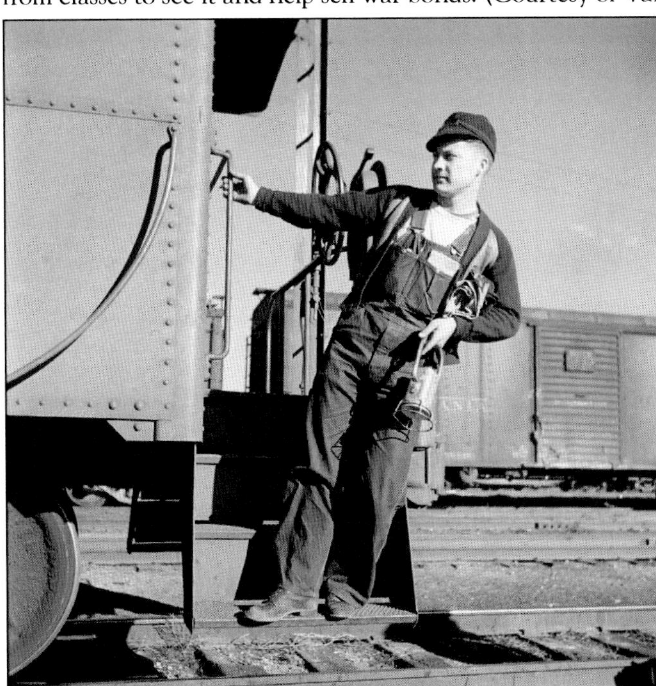

C.G. Kirkland, a brakeman on the Atchison, Topeka and Santa Fe Railway, is shown here getting off a caboose, the last car of a train. Jack Delano took this photograph in March 1943, when he visited Belen to document conditions for the New Deal Farm Security Administration. (Courtesy of Library of Congress, LC-USW3-020762-E.)

Four

A Growing Business Community

Prior to 1821, under Spanish rule, commercial trade was restricted to merchandise obtained via the Camino Real, or Royal Road, between Santa Fe, New Mexico, and Chihuahua, Mexico. With Mexican independence from Spain, trade continued along El Camino Real, but was also expanded to include goods brought over the Santa Fe Trail between St. Louis, Missouri, and Santa Fe.

In 1856, Jose Felipe Chaves moved from Bernalillo, New Mexico, to Belen and established a mercantile business with goods obtained from wagon trains on El Camino Real and the Santa Fe Trail. By 1860, he was listed as one of the five richest Hispanic merchants in New Mexico.

John Becker first came to Belen in 1873 to manage the store owned by Louis Huning of Los Lunas, New Mexico. In 1878, with financial assistance from Jose Felipe Chaves, he opened his own mercantile store. In 1903, John Becker was one of the founders of the First National Bank of Belen, and in 1910 he served as a delegate from Valencia County to the state constitutional convention.

In 1877, John Becker married Anna Vielstich of Milwaukee, Wisconsin. Anna's sisters all married men who worked for the John Becker Company. Johana Vielstich married John Becker's brother Frederick. Meta Vielstich married Carl Dalies, and Katherine Vielstich married Bernhard Reinken. These four families provided business and civic leaders to the community of Belen well into the 20th century. Other German immigrants who came to Belen and established businesses were Moses Sachs, Frederick Scholle, and Oscar Goebel. Two former clerks for the John Becker Company, Paul Feil and William Ellermeyer, later formed their own business in Belen, the Feil and Ellermeyer Company.

John Becker was instrumental in laying out the Belen Townsite Plan in 1903. In 1905, he joined forces with Jose Felipe Chaves to convince the AT&SF Railway to establish the western terminus of the Abo Canyon Cutoff in Belen. John Becker donated the land for the rail yard and depot to the railroad.

Beginning with the coming of the railroad to Belen in 1880, and accelerating with the opening of the Belen Cutoff through Abo Canyon in 1908, the Belen business community grew rapidly to meet the needs of a similarly growing population.

Businessmen, like Paul Feil, began working for John Becker at his mercantile store before branching out to open stores of their own. The railroad also brought opportunity to Bertha Rutz and Tom and Mary Seery when they opened hotels near the Belen Harvey House and the Belen Depot. Roy and Nelson Buckland opened a pharmacy, and several businessmen opened automobile dealerships.

The first newspaper in Belen was the *Hispano American*, owned and edited by Saturnino Baca. It was turned over to his son Elfego Baca in 1920 before it merged in 1947 with the *Belen News* to become the *Belen News Bulletin*. That newspaper is still published as the *Valencia County News Bulletin*.

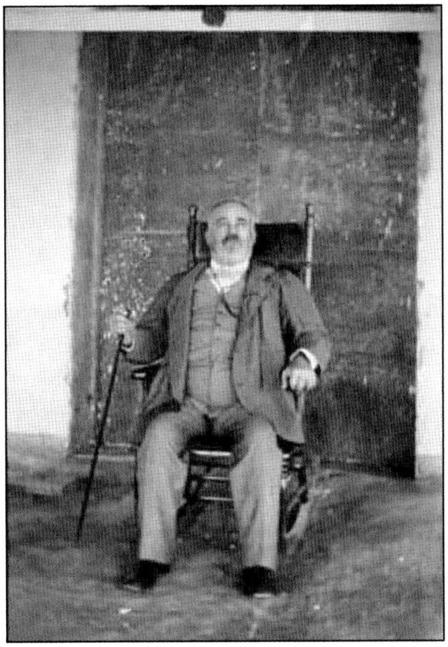

Jose Felipe Chaves (1835–1905) was an early merchant in Belen. With investments in many additional businesses, from banking to the New York Stock Exchange, Chaves was so successful and wealthy that he was known as "El Millonario." An 1870 list of the wealthiest Hispanic men in New Mexico had Chaves second in the territory. Jose Leandro Perea from Bernalillo was the wealthiest man. (Courtesy of Valencia County Historical Society.)

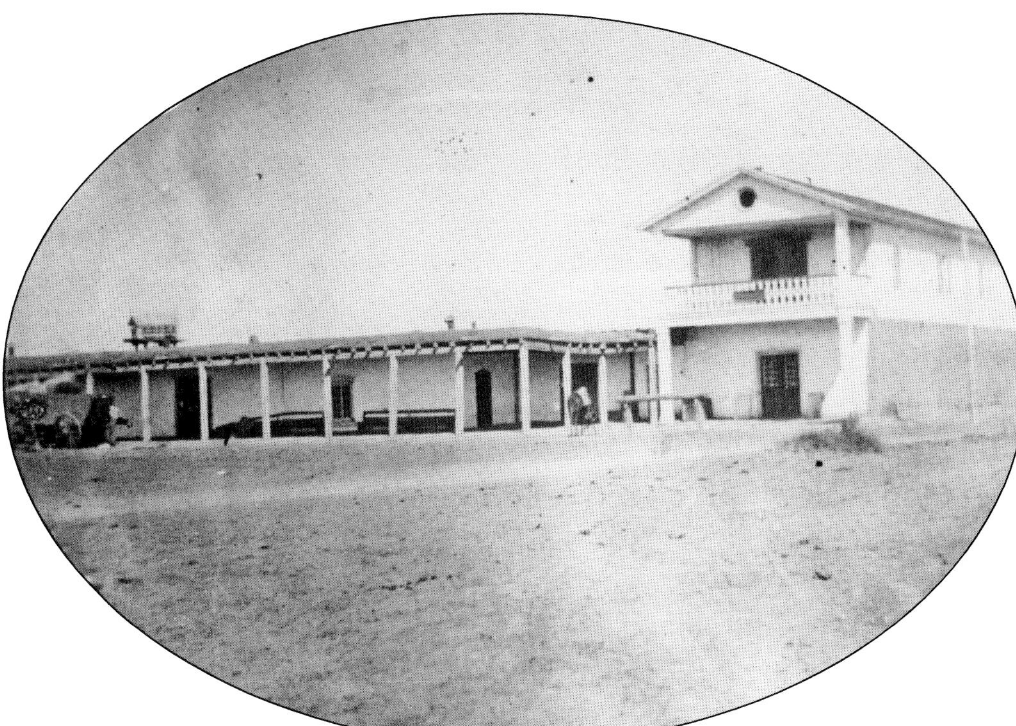

Jose Felipe Chaves's mercantile business was located where the Walgreens Drug Store on Main Street is today. The store was in the two-story building to the right in this photograph. The one-story buildings to the left were used for storage of hay, grain, and wool. (Courtesy of Valencia County Historical Society.)

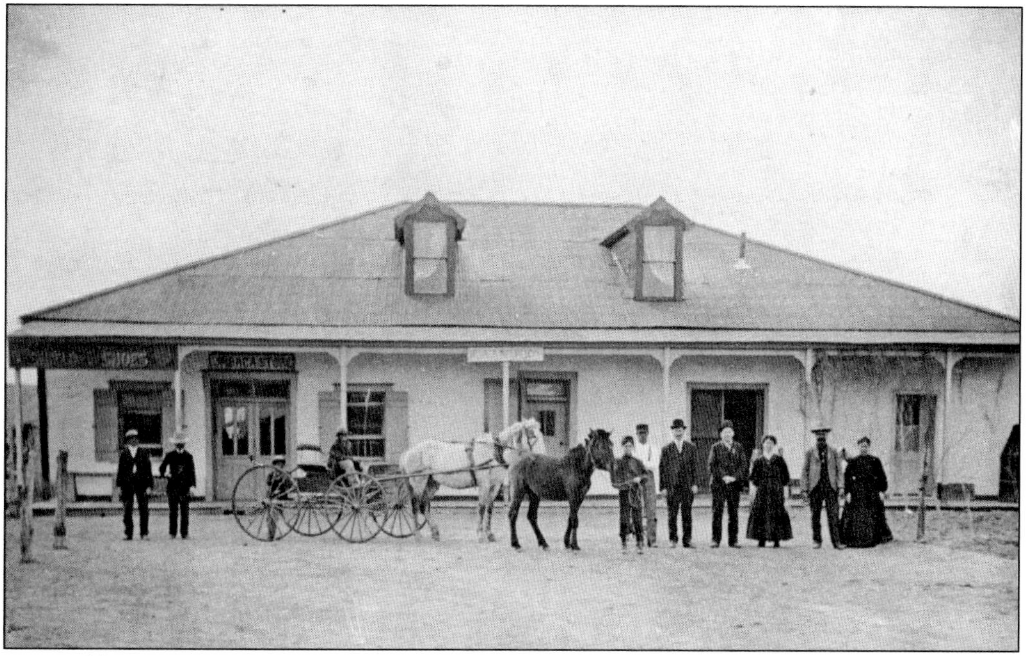

Pictured here is Juan Rey Baca's mercantile store, located to the south of Belen's central business area. This area of town was called Bacaville. The four people on the right are, from left to right, Tim B. Baca, Trinity B. Chavez, Juan Rey Baca, and Guadalupe Baca. (Courtesy of Valencia County Historical Society.)

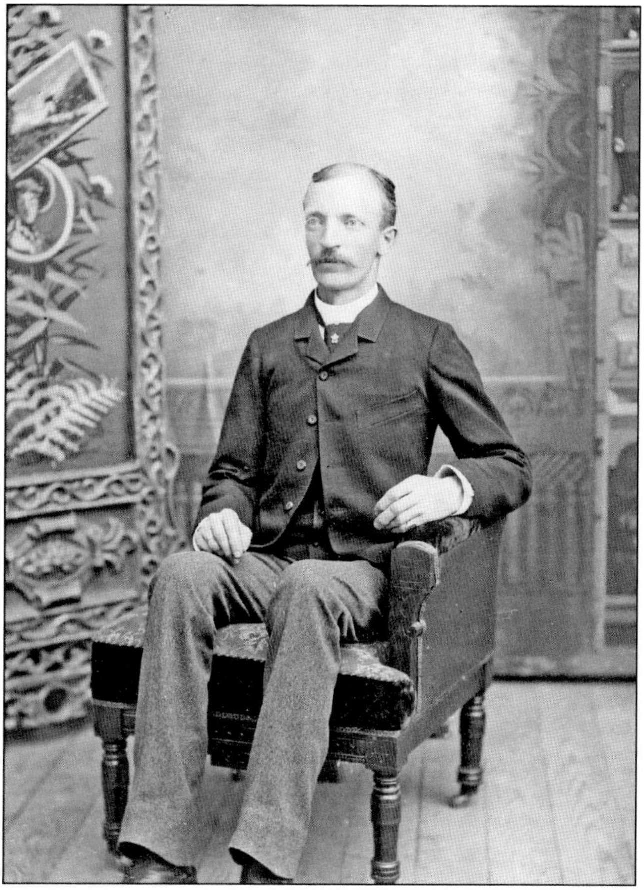

John Becker was born in 1850, in Hanover, Germany. Four Becker brothers came to the United States: John and Frederick to New Mexico, Gustav to Arizona, and Herman to Louisiana. John managed Louis Huning's store in Belen, starting in 1873. In 1877, with encouragement and financial support from Jose Felipe Chaves, he went into the mercantile business for himself. This photograph was taken by Mrs. Albright's Art Parlor in Albuquerque. (Courtesy Belen Harvey House Museum.)

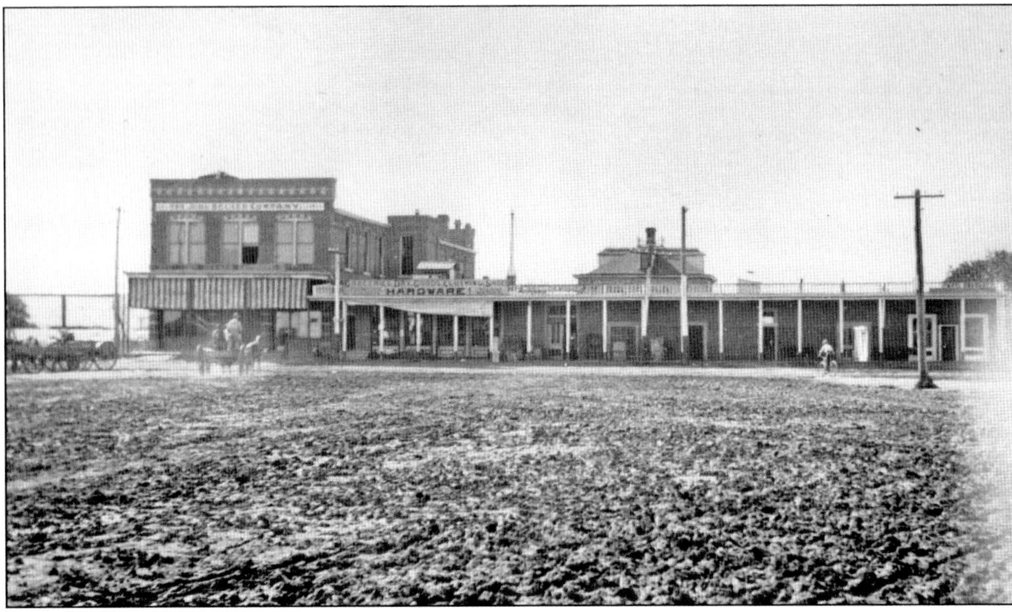

The John Becker Company included mercantile products, banking services, and a post office. John Becker, with several other stockholders, started the First National Bank of Belen in 1903 and located it inside his store. The only bank robbery in the history of the First National Bank of Belen occurred on Friday, January 15, 1904. The robbers eluded a posse of 50 men and escaped with an estimated $25,000. (Courtesy of Valencia County Historical Society.)

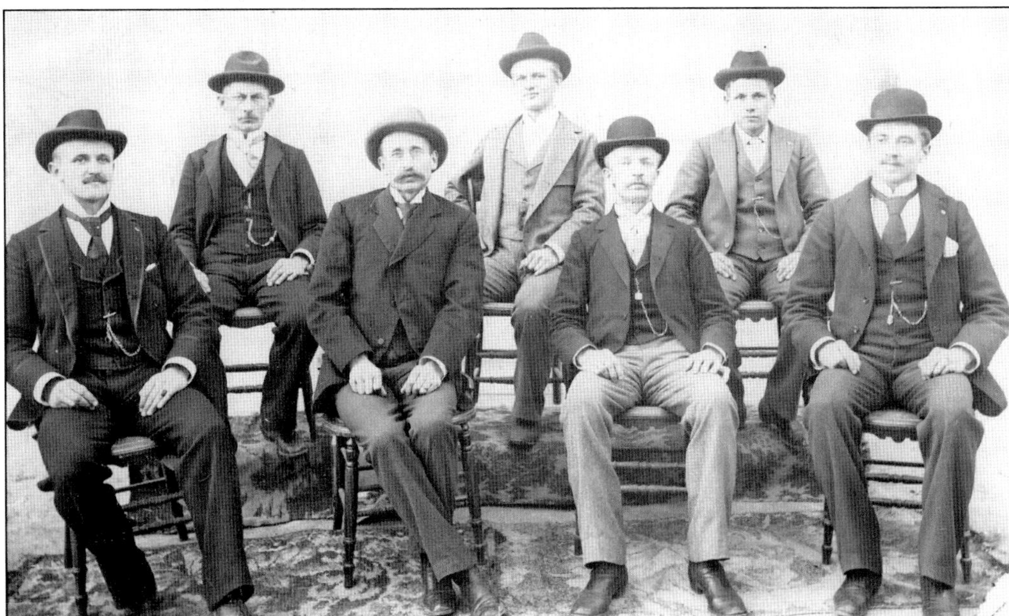

John Becker poses with his staff in 1896. From left to right are (first row) Paul Dalies, Theo Muenstermann, Becker, and Charles Reinken; (second row) John Douglas, Carl Dalies, and Louis Vielstich. Becker incorporated his business and shared his success with several of his faithful, long-time employees, including those pictured here. Becker, Reinken, Dalies, and Vielstich were all related by marriage. (Courtesy Belen Harvey House Museum.)

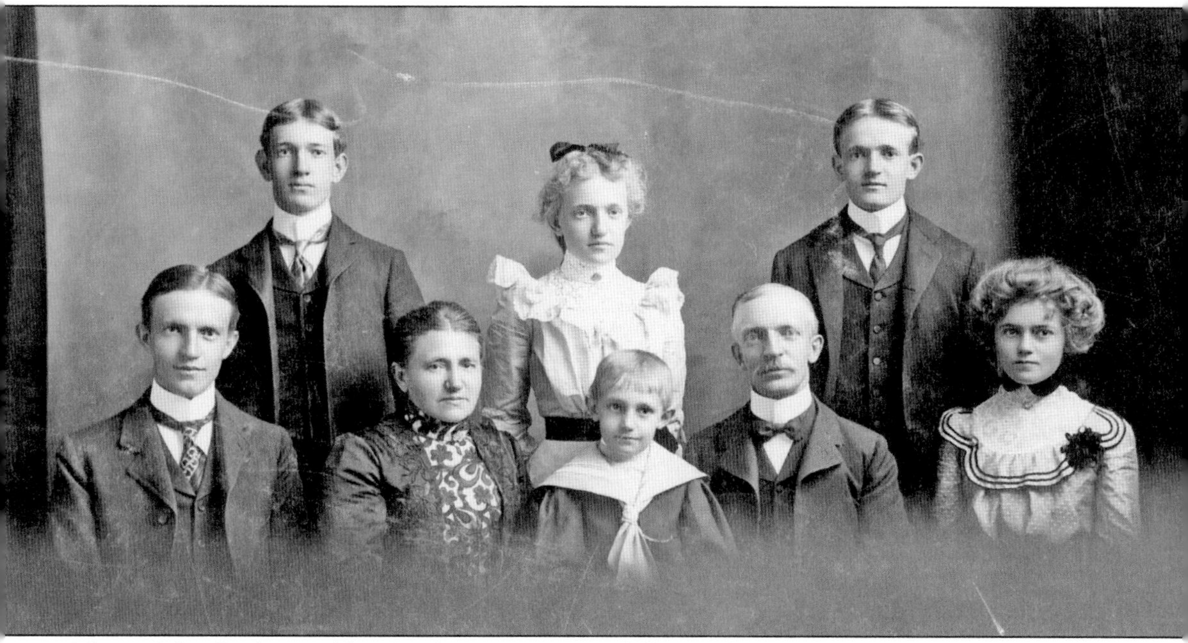

This is John Becker and his family in 1903. From left to right are (first row) Louis C., Anna Vielstich Becker, Ben, John Becker Sr., and Anita; (second row) Gustav, Lucie, and Hans. Anna worked in John Becker's mercantile store, and Hans was a partner with his father in the company. Louis C. spent his career working for the First National Bank of Belen. (Courtesy of Belen Harvey House Museum.)

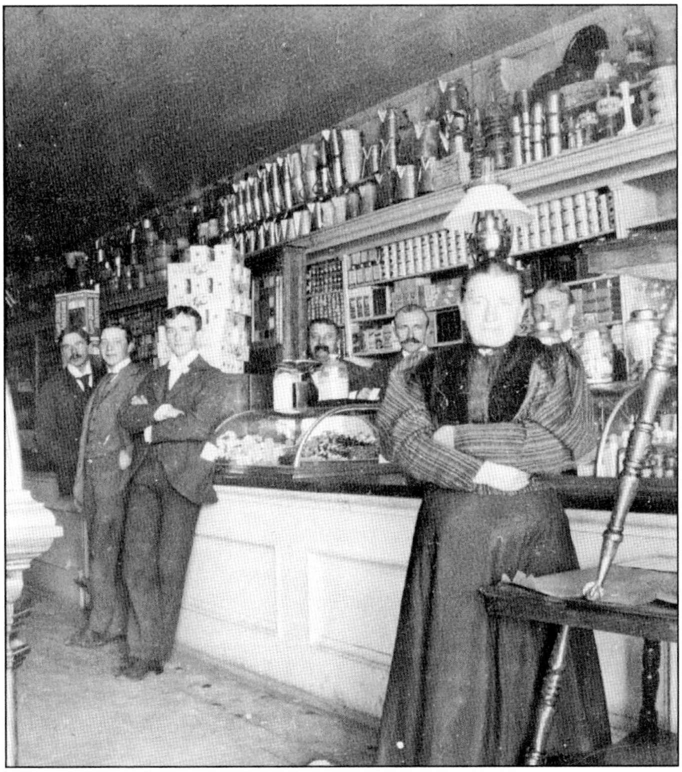

At left is the John Becker store interior around 1900. From left to right are Charles Reinken, unidentified, Hans Becker (John's son), unidentified, Carl Dalies, Anna Vielstich Becker (John's wife), and Paul Dalies. Below is another view of the interior of John Becker's mercantile store around 1900. The extensive range of products sold at the store included groceries; hardware; men's wear; shoes for men, women, and children; ready-to-wear clothing; furniture; pharmaceuticals; wine; whiskey; hay; lumber; coal; firewood; flour; wool; livestock feed; gas; oil; grease; and later automobiles, tractors, and caskets. (Both courtesy of Valencia County Historical Society.)

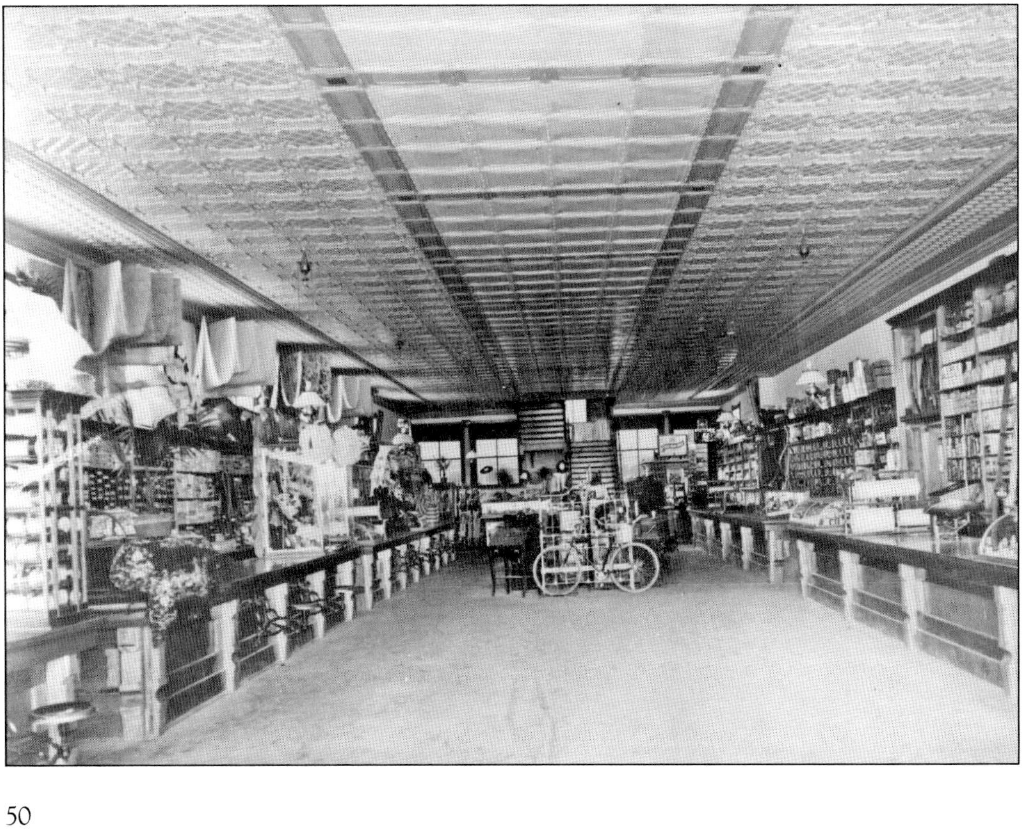

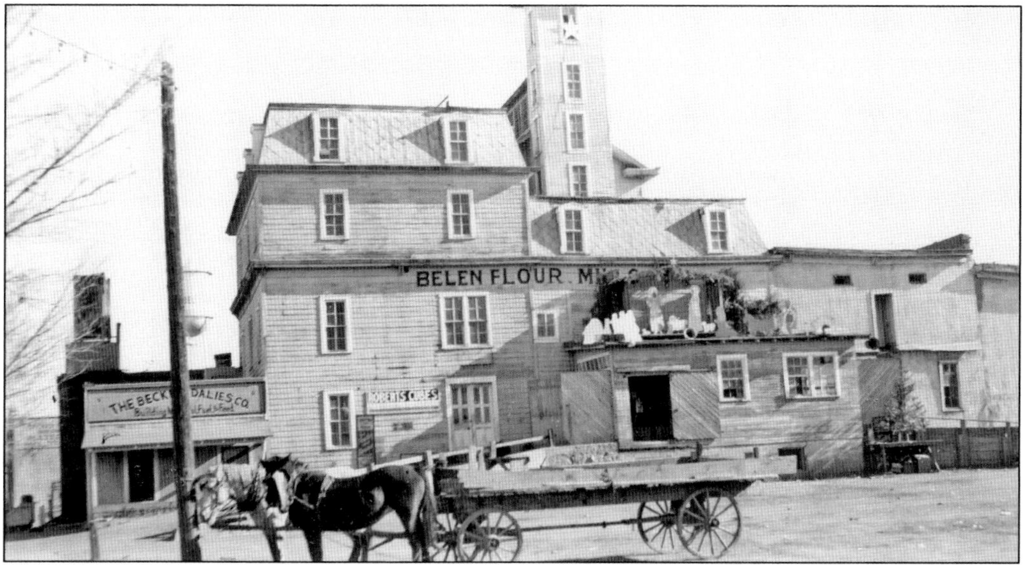

John Becker erected this steam-powered flour mill, located directly across Main Street from his mercantile store, in 1884. Local farmers would exchange 100 pounds of wheat for 50 pounds of flour. The mill is pictured here in 1937, decorated for the Christmas holidays. (Courtesy of Belen Harvey House Museum.)

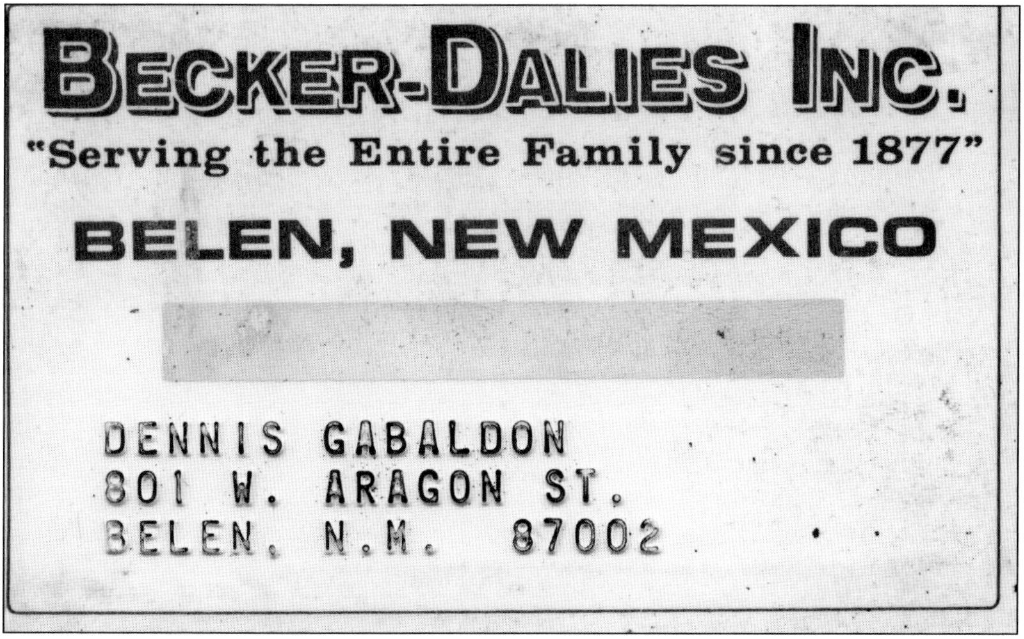

As the company that John Becker started in the 1870s entered the 20th century, it evolved to bring new products and services to customers in Belen and the surrounding area. The Becker Dalies Company had always extended credit, keeping accounts in hand-posted ledgers. In the 1960s, the company began using credit cards, like the one shown here issued to Dennis Gabaldon. (Courtesy of Theresa Gabaldon Baca.)

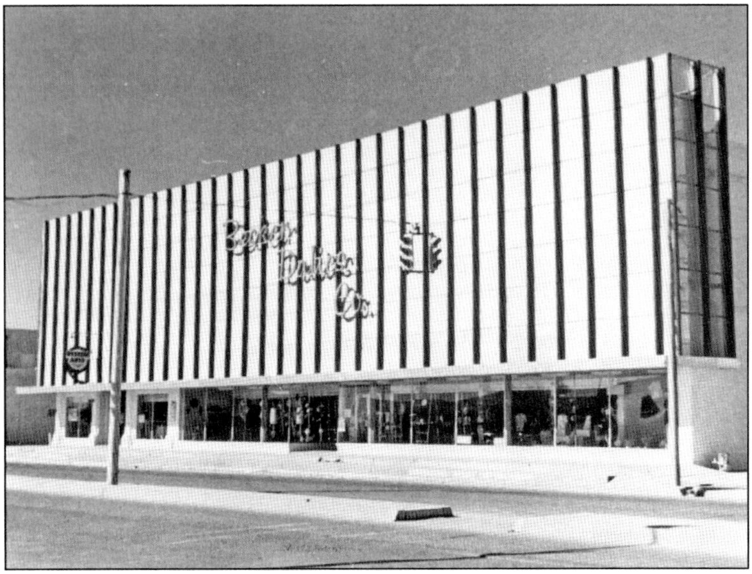

In the 1960s, the John Becker Company, reincorporated as the Becker-Dalies Company, was given a face-lift. Sidewalk-level display windows were added, along with a wire-mesh façade. Incorporation allowed John Becker to share the company's success with his employees and other investors. (Courtesy of the Valencia County Historical Society.)

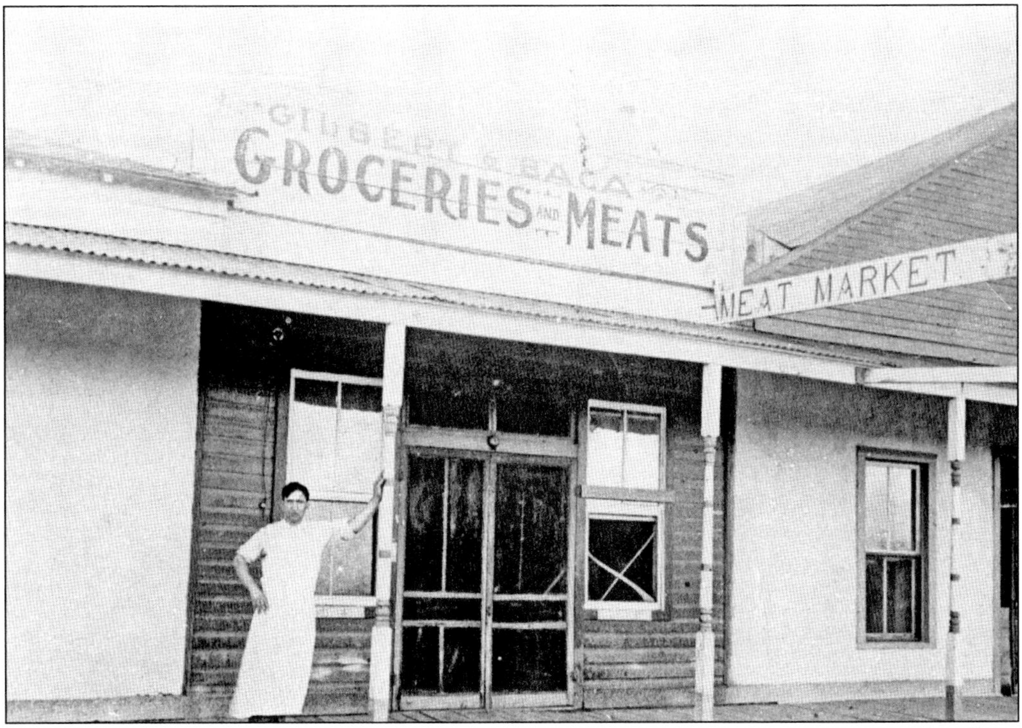

Antonio Gilbert's meat market, pictured here in 1920, was located on Main Street. Behind the store was his cousin Andres Garcia's original meat market. In true family tradition, when supplies were low and there was a paying customer, the families would meet the other's needs. It was not uncommon for meat to leave Garcia's store and go in the back door of Gilbert's. (Courtesy of Belen Harvey House Museum.)

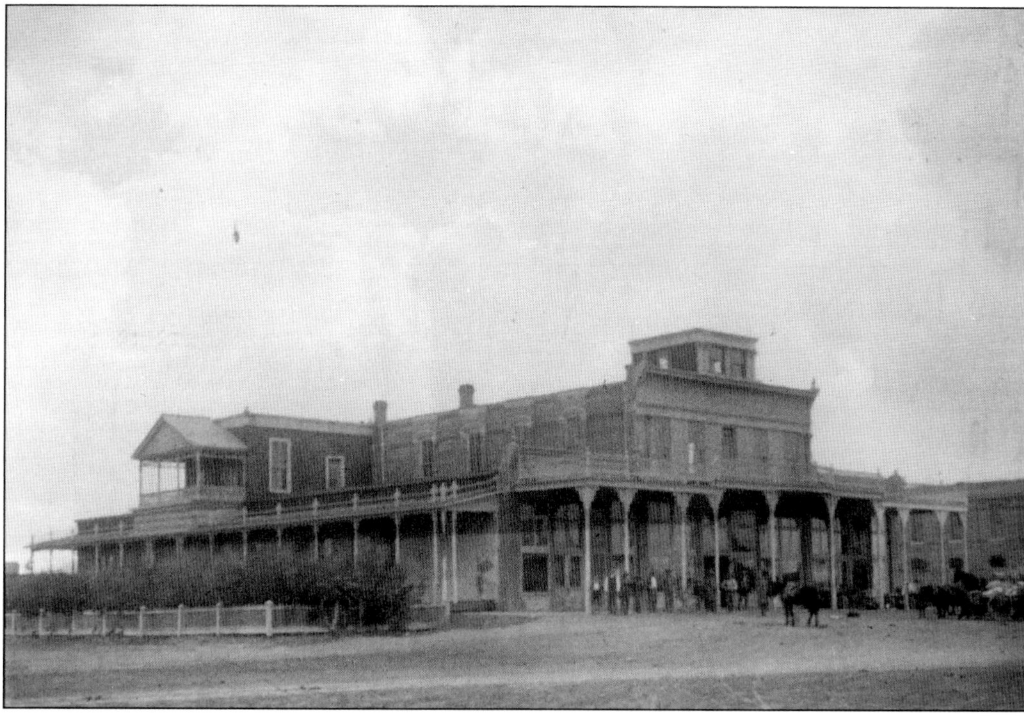

Fred Scholle immigrated to Belen from Germany in the 1880s. Like John Becker before him, he managed Louis Huning's Belen store. When he built his own mercantile store on Main Street, he modeled it after a Swiss chalet. The store was later purchased by William Ellermeyer and Paul J. Feil. (Courtesy of Valencia County Historical Society.)

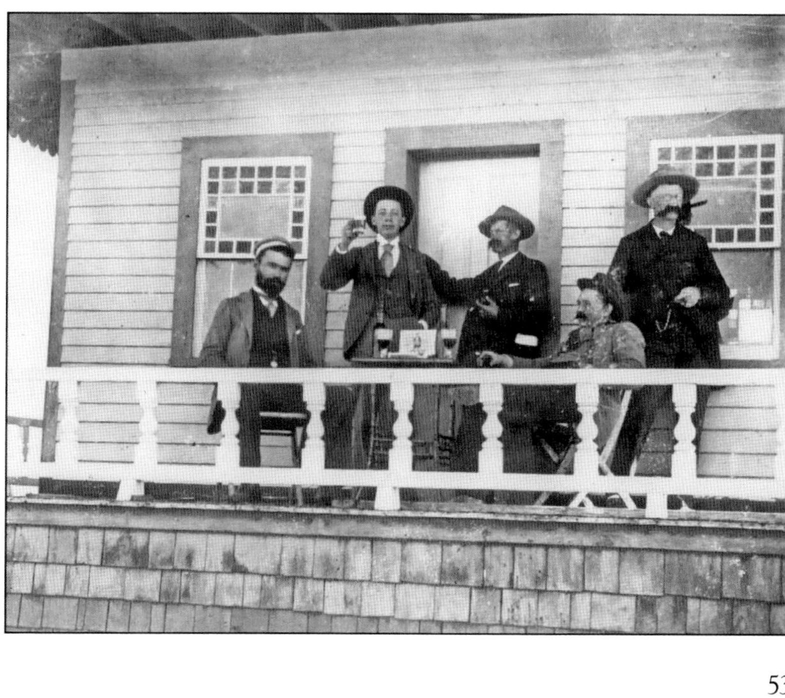

The cupola on top of the Scholle building was a popular place for young businessmen to gather and drink beer at the end of the day. Pictured here around 1890 are, from left to right, Chris Scholle, Carl Becker, Bill Speckman, Arthur Goebel, and Theo Muenstermann. (Courtesy of Valencia County Historical Society.)

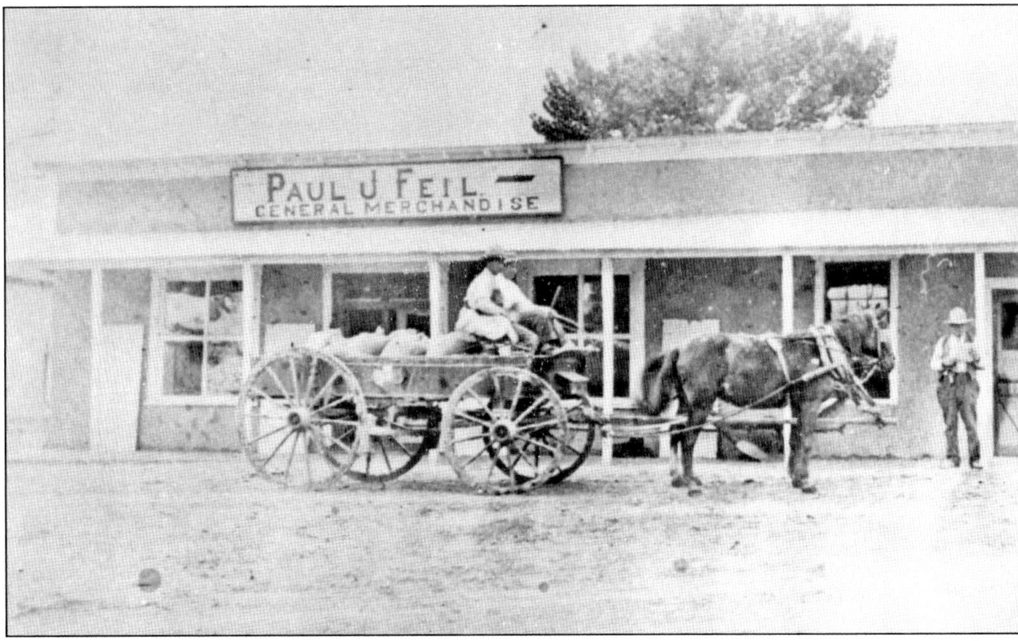

Paul J. Feil's first store was located at Jarales in 1913. Sitting on the wagon are Jose D. Olguin and Eduardo Sanchez, both grandchildren of Nicolas S. Sanchez, who stands by the porch post reading the newspaper. Feil soon joined William Ellermeyer and moved the mercantile business to Fred Scholle's store in Belen in 1919. (Courtesy of Valencia County Historical Society.)

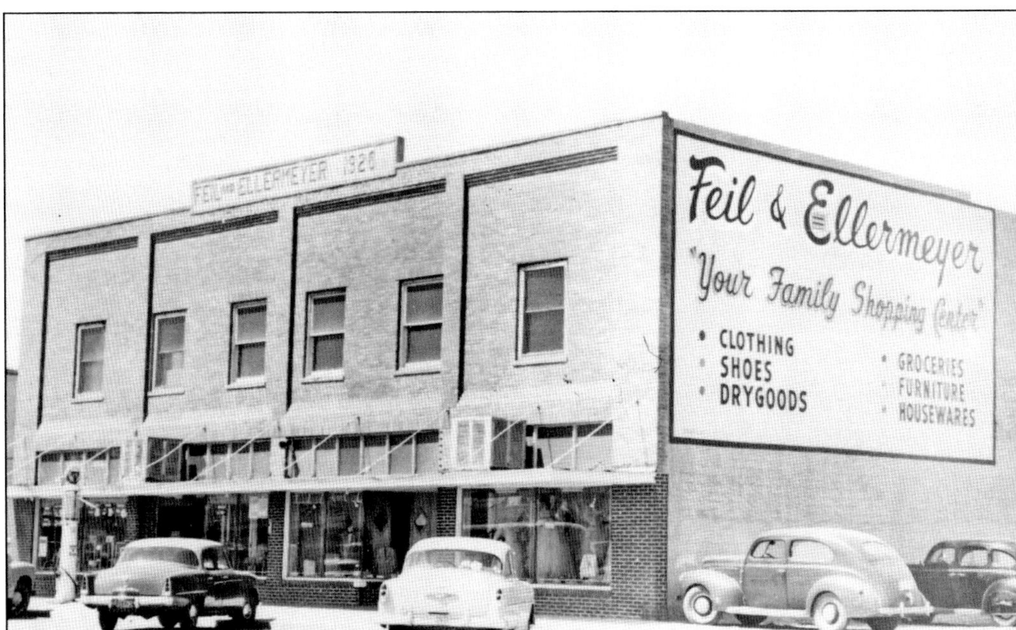

Paul J. Feil and William Ellermeyer had their mercantile business in Fred Scholle's Swiss chalet–style building from 1919 until 1928, when they constructed this two-story brick building. It is shown here in the early 1950s. (Courtesy of Valencia County Historical Society.)

German immigrants came to America traveling on trans-Atlantic steamships. Luise Feil Ellermeyer is the woman on the far right with shipboard friends on her first passage to the United States in January 1912. (Courtesy of Valencia County Historical Society.)

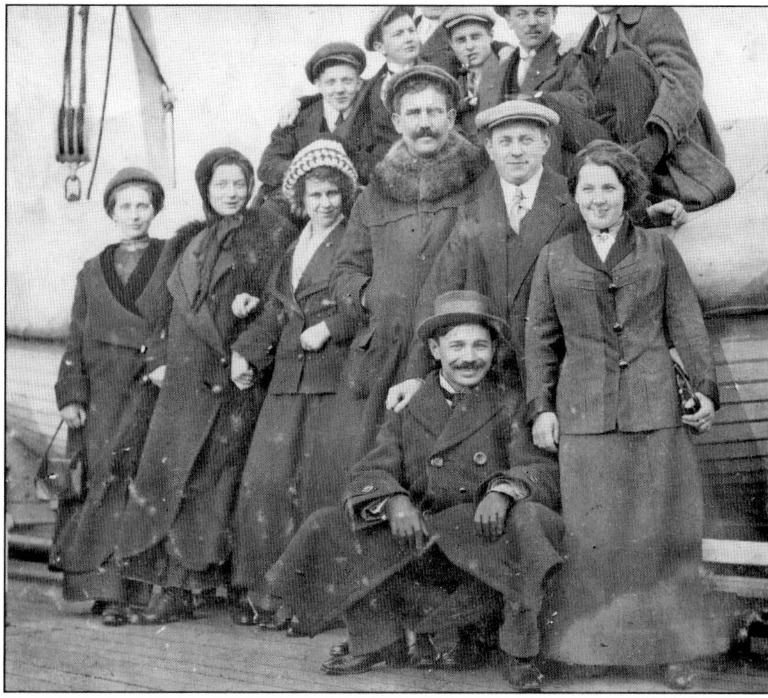

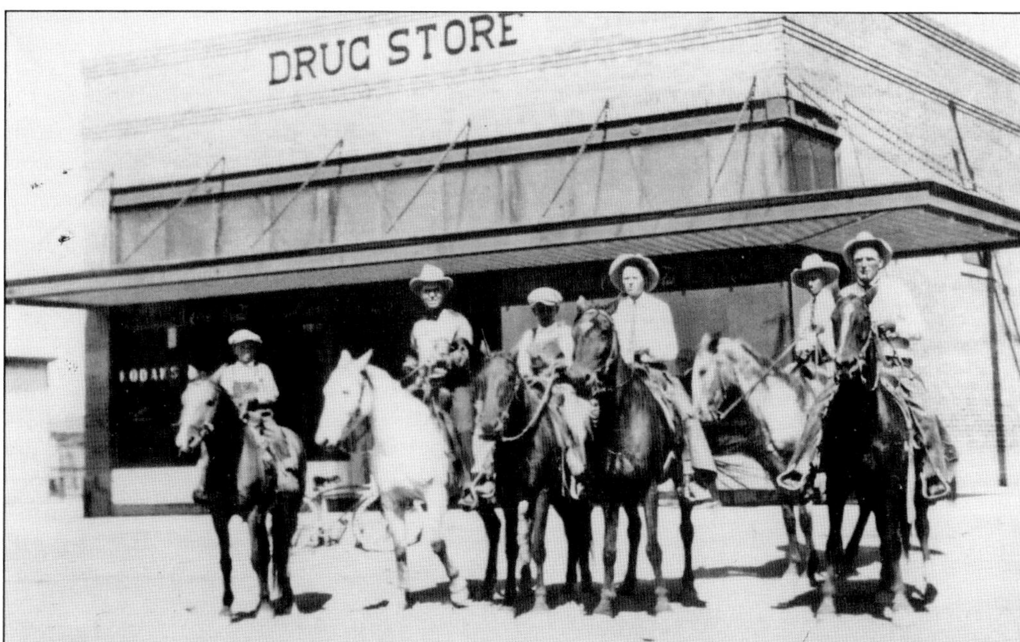

Roy Buckland and his brother Nelson wanted to open a drugstore in Belen. John Becker viewed them as competition and refused to sell them property. While John was on a trip to Germany, his son Hans got into a poker game with Roy and lost the property Buckland wanted. Roy had the building constructed before John returned from Germany. (Courtesy of Valencia County Historical Society.)

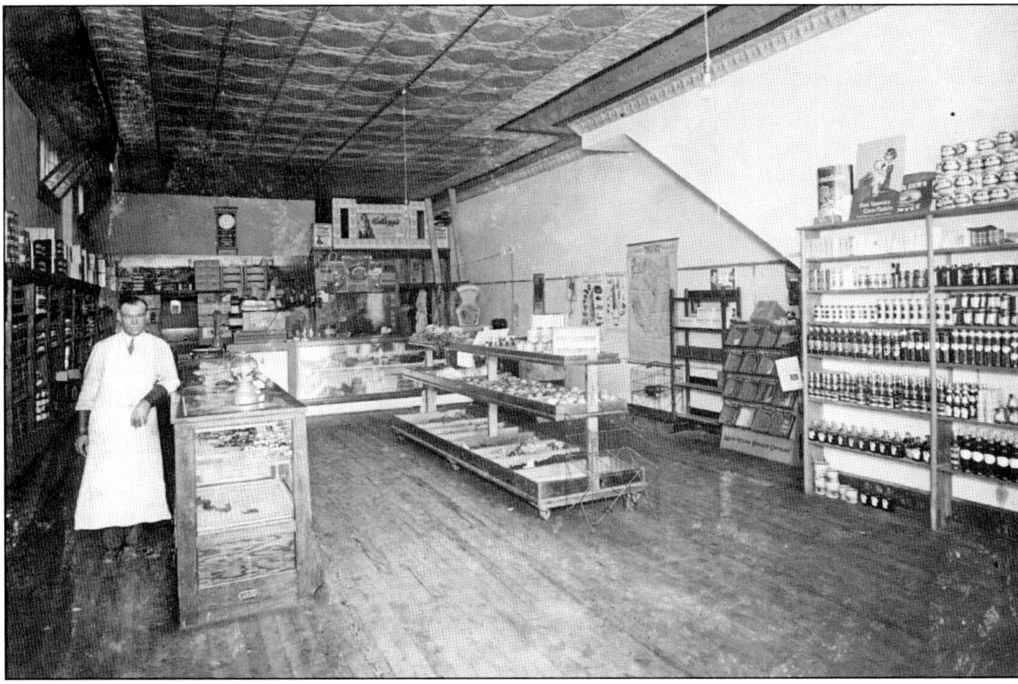

Harry Auge Sr. is shown inside the Midway Store, located at the corner of Second Street and Becker Avenue, in 1926. The store was later sold to Ike Billington. It was located in the Central Hotel building, later the home of Leo's Pool Hall and The Computer Place, a retail computer store. (Courtesy of Valencia County Historical Society.)

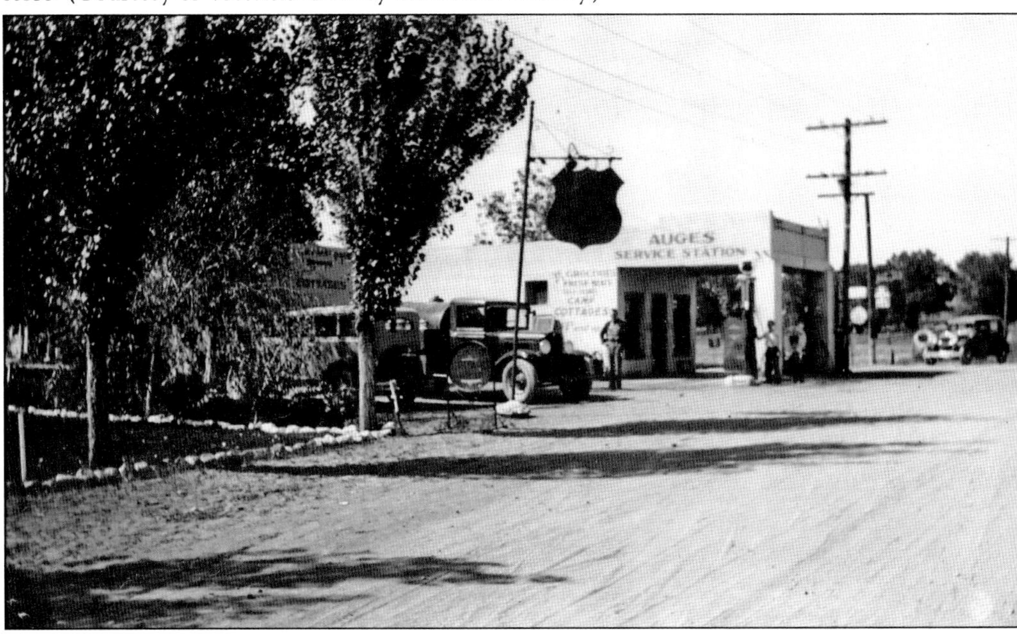

This is Auge's Service Station on River Road. Harry and Pearl Auge moved to Belen in 1923. Harry and Pearl's sons Harry Jr. and Lee opened an auto-repair and livestock-feed business at the same location in 1946. In 1951, Harry and Lee became Dodge dealers, and in 1971 they added Chrysler and Plymouth automobiles. (Courtesy of Belen Harvey House Museum.)

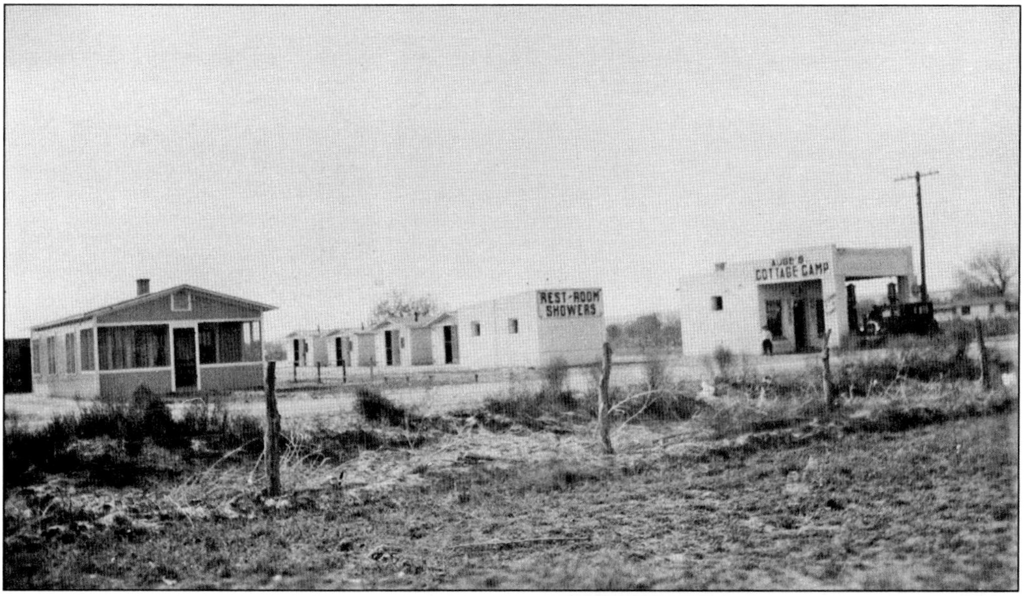

In addition to the grocery store, Harry Auge built apartments, tourist cabins, and a filling station on East River Road to provide for the needs of automobile travelers. Harry's grandsons Robert and Ed Auge later operated an automobile dealership at this location. (Courtesy of Valencia County Historical Society.)

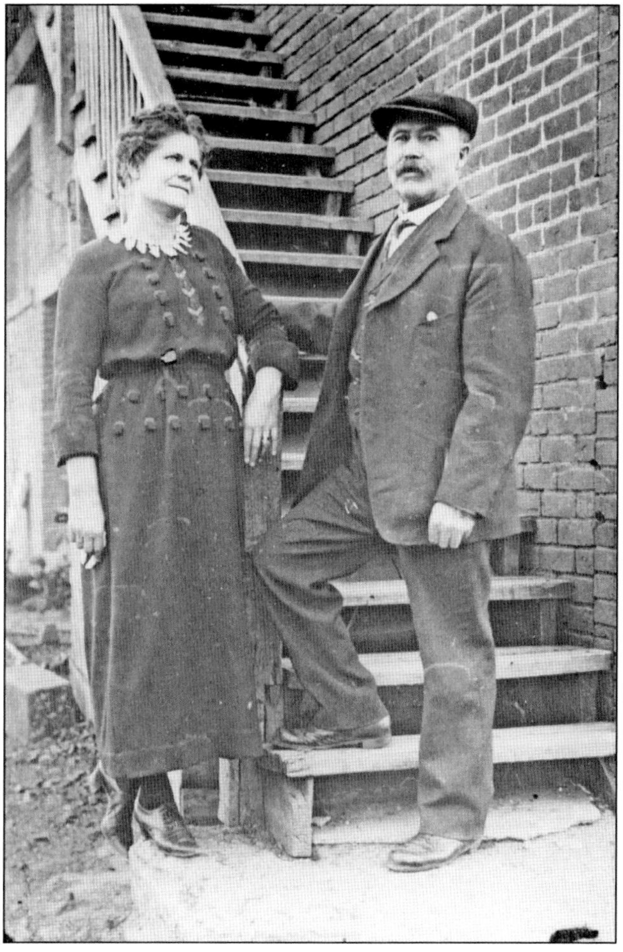

Katherine and Thomas Seery arrived in Belen in 1903. Thomas worked for the AT&SF Railway until his retirement in 1930. They had 10 children, and in 1948 and 1949 Katherine was chosen as the New Mexico Mother of the Year. The Seery's owned and operated the Central Hotel at the corner of Second Street and Becker Avenue. (Courtesy of Valencia County Historical Society.)

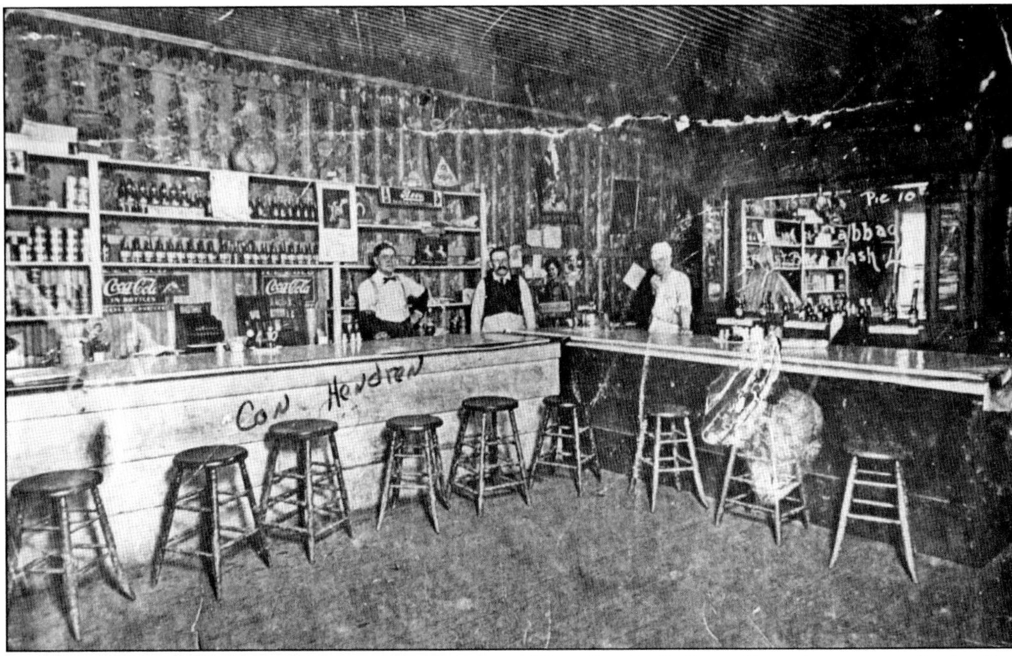

Con Hendren (far left) is shown at the counter of Hendren's Café on First Street, inside the Rio Grande Hotel (later called the Central Hotel) and across the street from the railroad depot. The café also featured a full bar, which helped attract customers from the town of Belen as well as the railroad. (Courtesy of Valencia County Historical Society.)

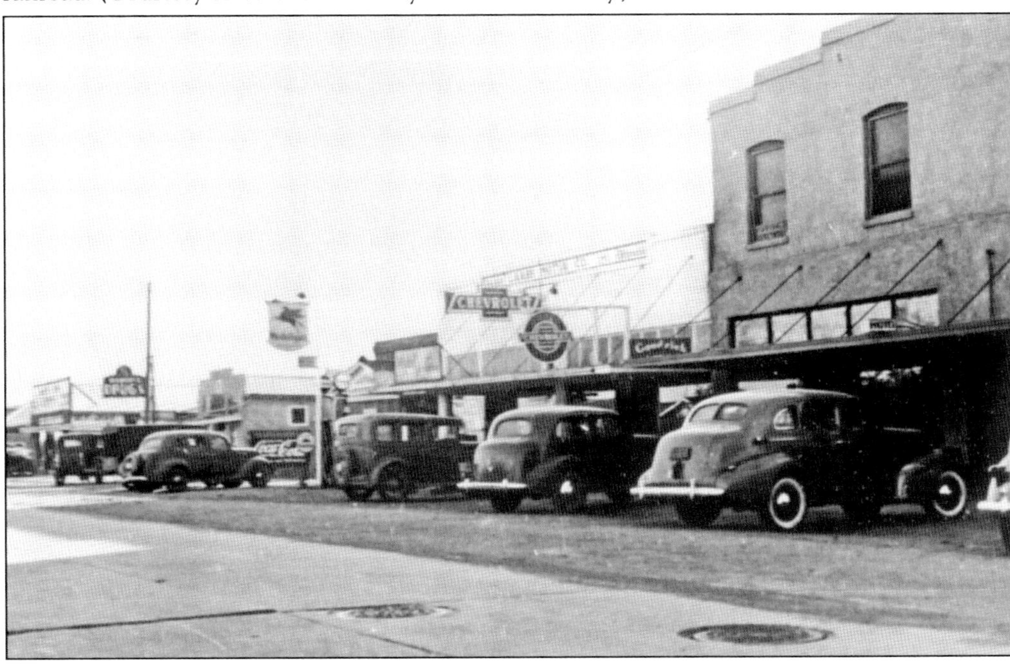

Several automobile dealers operated in Belen through the years, including Garrison Motors (Desoto-Plymouth), Laabs Motor Company (Chevrolet), Auge Sales and Service (Dodge-Chrysler), Caldwell Motors (Buick-GMC), and Leupold Motors (Ford). Pictured here is Laabs Motors on South Main Street in the mid-1930s. (Courtesy of Valencia County Historical Society.)

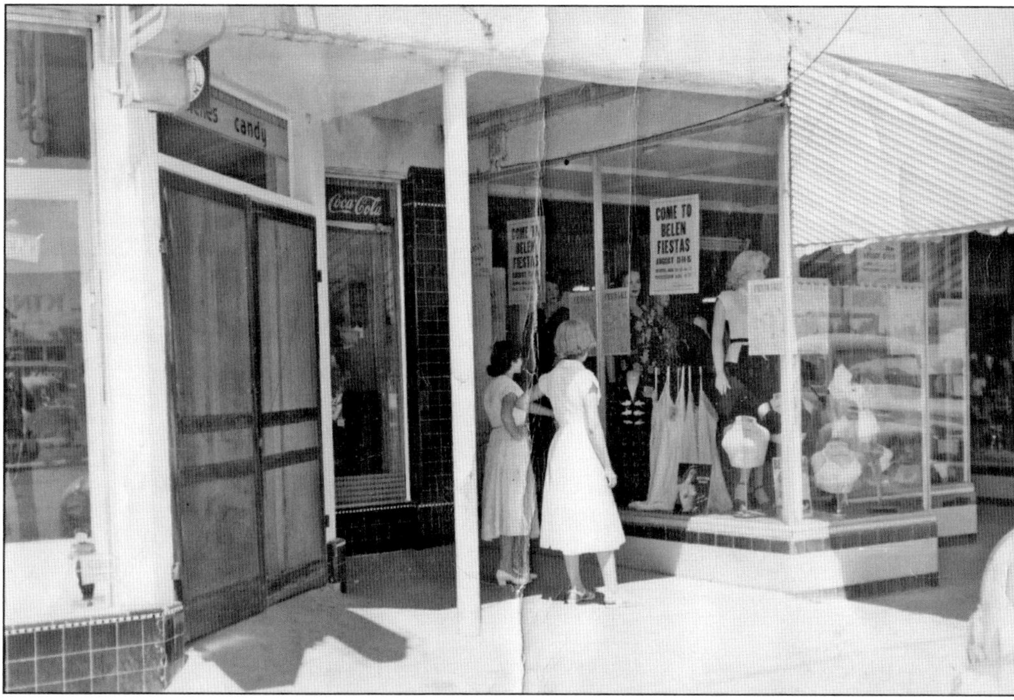

The Fair Store on Main Street in Belen was started by Ben Marcus and was managed by Karl Sternberg. This photograph, taken on August 4, 1950, is by Beavers Studio in Belen. Note the advertisement for the Belen Fiesta in the window. (Courtesy of Valencia County Historical Society.)

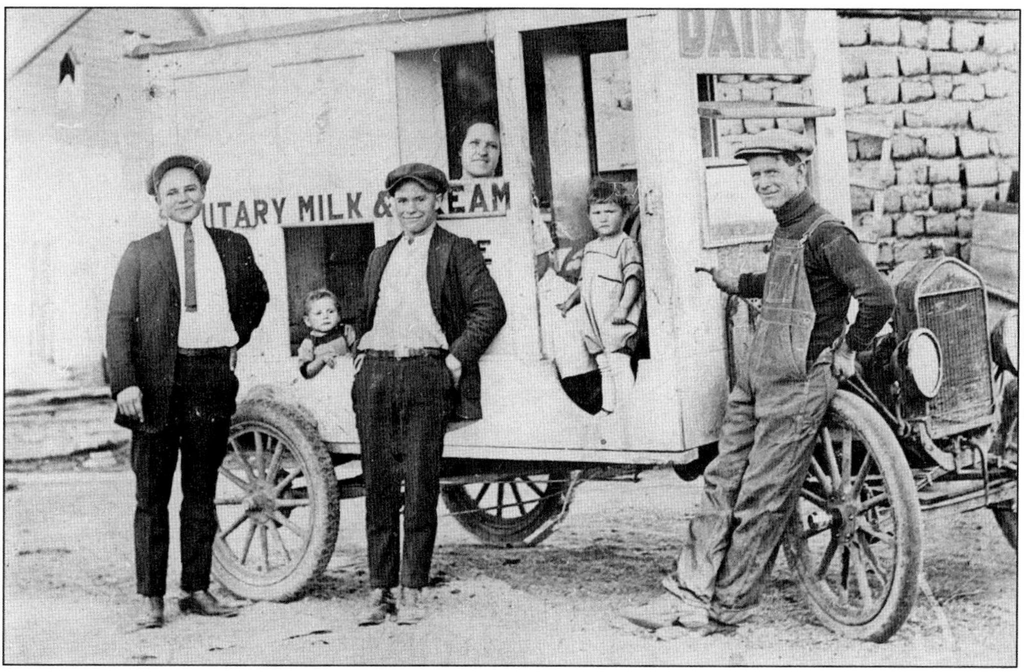

This is a c. 1925 photograph of the Sanitary Milk and Cream truck. It was a sign of increasing urbanization that many families no longer kept dairy cows and thus depended on the milk truck to deliver dairy items and ice. (Courtesy of Valencia County Historical Society.)

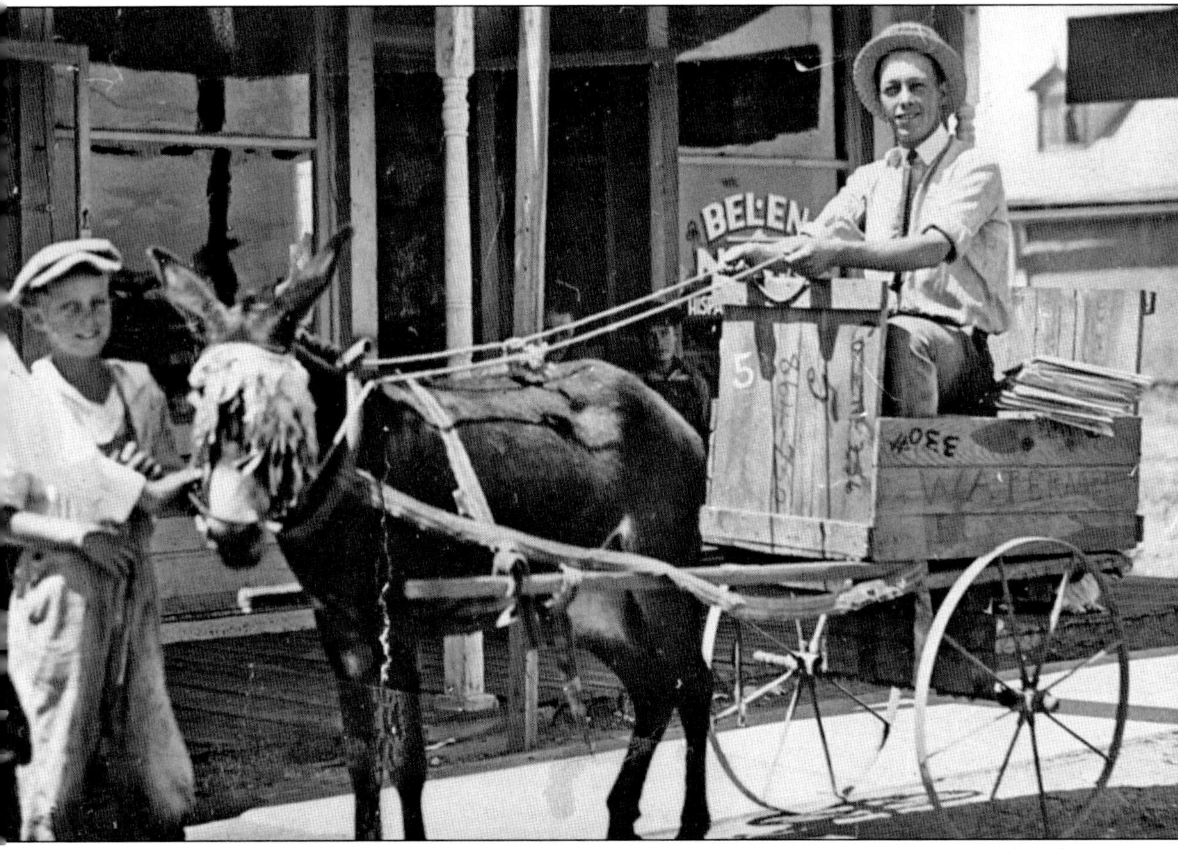

Elfego Baca, (no relation to the famous Socorro, New Mexico, sheriff of the same name) is shown here around 1920 as he delivers newspapers. Saturnino Baca, Elfego's father, was the editor and publisher of the newspaper *El Hispano Americano.* In 1920, Elfego took over the business with his brother Ignacio Baca. They continued the newspaper, later named the *Belen News*, until 1946. (Courtesy of Valencia County Historical Society.)

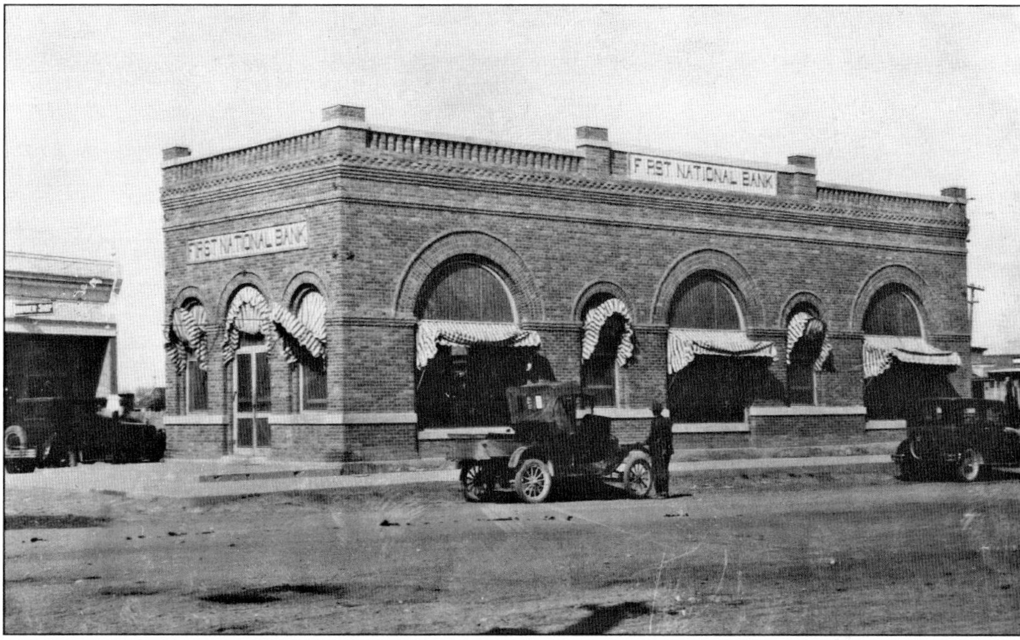

The First National Bank of Belen was founded by John Becker and was initially housed inside his mercantile store. Fearing the financial power banking services within merchant's stores gave men like John Becker, the territorial legislature passed a law prohibiting banks within stores. After moving the bank to a building next to his store, Becker eventually had this impressive brick building constructed across the street. The photograph below is of the interior of the First National Bank of Belen in 1917. (Both courtesy of Valencia County Historical Society.)

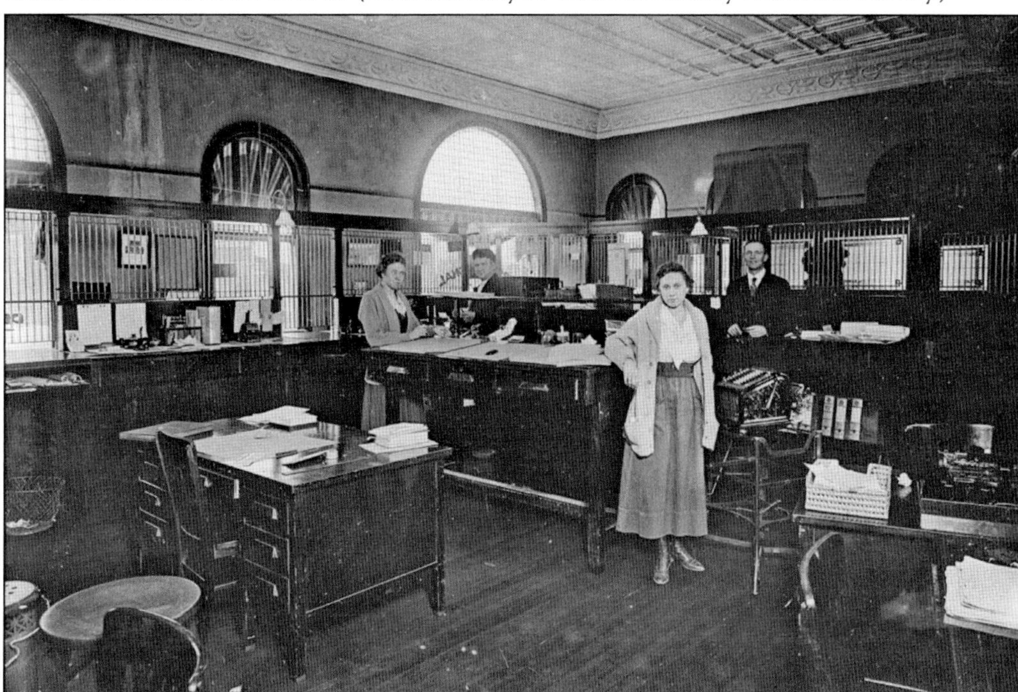

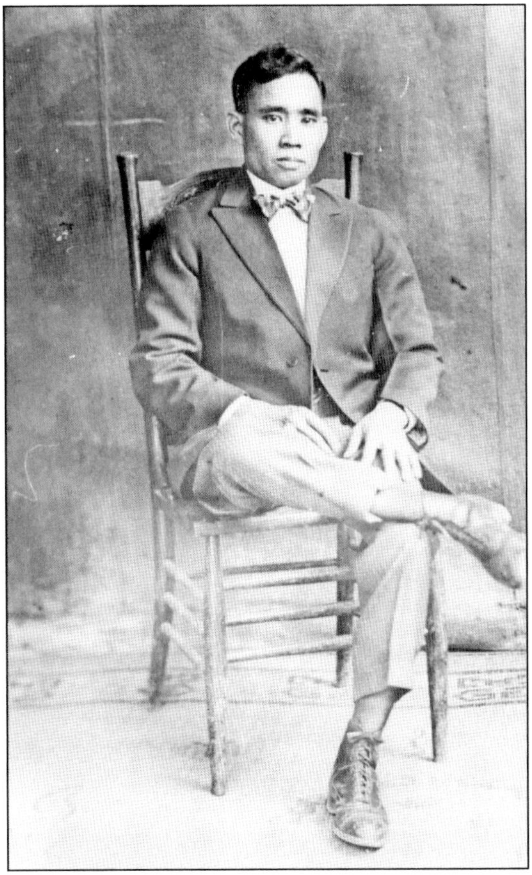

Frank Kaneshiro was born in Okinawa, Japan, in 1886 and came to Belen in 1915. He established the O.K. Cleaning Works, Belen's first dry-cleaning business. It was located in a two-story building across the street from city hall on Becker Avenue. For many years, he did all of the pressing and alterations for Becker, Dalies, Feil and Ellermeyer, the Fair Store, and other stores with clothing departments. (Courtesy of Valencia County Historical Society.)

Howard and Frank Wilson started the first truck line in the state of New Mexico in 1917. They operated out of Frank Wilson's kitchen in Belen with three Model A trucks from International and Diamond Rio. The hills were so steep near Isleta Pueblo that the trucks had to use the reverse gear and go up the hill backwards. (Courtesy of Valencia County Historical Society.)

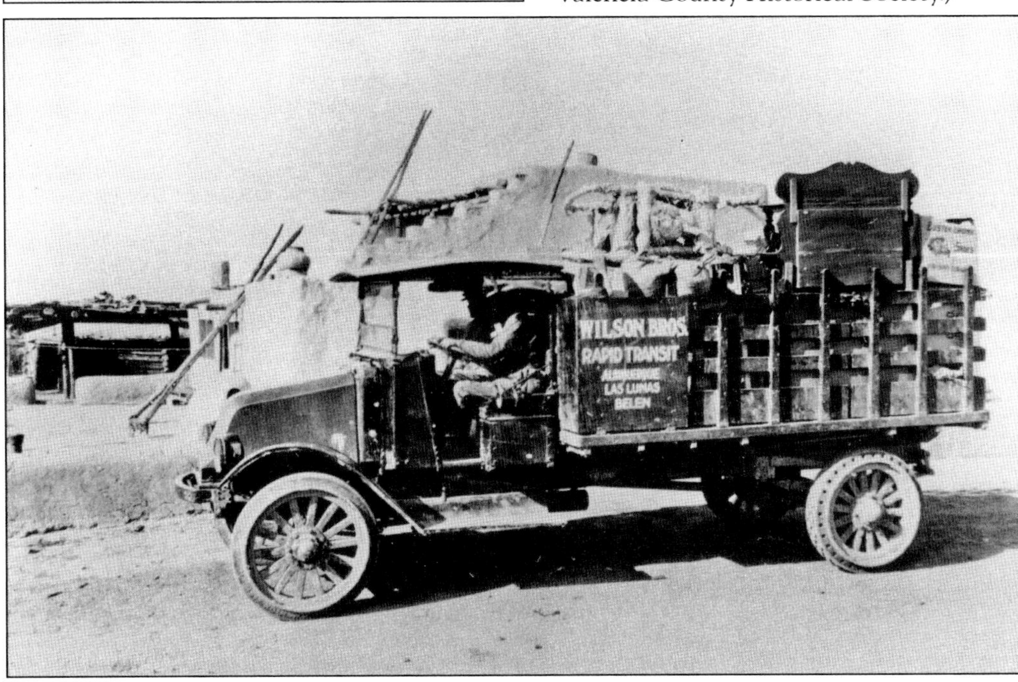

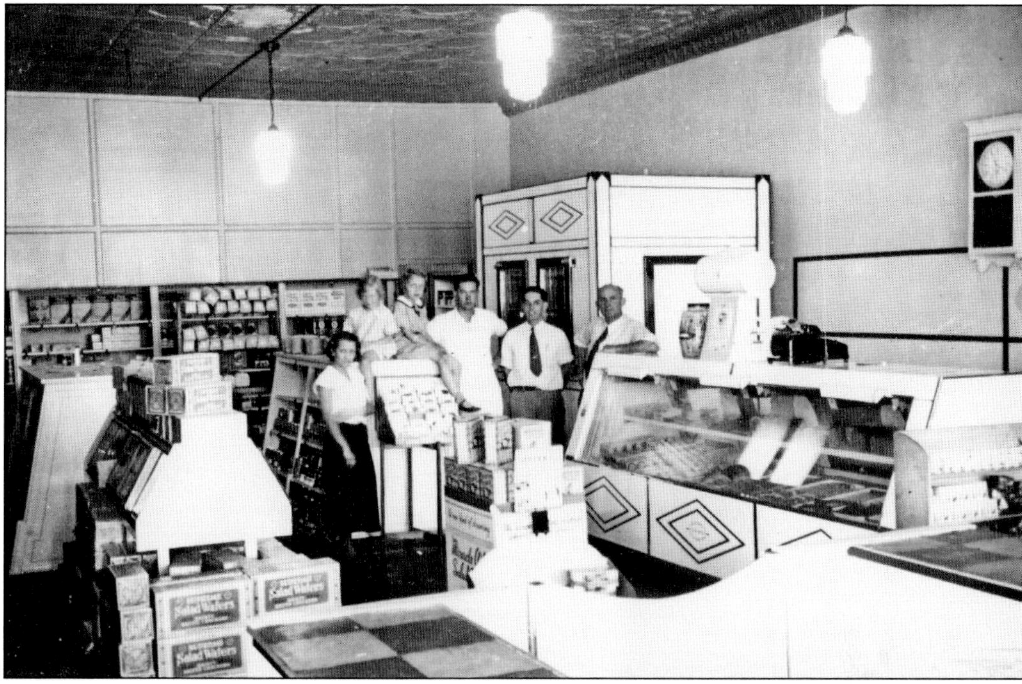

This is the Midway Market in 1932. Located on Becker Avenue, the market was owned by Ben Heady. Shown from left to right are Mary (Mrs. Ben) Heady, daughters Delores and Marilyn Heady, Gordon Platter, Cliff Platter, and Bishop Crawford. (Courtesy of Belen Harvey House Museum.)

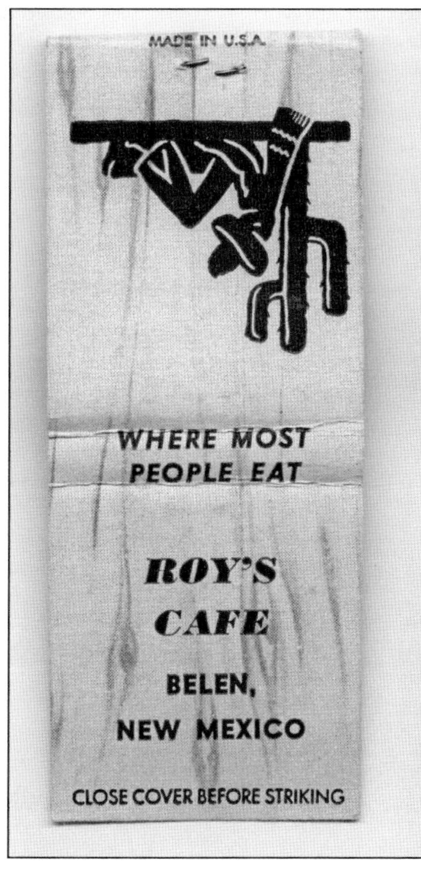

This matchbook cover advertises Roy's Café in Belen. The café was located on Main Street at the site of the present Hoover Vacuum Cleaner Repair Shop. Roy's Café was one of the few places that personnel from Los Alamos, New Mexico, were authorized to stop when they traveled to White Sands as they prepared for the first atomic bomb test in 1945. (Courtesy of Richard Melzer.)

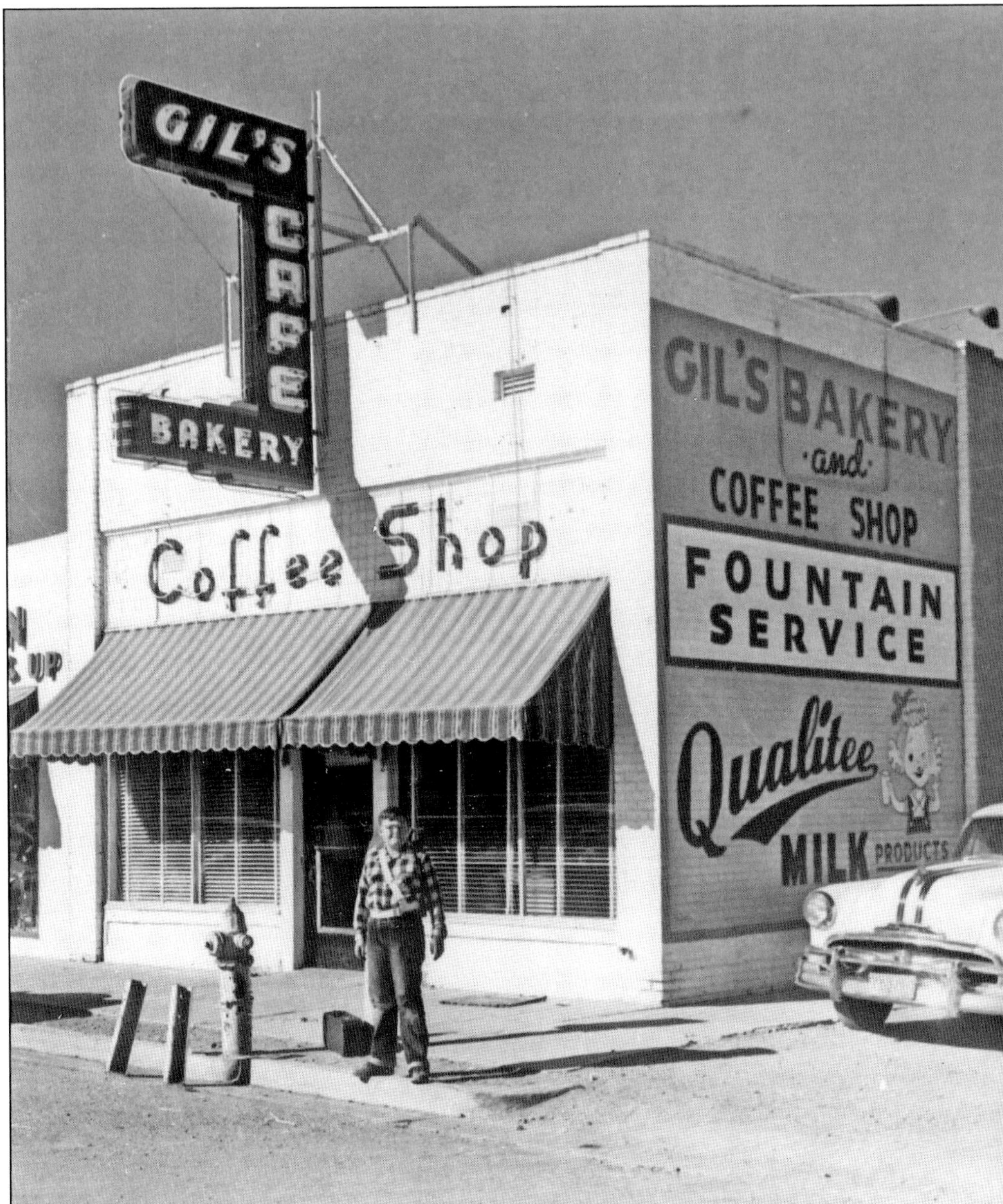

This is Gil's Bakery and Café around 1950. Gil Sanchez opened the business in 1947. Gil served as a community leader and local judge for many years. Born the fifth of 10 children on September 20, 1917, in Jarales, Gil graduated from Belen High School in 1935. He later served on the Belen Board of Education for more than 25 years. (Courtesy of Valencia County Historical Society.)

Gil Sanchez (shown here in 1955) worked at Harrell's Bakery for 11 years, starting in 1931 and lasting until 1942, and was employed by the Hawthorne Bakery in Nevada from 1942 until 1947, when he returned to Belen to open his own business. He purchased the Henry Sachs building at the corner of Main Street and Reinken Avenue. Gil specialized in elaborate cakes. (Courtesy of Valencia County Historical Society.)

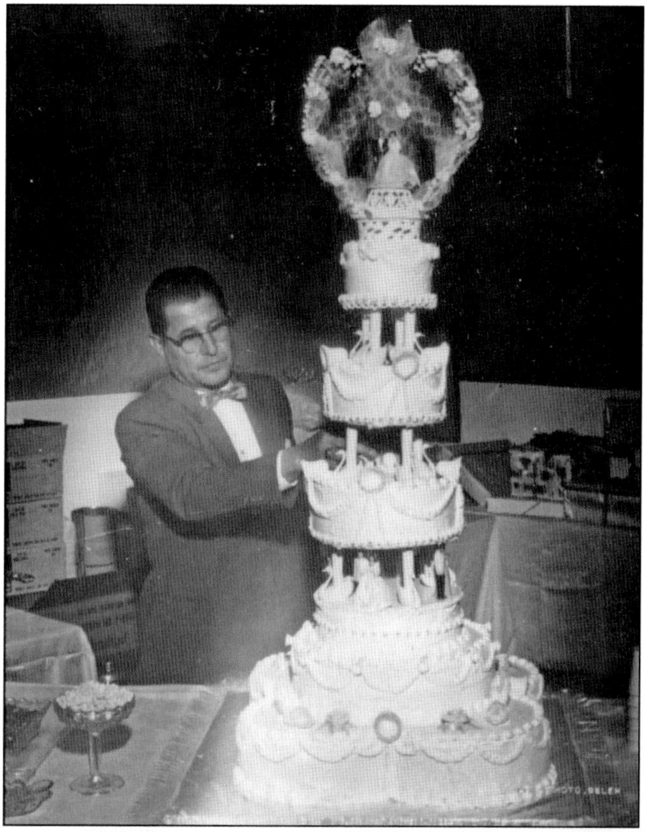

A parade was part of the Our Lady of Belen festivities. Many local businesses created floats, and marchers representing these businesses took part in the Fiesta Parade. These young bakers showcase the artistic baking talents of Gil Sanchez and Gil's Bakery and Café. (Courtesy of Valencia County Historical Society.)

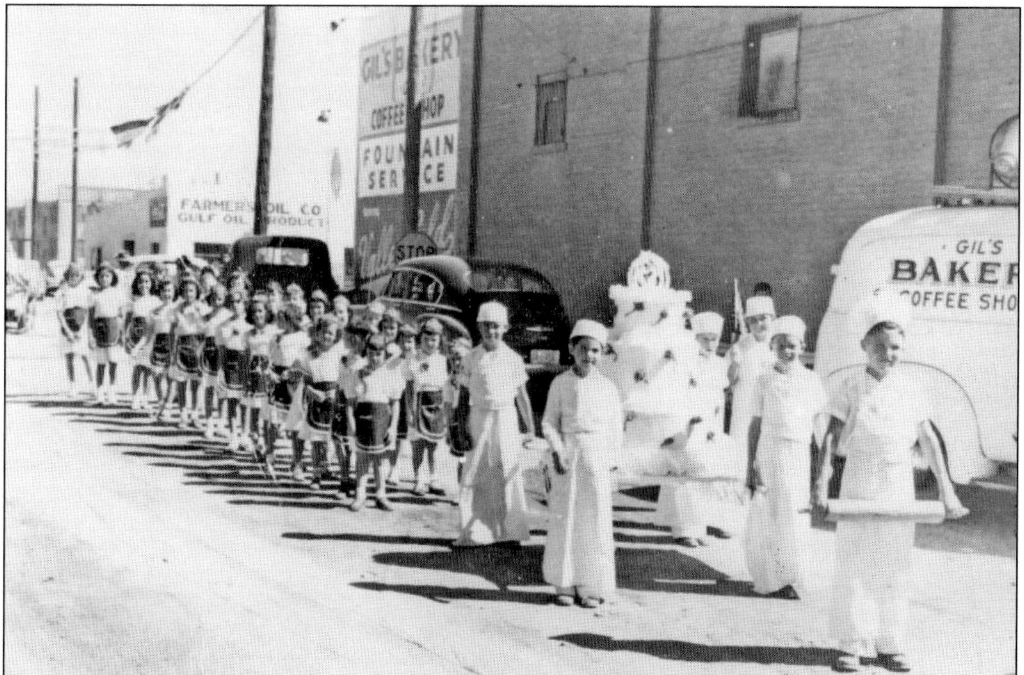

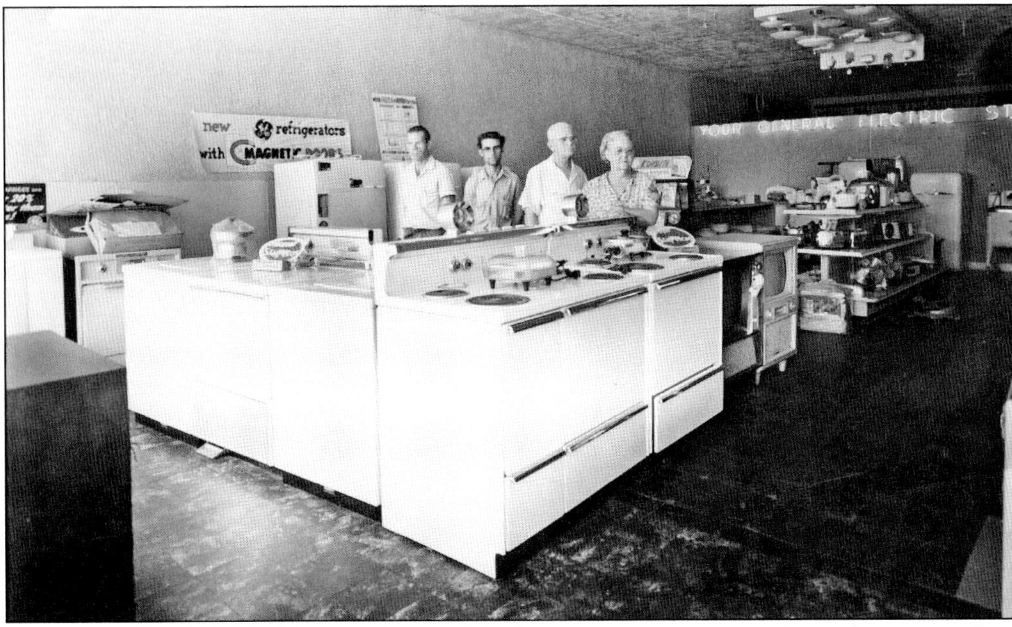

This is the interior of Dils Electric Company around 1960. Fred Dils moved to Belen in 1909 from Mountainair, New Mexico. He married Corra Newell in 1924. Fred started the Dils Electric Company in 1943 and did the majority of the residential and commercial electrical contracting in Valencia County in the 1940s through the 1960s. (Courtesy of Valencia County Historical Society.)

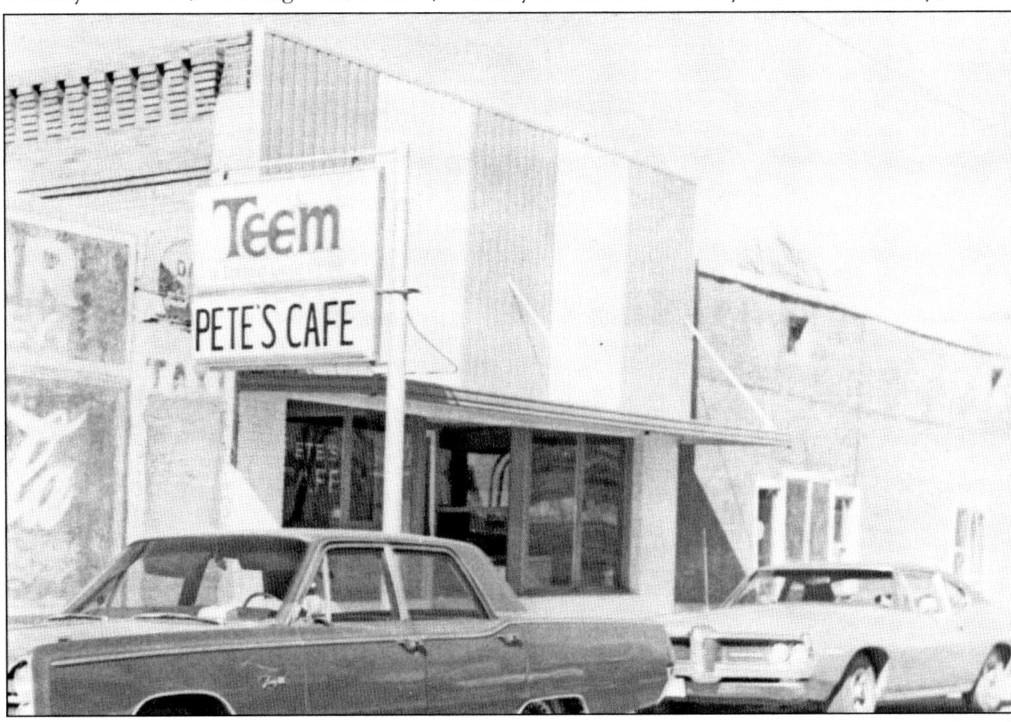

Pete Torres, son of Pedro Torres Sr. and Mercedes Gurule, founded Pete's Café in 1949. Although it started small, the restaurant was enlarged and remodeled and became very successful. It is currently operated by the third generation of the Torres family. (Courtesy of the Torres family.)

Eligia Torres is shown here in 1955 preparing chile at Pete's Café. Eligia and her husband, Pete, shared duties at the restaurant. Over the years, Torres family members from three generations spent time working at Pete's. Many of the recipes served since the restaurant's inception have endured. (Courtesy of the Torres family.)

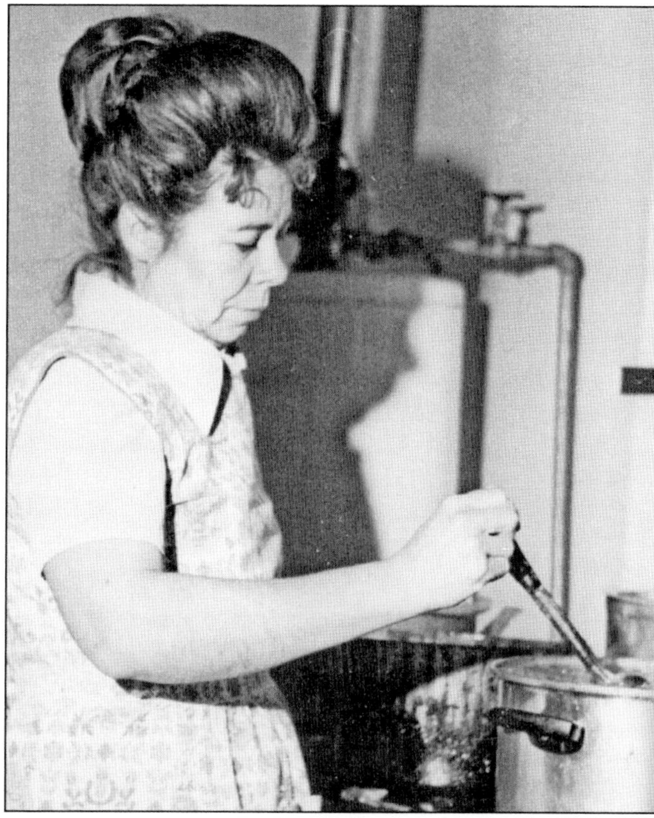

Pete Torres is shown here in 1972. When he and his wife started the business, Eligia would cook and operate the restaurant during the day, and Pete would come in after work at the Gas Company of New Mexico to handle the evening shift. The motto of Pete's Café today is "It's not best because it's the oldest, it's oldest because it's the best!" (Courtesy of the Torres family.)

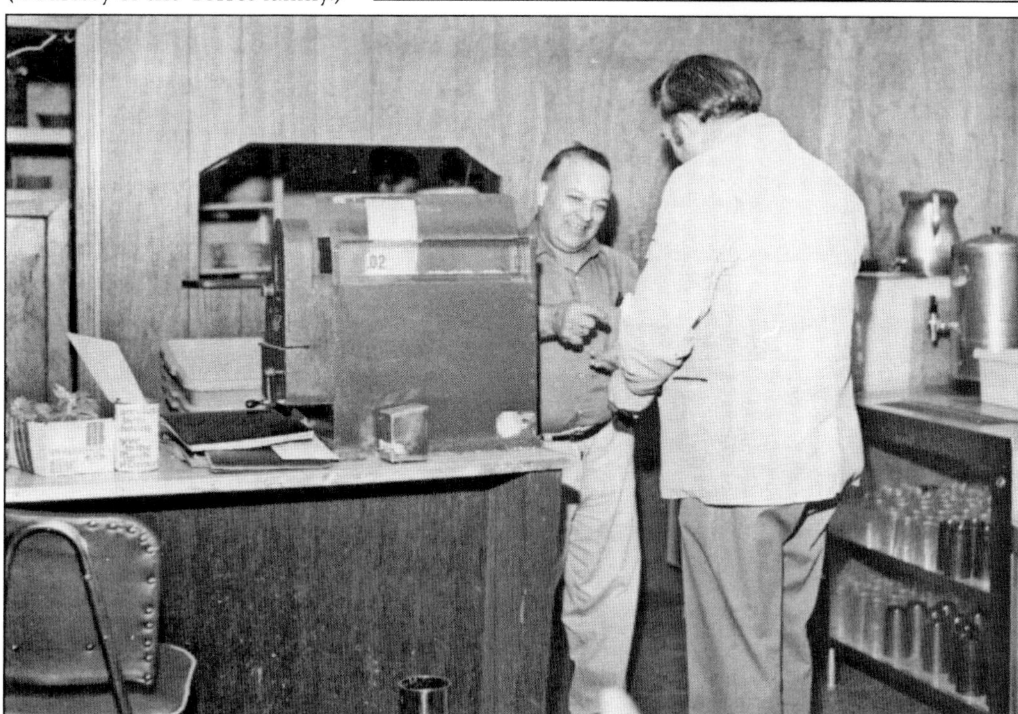

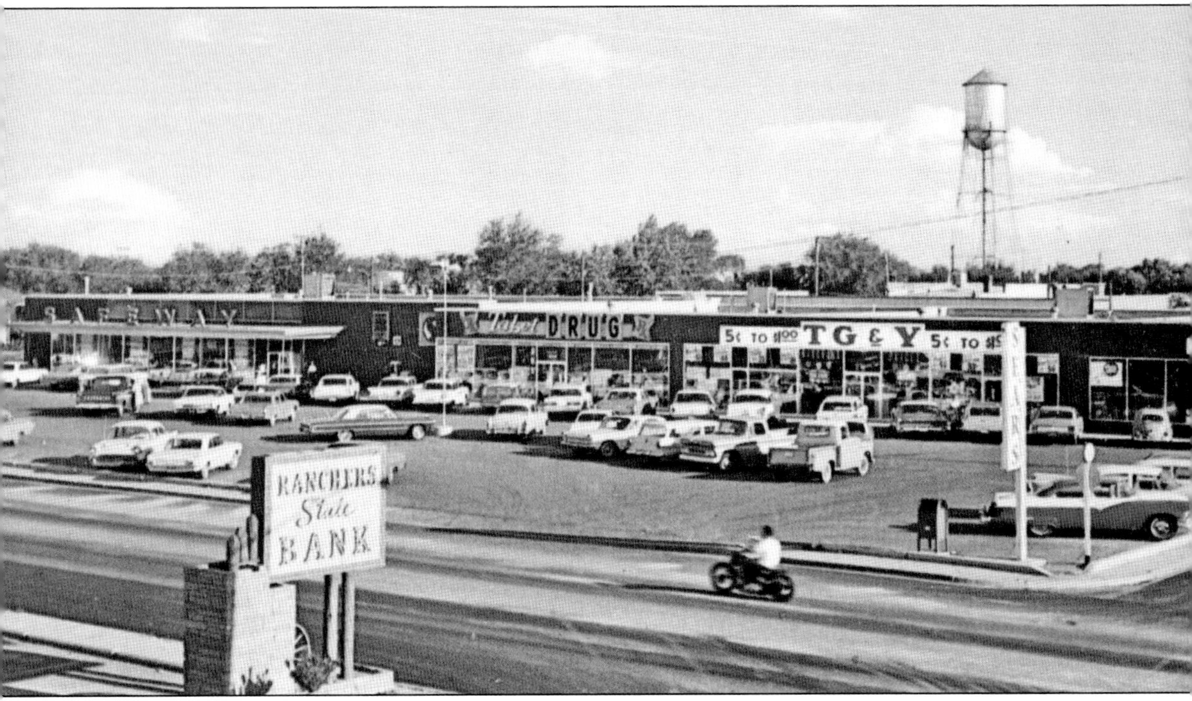

This is the Tabet Center on Reinken Avenue in Belen. Carlos Tabet came to the United States at age 16 and worked his way from New York to New Mexico by selling pots and pans. In 1905, he married Onesima Garcia, and they had 11 children. In 1927, he opened a grocery store on South Main Street in Belen, which he operated until he retired in 1947. (Courtesy of Richard Melzer.)

Five

PUBLIC SERVICE

The village of Belen was incorporated in 1918. The population was about 1,500, and the village was governed by a board of trustees. Bernard Jacobson (1918–1922) was the first mayor. During his administration, Belen acquired its first fire truck, and the first electricity service was provided.

Manuel Garcia (1922–1930) was the next mayor. His administration installed a water and sewer system and established uniform street names and lot numbers. It was during the Garcia administration that John Becker donated the land in 1927 that would become Anna Becker Park. A building code was adopted in 1929, and several new buildings were constructed along Main Street. Belen's population in 1930 was 2,116.

Con Hendren (1930–1932) was Belen's next mayor, with Mel Tate (1932–1940) following him. During Tate's administration, a traffic light was installed at Main Street and Becker Avenue in 1935. In 1937, village offices were located at 503 Becker. Natural gas service started in 1939.

When Waite Keeney (1940–1942) became mayor of Belen, the population was 3,038. That year, Belen changed its status from a village to a township. Keeney was followed in office by Don Redebaugh (1942–1946), and when ill health forced his retirement, John Becker's son Louis C. Becker (1946–1950) filled the position of mayor. Between 1940 and 1950, the hospital was built, street lights were installed, garbage collection began, a new fire truck was purchased, and an airport was located near the fairgrounds.

Earl Peter (1950–1956) was followed as mayor by Neel Alexander, who served a remarkable 20 years in office (1956–1960, 1962–1966, and 1968–1980). During Mayor Alexander's tenure, a new swimming pool and recreation facilities were built, additional stoplights were installed, and Rio Grande Estates was developed. The population of Belen in 1960 was 5,031. In 1966, Belen's status again changed, this time from a township to a city. By the year 2000, Belen's population had grown to 6,901.

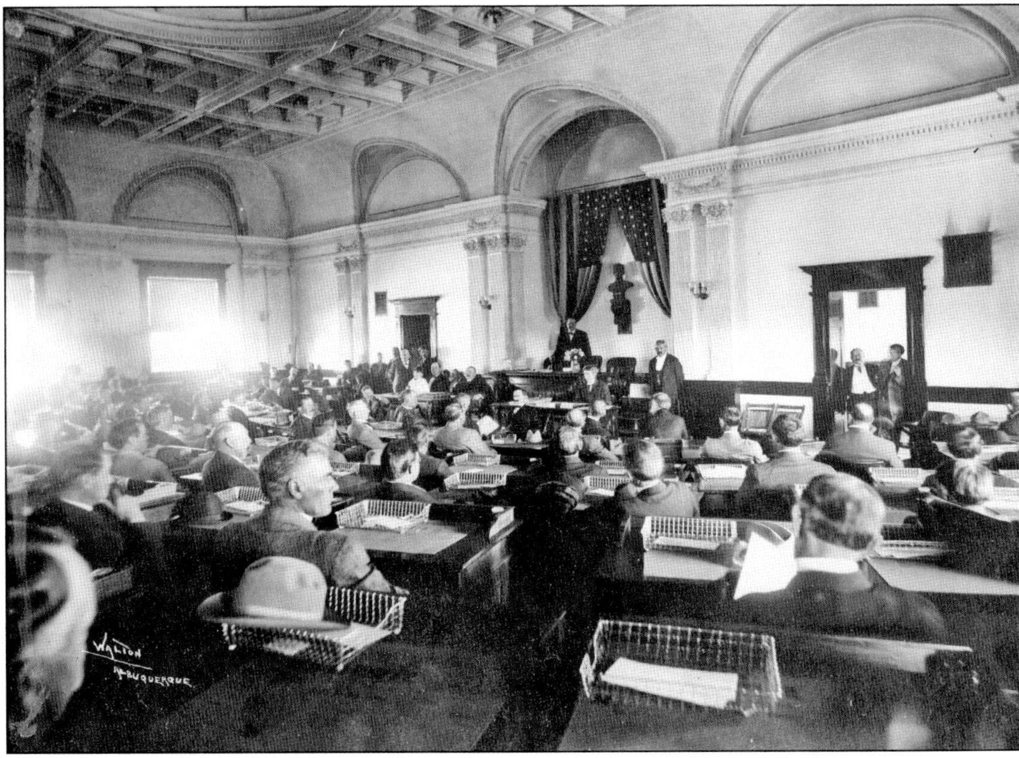

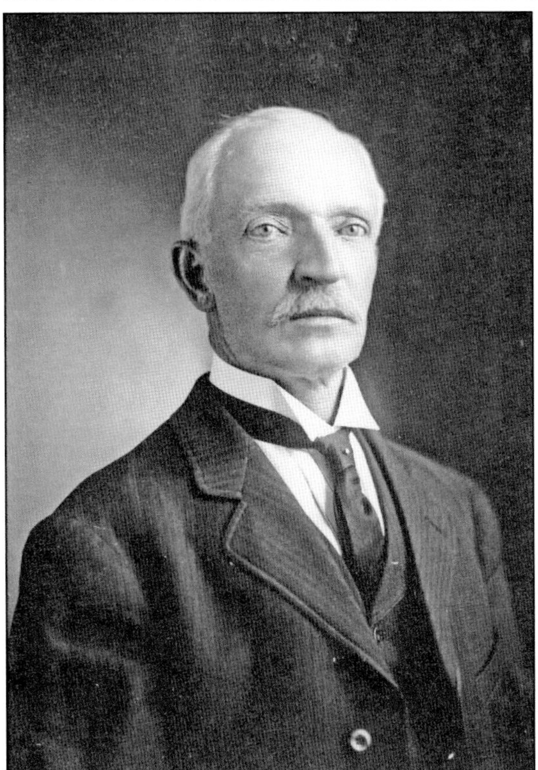

The New Mexico Constitutional Convention, leading up to statehood for New Mexico, was held in Santa Fe during October and November 1910. John Becker, at left, was one of the delegates to the convention from Valencia County. It was his only political role. Solomon Luna from Los Lunas and Sylvestre Mirabal from San Mateo were the other two delegates. The state constitution that resulted from this convention made statehood for New Mexico possible. The photograph above shows some of the 100 delegates in session at the territorial capitol. (Above, courtesy of Belen Harvey House Museum; at left, Valencia County Historical Society.)

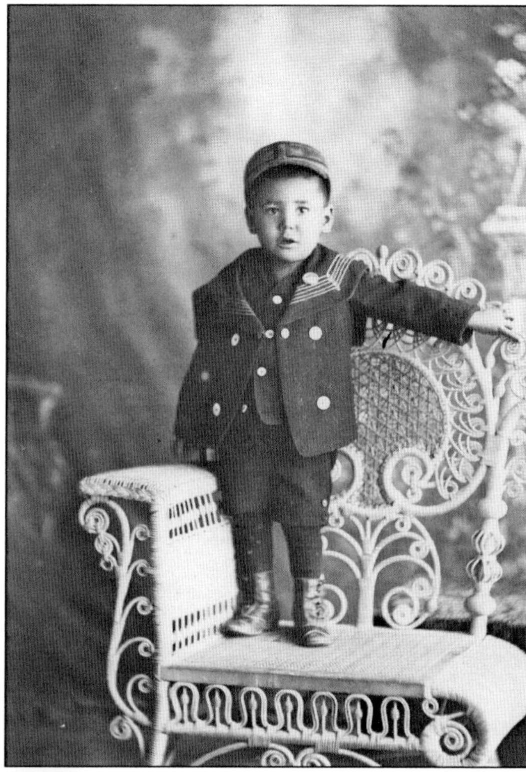

US senator Dionisio "Dennis" Chavez was born in Los Chavez in 1888, but his family moved to Albuquerque when he was still young. Dennis was a direct descendant of the founder of Los Chavez, Don Nicolas Duran y Chavez. Dennis was elected to the US House of Representatives in 1930 and served two terms. He ran for the US Senate in 1934 but was defeated by Bronson Cutting. When Cutting died in an airplane crash in 1935, New Mexico governor Clyde Tingley appointed Chavez as his replacement. Chavez was reelected in 1936, 1940, 1946, 1952, and 1958. Senator Chavez introduced the first federal legislation to protect the rights of Hispanics and Native Americans. (Both courtesy of Valencia County Historical Society.)

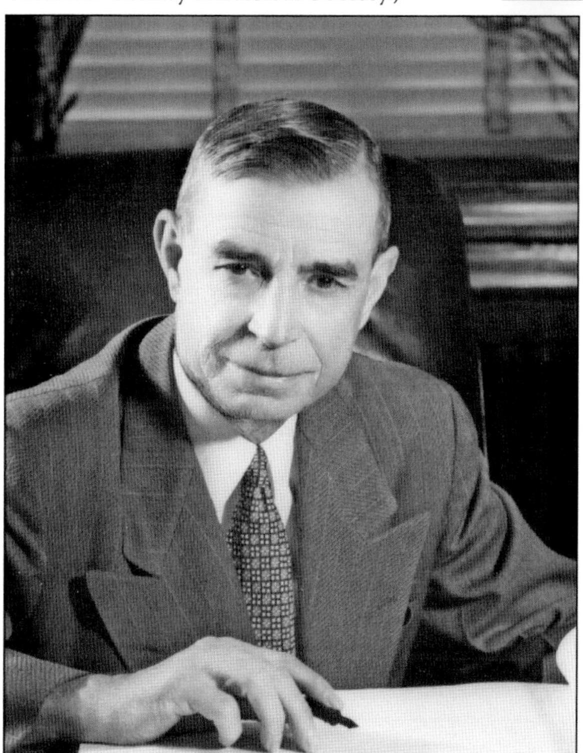

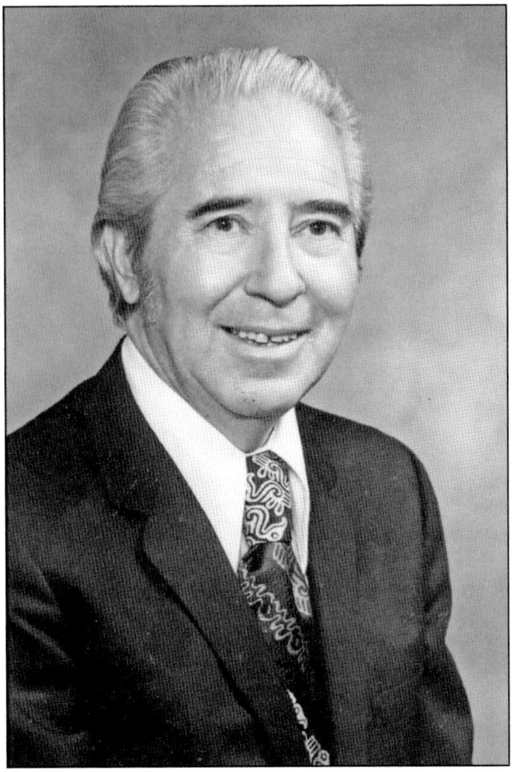

Judge Tibo Chavez was born in Belen in 1912. He was a cousin of Sen. Dennis Chavez and was lieutenant governor of New Mexico from 1951 to 1954. He also served for 22 years as a state senator. He was a 13th Judicial District Court judge from 1979 until his death in 1991. Judge Chavez was a founding member of the Valencia County Historical Society. (Courtesy of Los Lunas Museum of Heritage and Arts.)

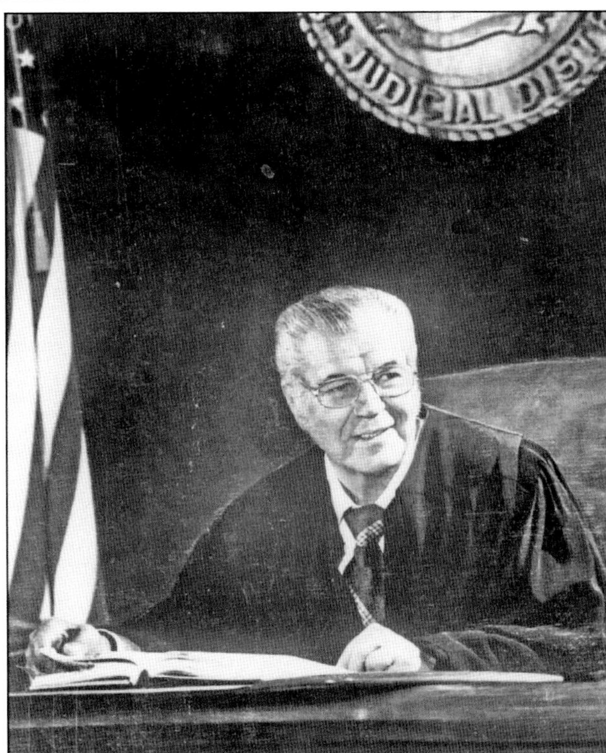

This is Judge Filo Sedillo around 1975. He graduated from Georgetown University Law School in 1933 and began practicing law in Belen the following year. He was active in the Democratic Party in Valencia County (chairman for 30 years), as well as the state and national political scene. He was elected attorney general of New Mexico and served from 1939 to 1940. (Courtesy of Valencia County Historical Society.)

Judge Mayo T. Boucher is seen here around 1975. Judge Boucher was born in Texas and was working for the railroad to save money for law school when he moved to Belen. He graduated from the University of New Mexico Law School in 1952. He served in the state legislature as a representative from Valencia County for four consecutive terms. He was a judge in the 13th Judicial District Court. (Courtesy of Valencia County Historical Society.)

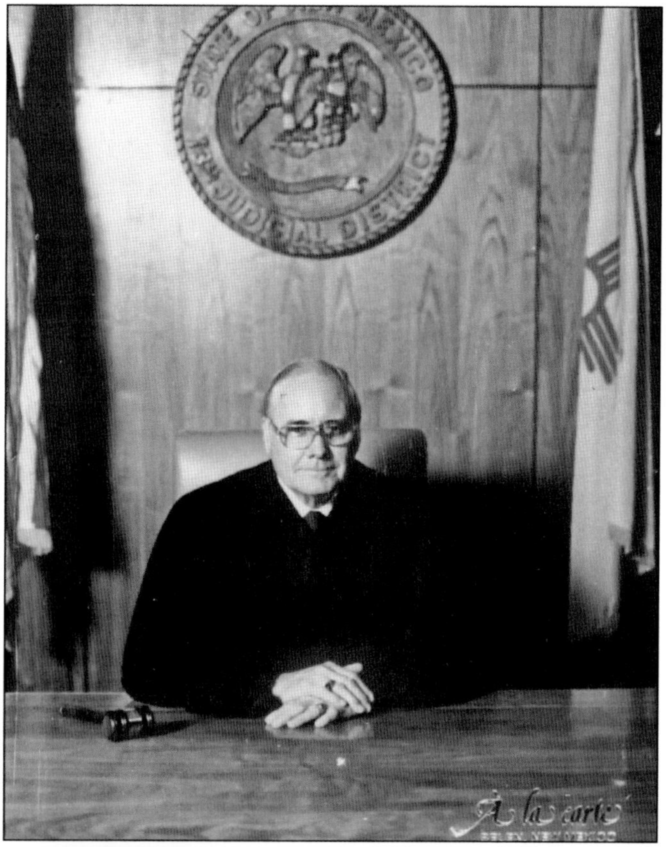

Officers and staff of the Belen Police Department are pictured outside the police department around 1950. The raised box on the left contains a siren that was blown to signal curfew. The siren was also used to signal emergencies and as an air-raid warning. (Courtesy of Valencia County Historical Society.)

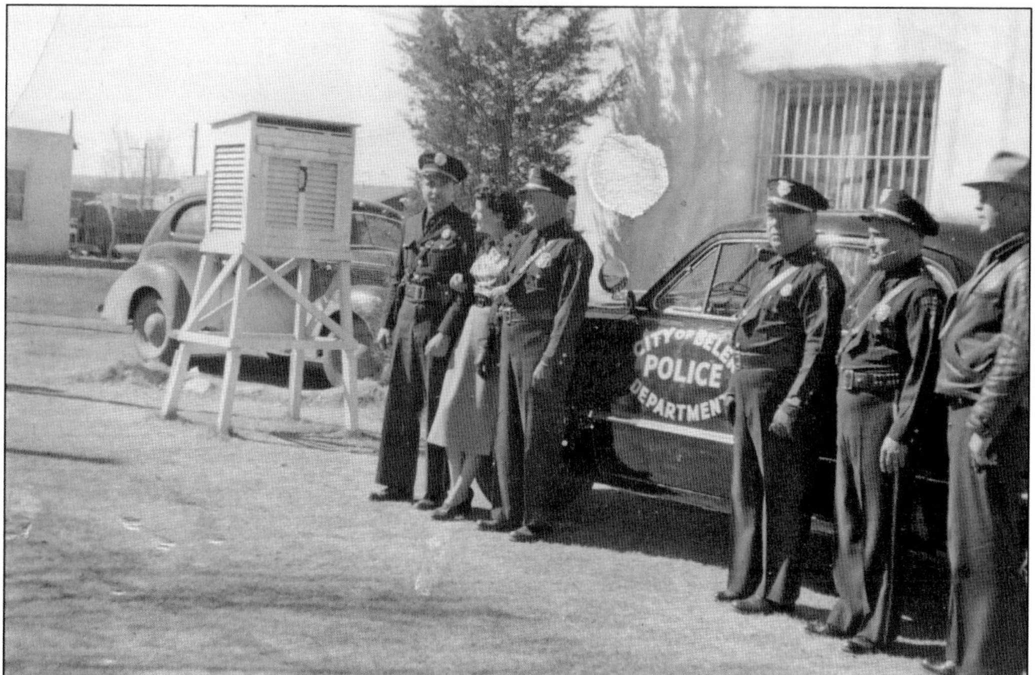

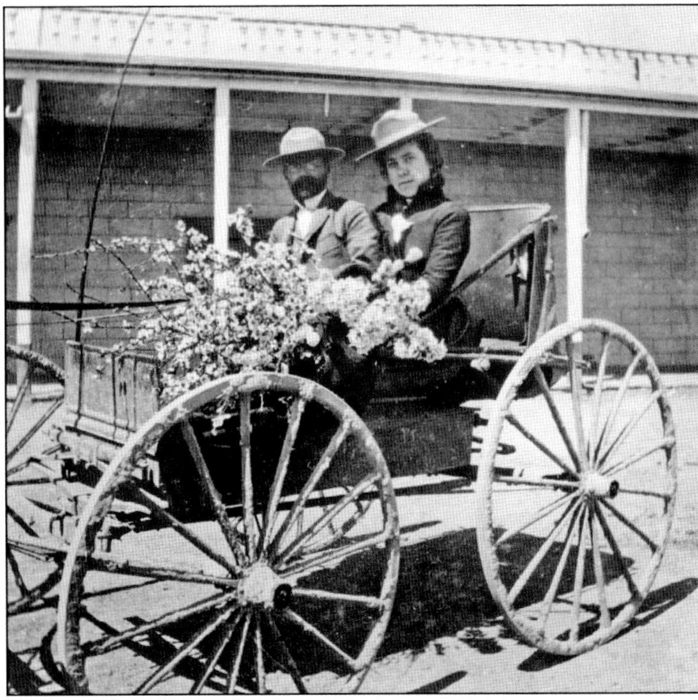

Dr. William D. Radcliffe Sr. and Laura Zinth are pictured here around 1900. Radcliffe was John Becker's nephew and was probably the first medical doctor in Belen. He arrived in the 1880s and worked until his death in 1942. His son William Radcliffe Jr., who also became a doctor, was born in Belen in 1907. (Courtesy of Valencia County Historical Society.)

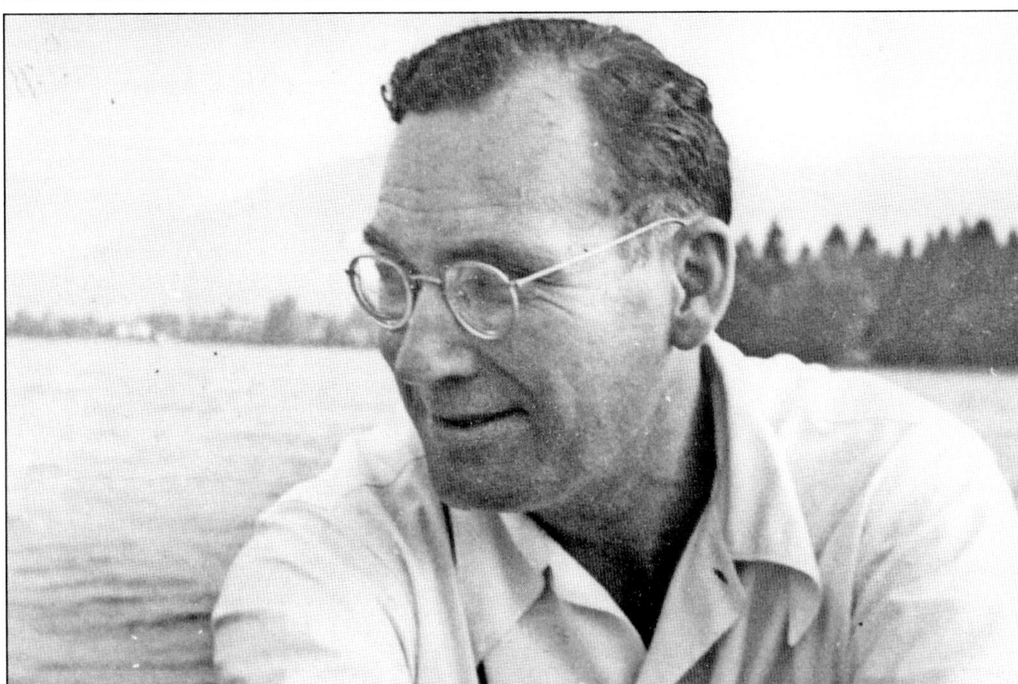

Dr. William Radcliffe Jr. received his medical degree from the University of Southern California School of Medicine in 1934. After distinguished military service during World War II, he returned to Belen in 1950 and established a private medical practice. He continued the practice until his death in 1969. Father and son served the medical needs of Belen for almost a century. (Courtesy of Valencia County Historical Society.)

Dr. Samuel Wilkinson first arrived in Belen around 1910 to serve as a railroad doctor. He came to New Mexico with tuberculosis and, once recovered, he practiced medicine in Belen and Valencia County for almost half a century. In 1908, he married Augusta "Gussie" Holder, who later worked for the Becker Dalies Company. (Courtesy of Valencia County Historical Society.)

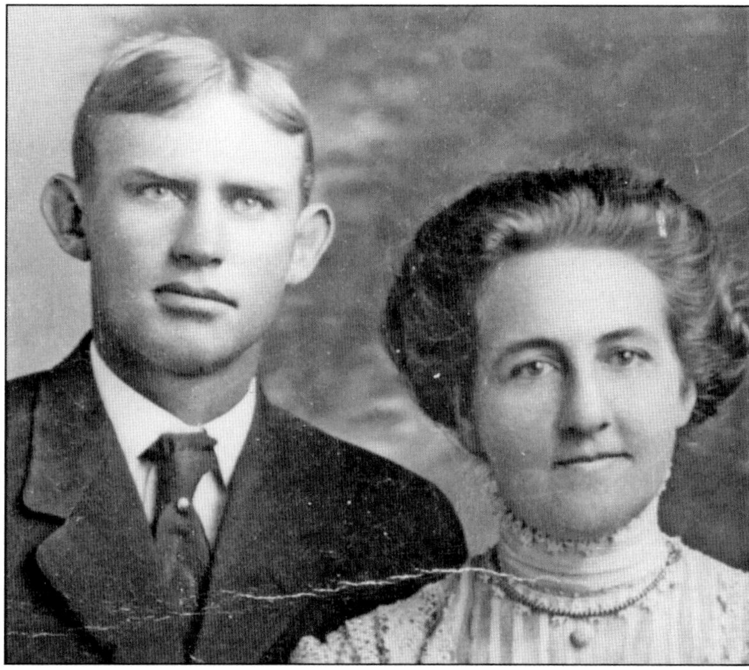

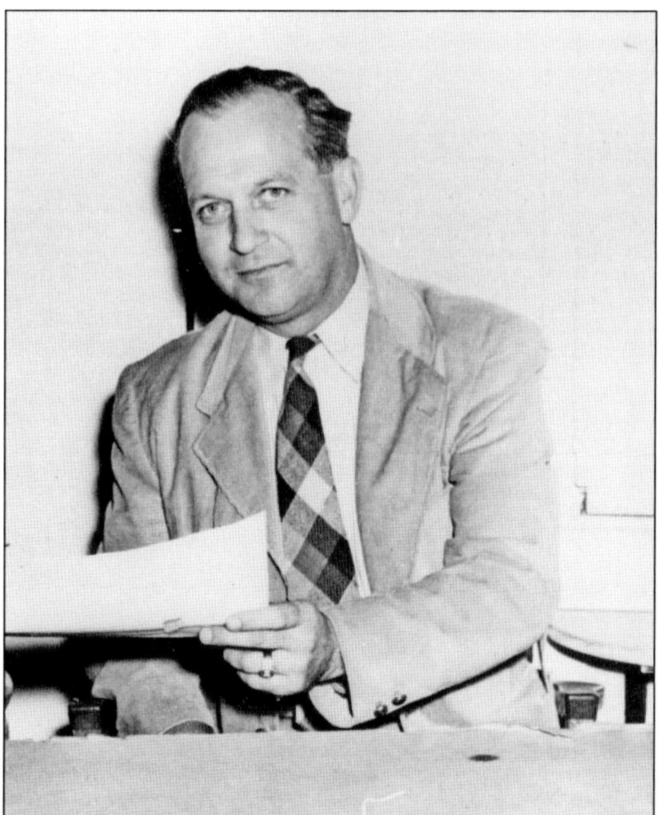

Earl E. Peter Sr. served four consecutive terms as mayor of Belen, from 1948 through 1956. While Earl was mayor, Belen replaced most of the town's sewer system, and garbage pickup service was initiated. He was instrumental in building the present bridge across the Rio Grande. Earl was also the founder of Ranchero Builders Supply Company. (Courtesy of Valencia County Historical Society.)

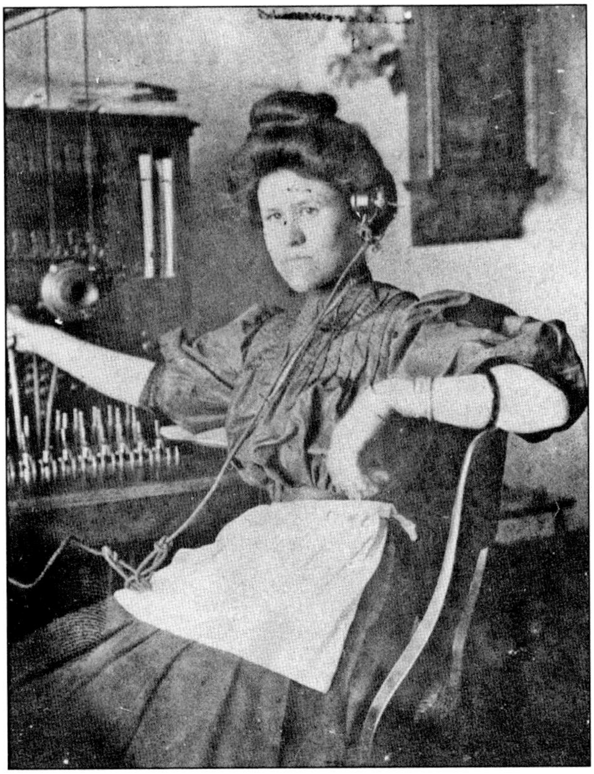

Quirina Baca Lovato, Belen's first telephone operator, is pictured here around 1915. Quirina Baca married Selso Lovato, who worked for the railroad and served as a Valencia County Commissioner. The first telephones were installed in Belen around 1910. By 1916, there were more than 100 telephones in service in the town. In the early 1920s, telephone service in Belen was taken over by a Colorado company. (Courtesy of Valencia County Historical Society.)

By the early 1920s, the telephone company in Belen was located in this residential building on Dalies Avenue, one block east of Buckland Drug Store. Three telephone company employees pose on the front steps. Telephone service was provided by the Mountain States Telephone and Telegraph Company. (Courtesy of Michael Jaramillo.)

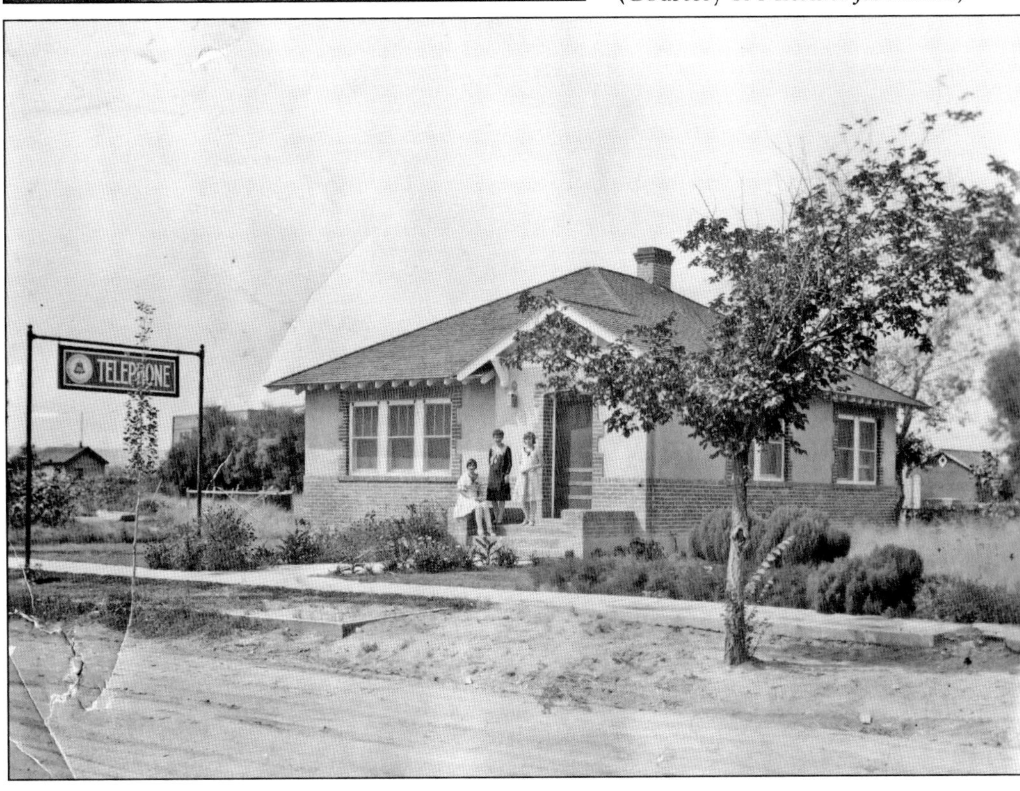

BELEN, N. M.

J. B. REYNOLDS, District Manager, Albuquerque.
W. J. DAVIDSON, Exchange Manager, Belen.

A

A T & S F Ry Co, Depot	18 J
A T & S F Ry Co, Round House	18W
Abell H L, r	24

B

Baca Miguel E, Gen Mdse, Adelino	54-2 J
Baca Saturnino, r	76W
Becker Adolph, r	22W
Becker F A Jr, r	22 J
Becker The John Co,	
Lumber, Coal, etc	15
Office	11
Store	61
Order Department	60
Becker John Jr, r	65 J
Becker L C, r	31
Becker Lucie, r	59
Belen Bar	69
Belen Cleaning Works & Hand Laundry, S Kasuya	43
Belen Commercial Club, L C Becker Pres	7W
Belen Commercial Co, Gen Mdse	14
Belen Hotel, Bertha Rutz Prop	62
Belen Machine & Auto Works, Tony Brick, Prop	49
Bowland Thos H, r	79
Brown H M, r	82
Buckland Bros, Druggists	7 J
Budweiser Bar, Etiennie Didier Prop	64
Byers H E, r	45W

C

Campbell Ranch	29 J
Cash E G, r	46
Cassel E R, r	36
Castillo Felipe S, Blacksmith Shop, Jarales	28-3 J
Charles Albert S, r	70
Chaves Bros Livery Co, Chaves Bros, Props	51
Chaves Jose E, r	13
Cotton S K, r	25W
Cut Off Saloon, E G Cash Prop	10

D

Dalies Paul B, r	3 J
Davidson J L, r	52W
Delgado F A, r	84
Didier A, Cash Store	4
Dudley I A, Ranch	71-2W

E

Eaker C L, r	80

F

Feil & Ellermyer, Gen Mdse, Jarales	28-2 J
First National Bank	67
Fischer Frank G, r	3W
Fraser Carl W, r	94

G

Garcia Andres, Ranch, Jarales	28-3W
Garcia J M, Meat Market	8-W
Garcia Livery Co, D Garcia Prop	2
Gilbert & Sons, Meats, Groceries	19 J
Goebel Edgar, Ranch	54-2W

H

Harvey House	41 J
Hicks Mrs L W, r	93
Hispano Americano Pub Co	34
Hobbs G, r	48

I

Imperial Hotel, Mrs R C Kuhn Prop	50

J

Jarales Trading Co The, Gen Mdse, Jarales	28-2W
Jefferson H, r	37

K

Kennebeck H B, r	45 J
Kronig A R, r	39W

L

Lawler Mrs G M, r	97
Le Brun Wm E, r	30 J
Lynch W L, r	89

M

Mallow W P, r	85
Mason Roy A, r	56
McGrath Mrs W E, r	78
Moore C A, r	41W
Moore F B, Contractor	30W
Moore M L, r	81
Mountain States Telephone & Telegraph Co—	
Manager's ofc	0
Public ofc	75
Davidson W J, Exch Mgr, r	16

N

Neill E O	57
New State Tailors & Cleaners,	
J. L. Ashinhurst Prop	99

O

O K Cleaning Works, Frank Kaneshiro Prop	98

P

Pargas Emilio, r	23
Paul Sidney, r	29W
Pecolotto Frank	21
Peoples Lumber Co, B Jacobson	1
Picard Rev J A, r	5 J
Pohls Ranch, r	71-1 J
Postal Telegraph-Cable Co,	
To send a telegram call	"Postal"
For other purposes call	
Office	6
Preston A H, r	27 J
Prettner Richard C, r	71-1W
Public School	92

R

Radcliffe Wm D, MD	8 J
Raff Blacksmith Shop, F L Raff	53
Railways Ice Co The, G H Knowles Mgr	38
Reese E O, r	58
Riley C P, r	91
Rio Grande Saloon & Restaurant, Conrad Pahlisch	74
Rydholm Mrs C O, r	90

S

Sanchez Jesus, Gen Mdse, Adelino	54-3 J
Scholle Fred, Store	17
Servis S S, r	54-3W
Severns C, r	96
Silva Tomasita, r	55 J
Simmons P P, r	52 J
Spooner Mrs C B, r	35 J

T

Tate M H, r	32
Taylor Mrs C C, r	9
Torres Maria U, r	12 J

W

Weisinger H E, r	95
Wetmore H R, r	44
Wilkinson Dr S L, ofc	77
Wilson Claude N, r	25 J
Wilson Geo H, r	40
Witzel Geo, r	68

Z

Zeigler Rev John A M, r	65W

UNDERTAKERS Private Ambulance—Lady Assistant **Strong Bros.**

PHONES: OFFICE 75 -:- RESIDENCE 686

This is the entire 1916 telephone directory for the town of Belen. The John Becker Company had four telephones at the store. Some other Belen businesses that had telephones were Buckland Pharmacy, E.G. Cash's Cutoff Saloon, Feil and Ellermeyer Mercantile in Jarales, the Belen Harvey House, Frank Kaneshiro's O.K. Cleaning Works, and Fred Scholle's store. Two physicians, Dr. William Radcliffe and Dr. S.L. Wilkinson, also had telephones. More than 50 Belen residents had telephones in their homes. (Courtesy of Michael Jaramillo.)

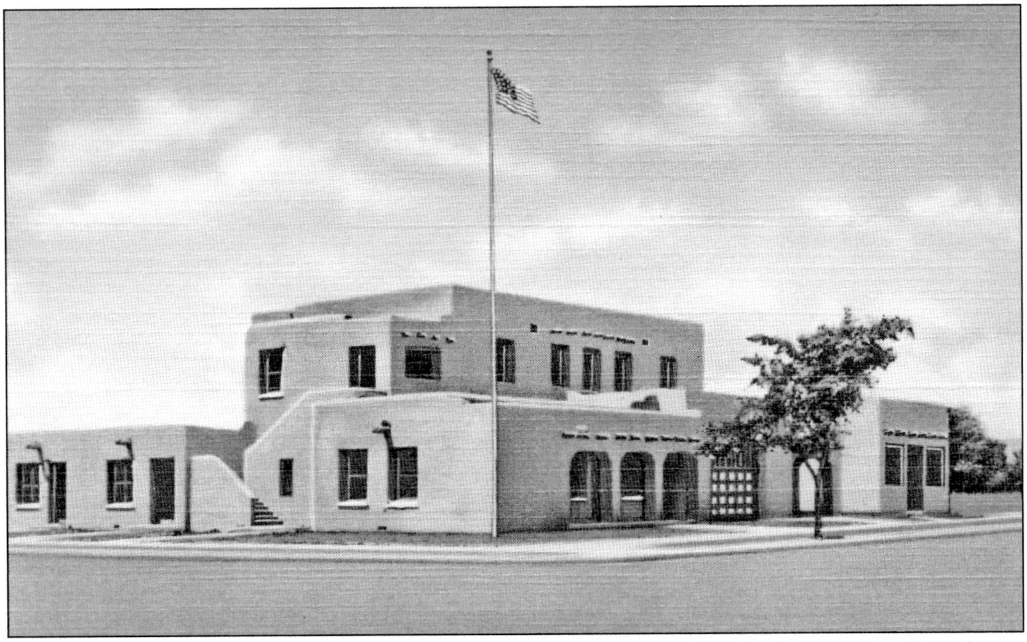

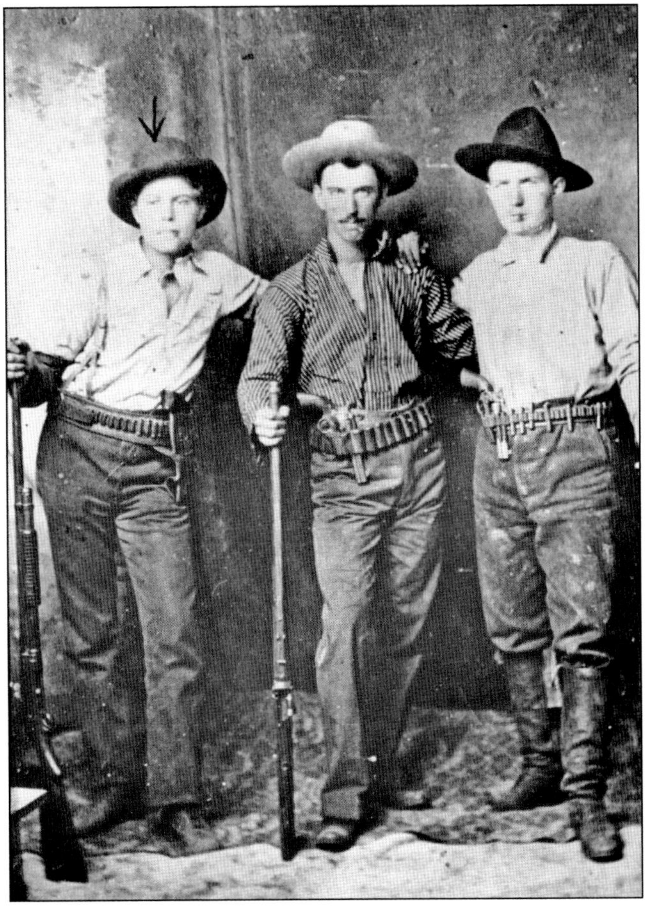

The old Belen City Hall and Police Department Building was constructed of adobe in 1938. It was a federal Works Progress Administration (WPA) project. Another WPA project across the street was the Welfare Building. Construction of these Pueblo Architecture–style buildings provided employment for many Belen residents during the Great Depression. (Courtesy of Richard Melzer.)

Con Hendren (left) served as mayor of Belen from 1930 to 1932. As a public official in Belen, he divided his time between running his business and responding to the needs of the town. The occasion for these wild-west costumes is not known. (Courtesy of Valencia County Historical Society.)

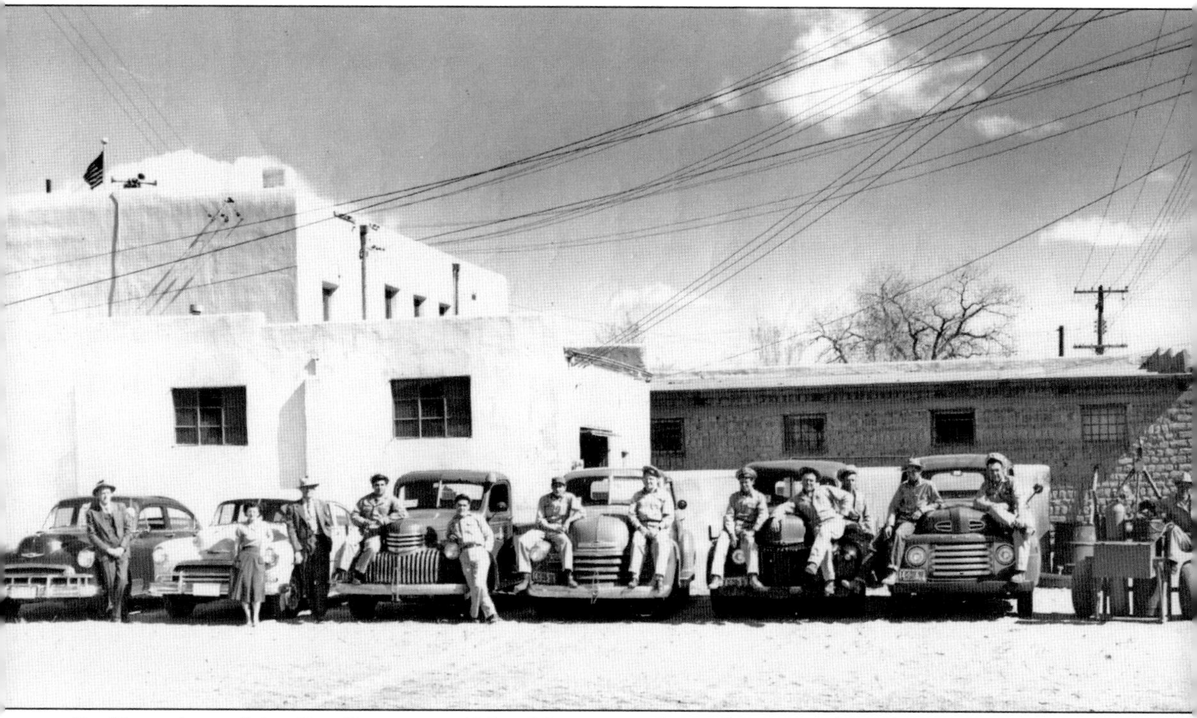

Staff members of the Gas Company of New Mexico are shown here in 1951 with company vehicles. From left to right are George Knecht, Theodora Sanchez, Bob Barton, Adam Sanchez, Ray Romero, Frank Sanchez, W.A. Burns, Amado Sanchez, Jose Jaramillo, Jess Whitten, Juan Chavez, Merrell Martin, and Daniel Garcia. By 1941, the company had nearly 400 customers in Valencia County, with two thirds of them in Belen. (Courtesy of Belen Harvey House Museum.)

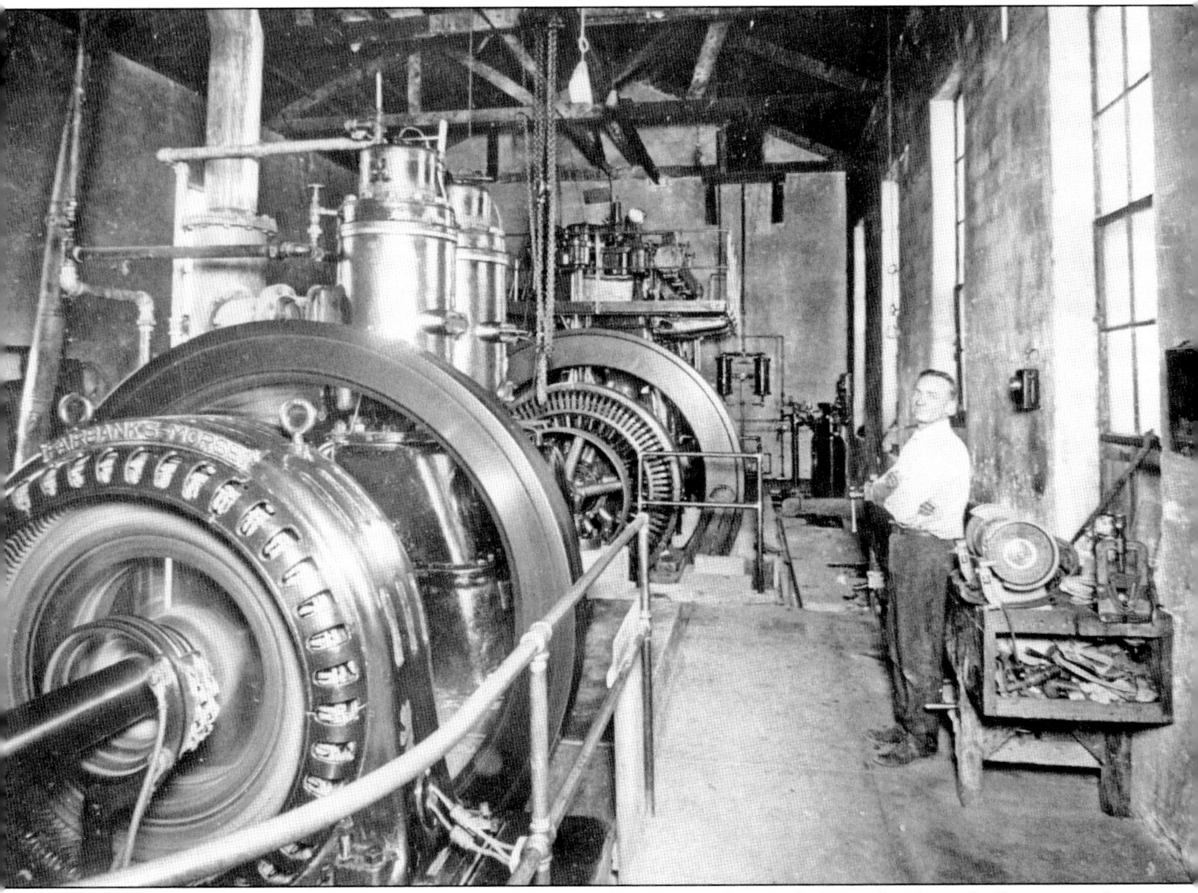

The Belen electricity-generating plant is seen here in 1930, with Tom P. Campbell posing for the camera. The plant was built in 1923 and featured diesel generators, later used in Belen for backup generating capacity in case of a utility-grid power failure. The electric plant was located on Second Street, about two blocks south of Becker Avenue. (Courtesy of Valencia County Historical Society.)

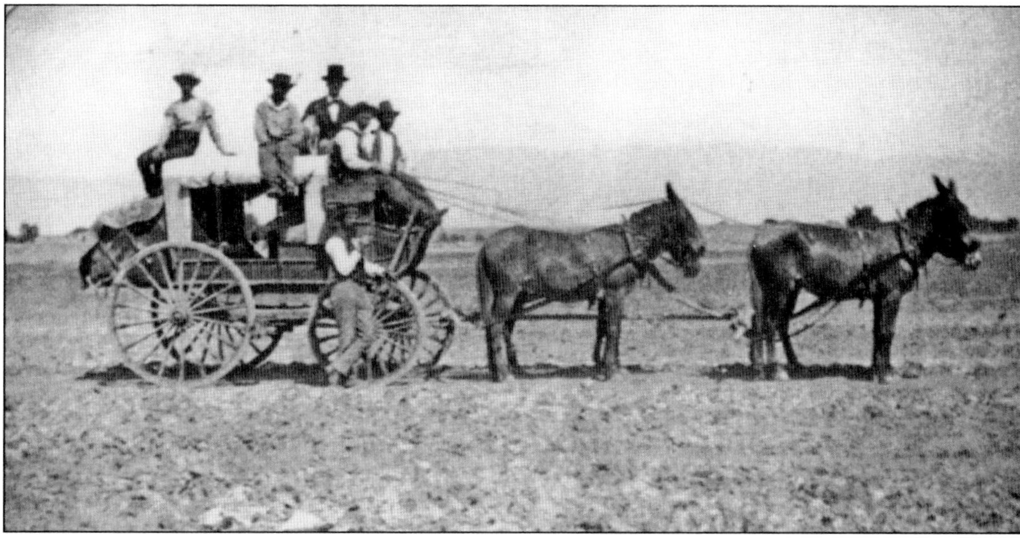

Stagecoaches provided public transportation in the Belen area until the early 20th century. This stagecoach, photographed around 1890, carried passengers between Belen and Los Lunas. The coach is being pulled by mules instead of horses. Residents could also rent horses and carriages from livery stables like the one run by Harry Byers. (Courtesy of Valencia County Historical Society.)

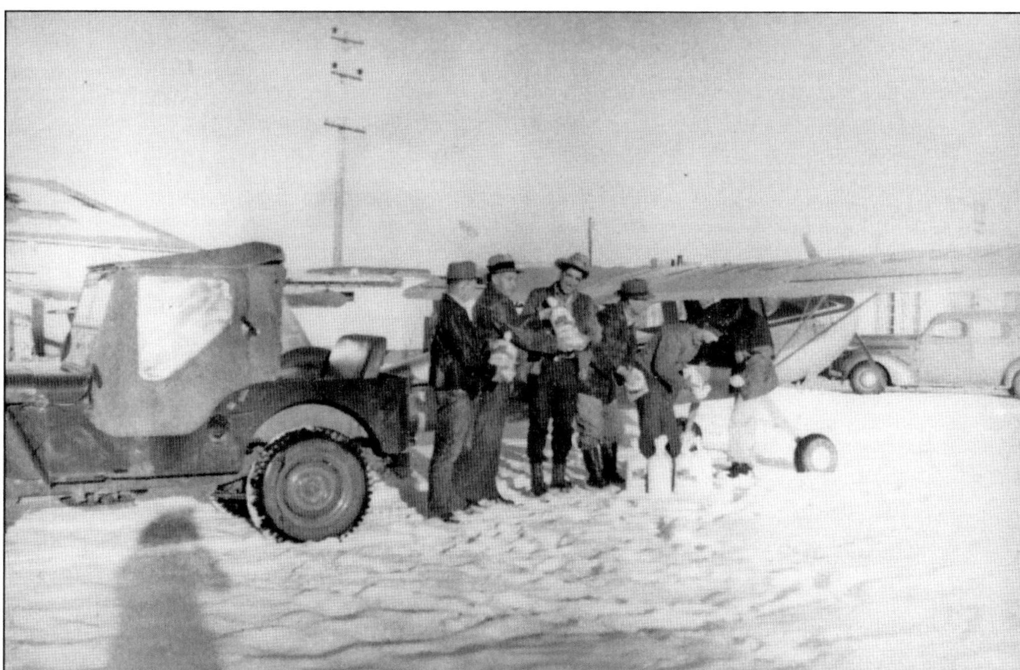

Belen's first airport was privately owned by Filo Sedillo and Hollis Wilson in the 1940s. It was located near where Ranchero Builders Supply is now. Wilson provided flying lessons and gave many Belen residents their first airplane rides. In 1922, the first plane to land in Belen ran out of gas and was forced to land near the railroad tracks. (Courtesy of Valencia County Historical Society.)

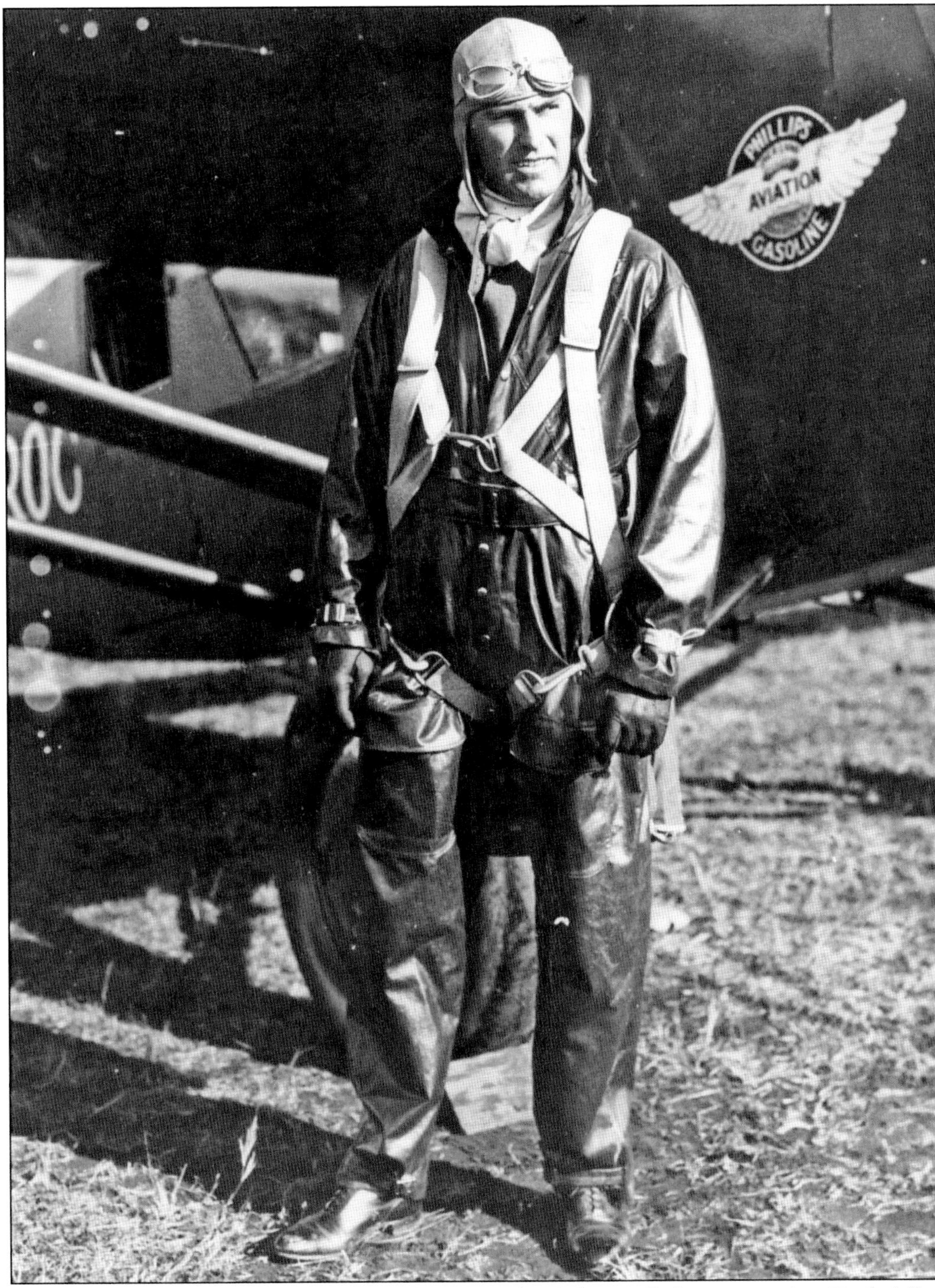

Inspired by Charles Lindbergh's solo flight across the Atlantic, Belen native Art Goebel flew the first nonstop flight from California to Hawaii—a distance of 2,400 miles—in 26 hours and 17 minutes in August 1927. Although the 31-year-old Goebel did not fly solo, he was dubbed the "Conqueror of the Pacific," just as Lindbergh had been called the "Conqueror of the Atlantic." (Courtesy of Valencia County Historical Society.)

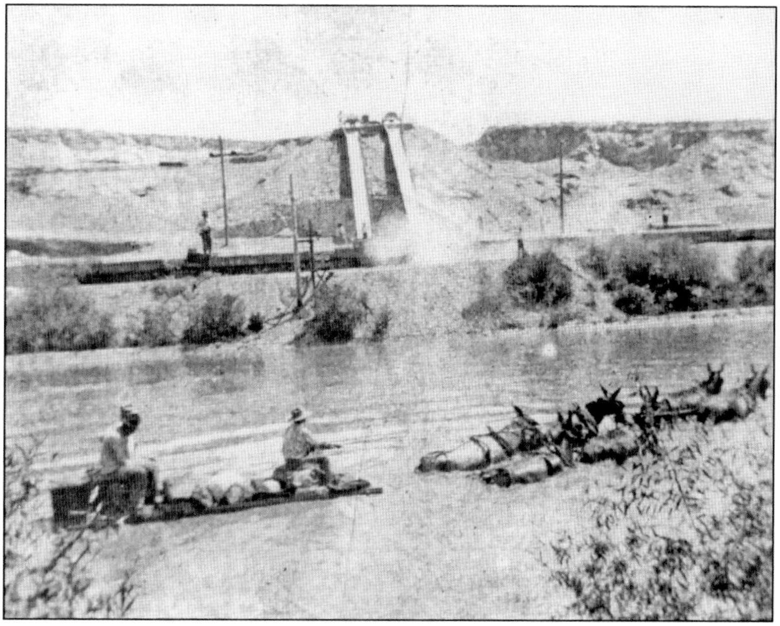

The Rio Grande was initially forded or crossed using small boats and rope-drawn ferries. The first bridges across the river were constructed of wooden timbers. In this photograph, a team of six mules is pulling a wagon loaded with large rocks that will be dropped in the river to form a pylon to support the bridgework. (Courtesy of Valencia County Historical Society.)

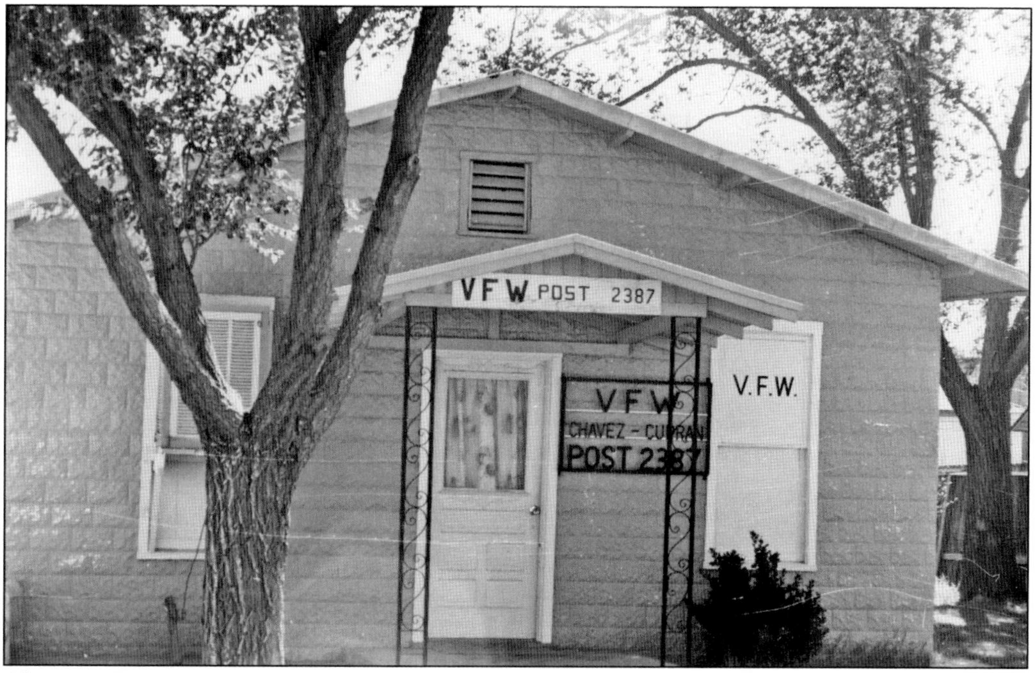

Chavez VFW Post No. 2387 was founded on April 20, 1945, with 26 charter members. It was named after Cpl. Horace Chavez, who was a prisoner of war and was killed at the Battle of Bataan during World War II. In 1976, the post's name was changed to Chavez-Curran to include honoring Capt. John Curran of Belen, a helicopter pilot killed in Vietnam. (Courtesy of Valencia County Historical Society.)

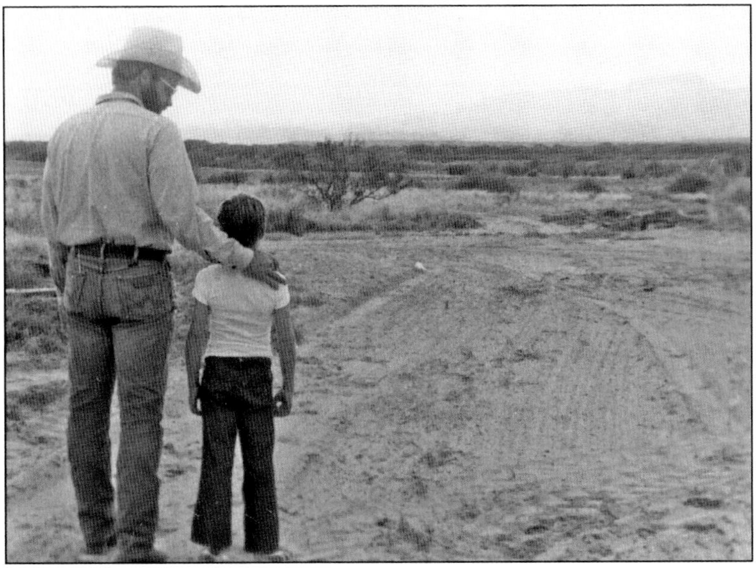

The New Mexico Boys Ranch, serving young men from broken homes, was started in 1944 by Al Buck and a group of Belen area businessmen. By the 1980s, the 2,350-acre Christian home had served more than 2,000 boys, supported by farming and ranching activities and private donations. The boys attended schools and churches in Belen. (Courtesy of Valencia County Historical Society.)

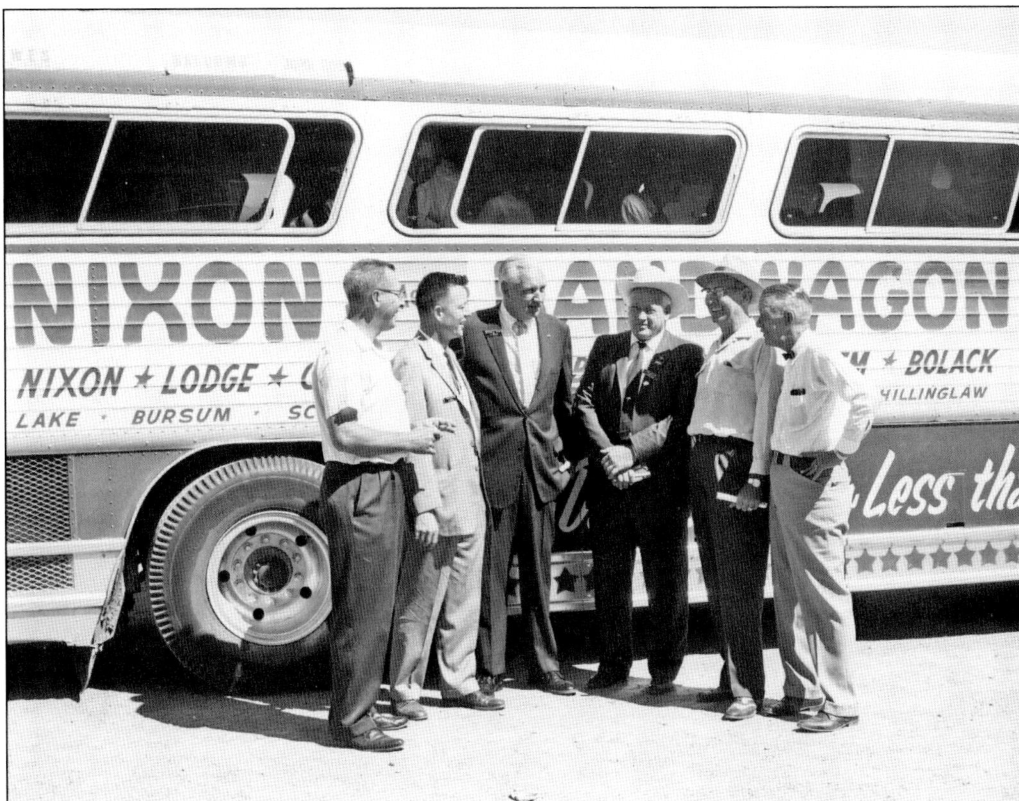

The 1960 presidential campaign came to Belen when the Richard Nixon "Bandwagon" pulled into town in September of that year. Pictured from left to right are Belen businessman Austin Lovett, two unidentified, former New Mexico governor Tom Bolack, J.B. Edmond, and *News Bulletin* editor Elfego Baca. (Photograph by Lenz Photo Shop, courtesy of Valencia County Historical Society.)

Six

Church Life in Belen

Religion has been important to the residents of Belen since the earliest days of the land grant. The title of the grant was, after all, Nuestra Senora de Belen (Our Lady of Belen), which also became the name of the Catholic church. The name Belen is Spanish for Bethlehem. The annual Our Lady of Belen Fiesta became the most important religious, as well as social, event of the year, and former residents often returned to Belen for the celebration.

Local Catholic priests served the community in many ways. Fr. Juan Anthony Picard was the priest at Our Lady Of Belen from 1901 to 1919. During this time, he was a member of the Commercial Club, a predecessor of the chamber of commerce. He also served on the Belen School Board and for a time was the town marshal. Our Lady of Belen Catholic Church has four active missions: Christo Rey in Bosque, San Isidro in Pueblitos, San Francisco Xavier in Jarales, and Our Lady of Guadalupe in Los Chavez.

John Becker and several other German merchants in Belen were members of the Evangelical Lutheran Church of Zion. Becker and his wife, Anna Vielstich Becker, were major contributors to the building of the Lutheran church at the corner of Reinken Avenue and North Fourth Street in 1911.

As more Protestants came to Belen, many of whom were employed by the Atchison, Topeka, and Santa Fe Railway, they established congregations of their own. Eventually, German Lutheran Church attendance declined, and the church building was subsequently used by a number of different Christian groups, including the Methodists and the Episcopalians. One of these groups was the First Federated Community Church of Christ. Preachers from as many as 19 different denominations preached at the church. This group occupied the former Lutheran church until 1964, when it became a Presbyterian church.

Religious observance is still an important part of life in Belen. In recent years, both the Presbyterians Methodists have built impressive new church facilities to serve their parishioners.

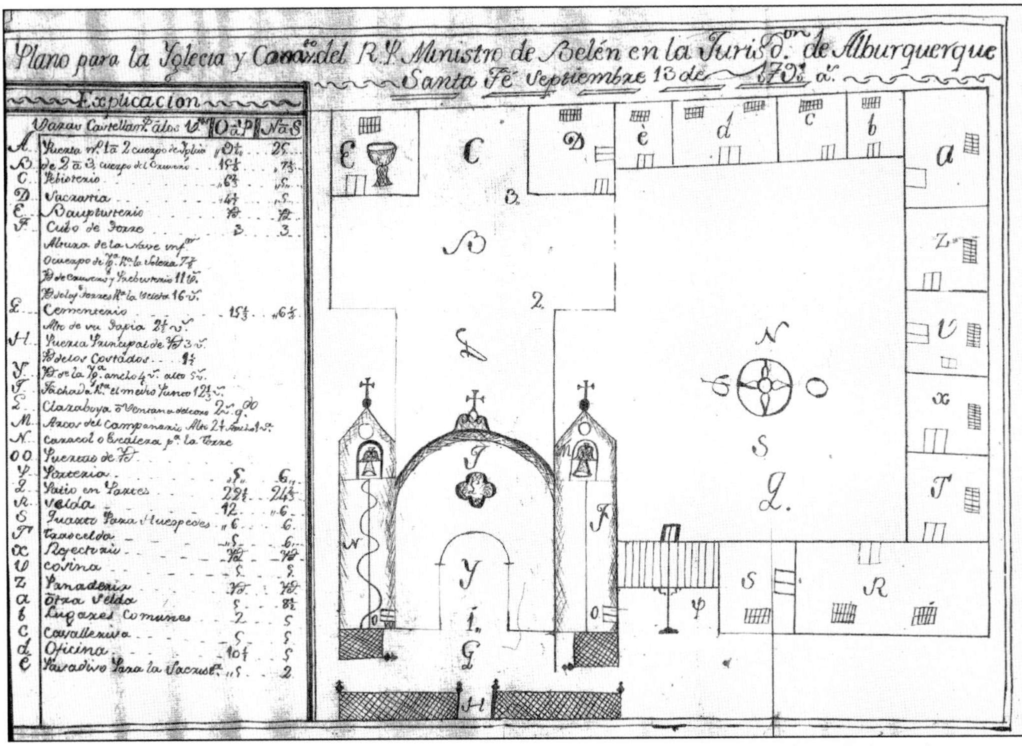

This is the plan of the original Our Lady of Belen Catholic Church, erected in 1793, at the present intersection of Ross and Wisconsin Streets. It was destroyed by a flood in 1855. The resulting dispute over a new location for the church created ill feelings among parishioners that lasted for many years. (Courtesy of New Mexico State University Archives.)

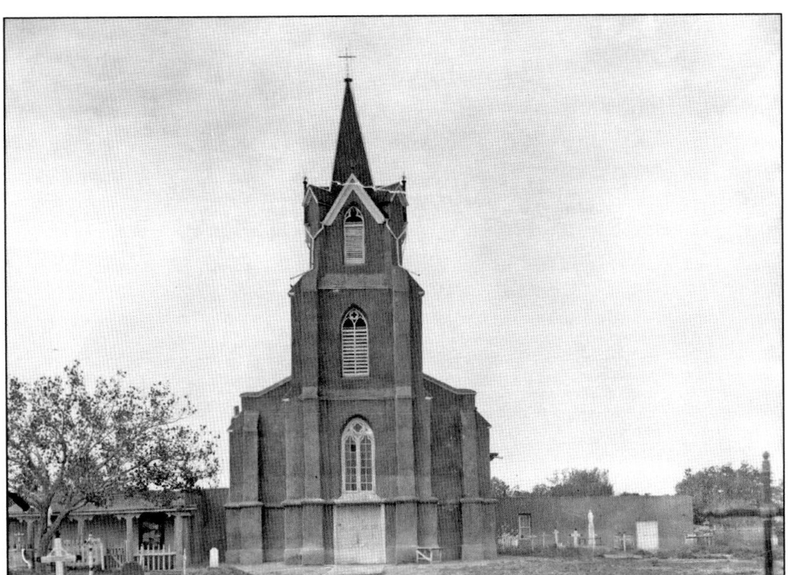

This photograph of the second Our Lady of Belen Catholic Church was taken in 1890. The church had twin spires when it was built in 1860, but they were replaced with a single, taller spire in 1875 to give the church a more Gothic appearance. (Courtesy of Valencia County Historical Society.)

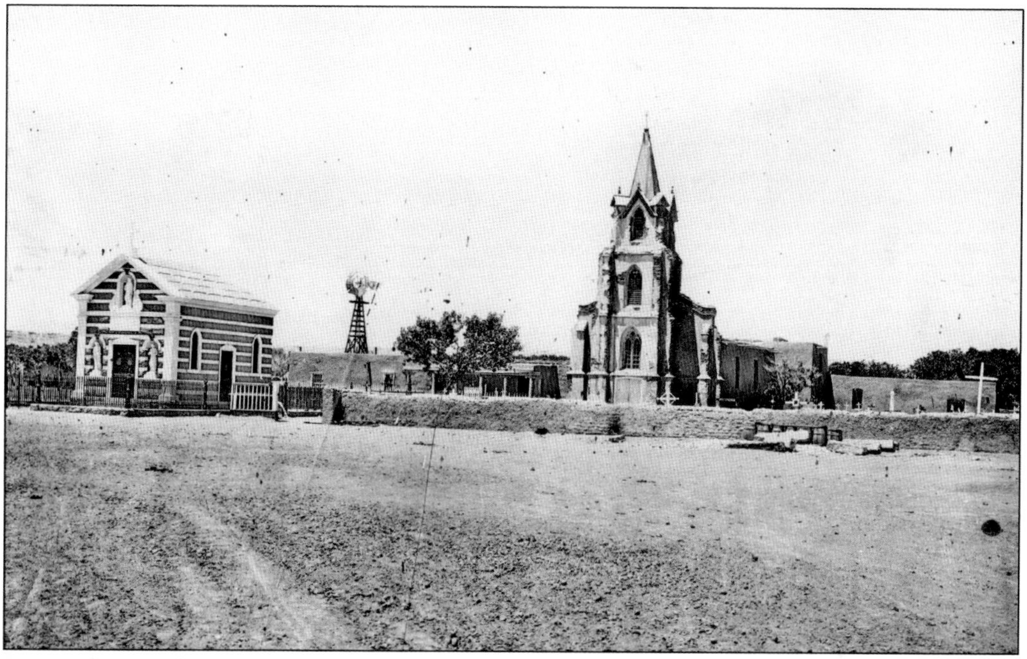

Pictured around 1920, Our Lady of Belen Catholic Church stands to the right of the Jose Felipe Chaves mausoleum. Closer inspection also reveals the poor condition of the plaster covering the adobes used to construct the main church building. (Courtesy of Valencia County Historical Society.)

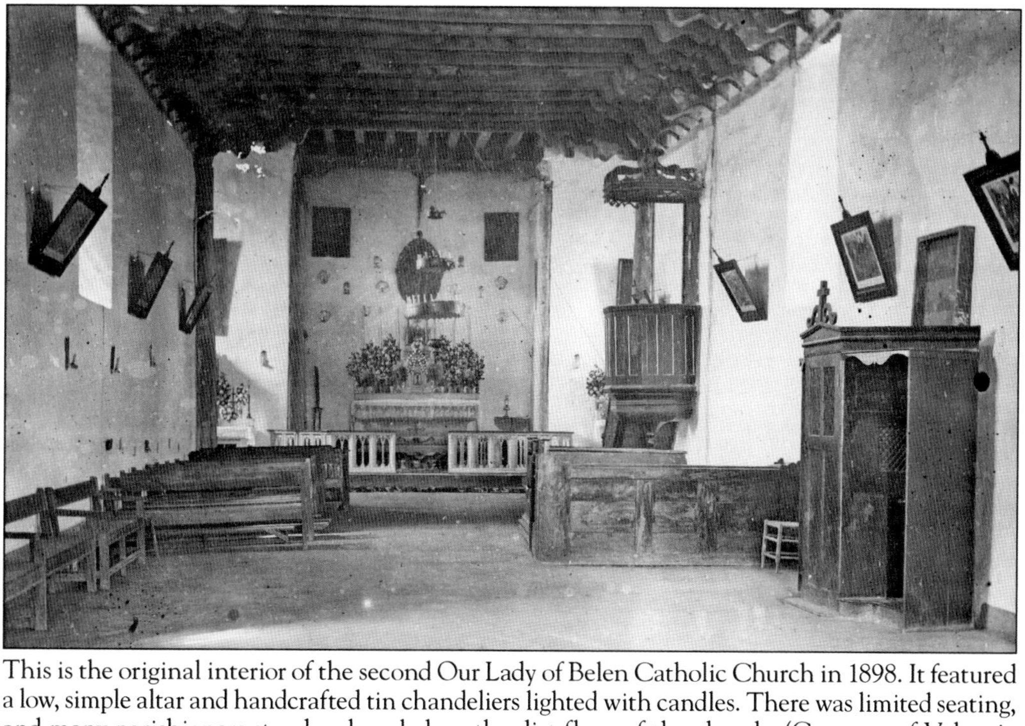

This is the original interior of the second Our Lady of Belen Catholic Church in 1898. It featured a low, simple altar and handcrafted tin chandeliers lighted with candles. There was limited seating, and many parishioners stood or kneeled on the dirt floor of the church. (Courtesy of Valencia County Historical Society.)

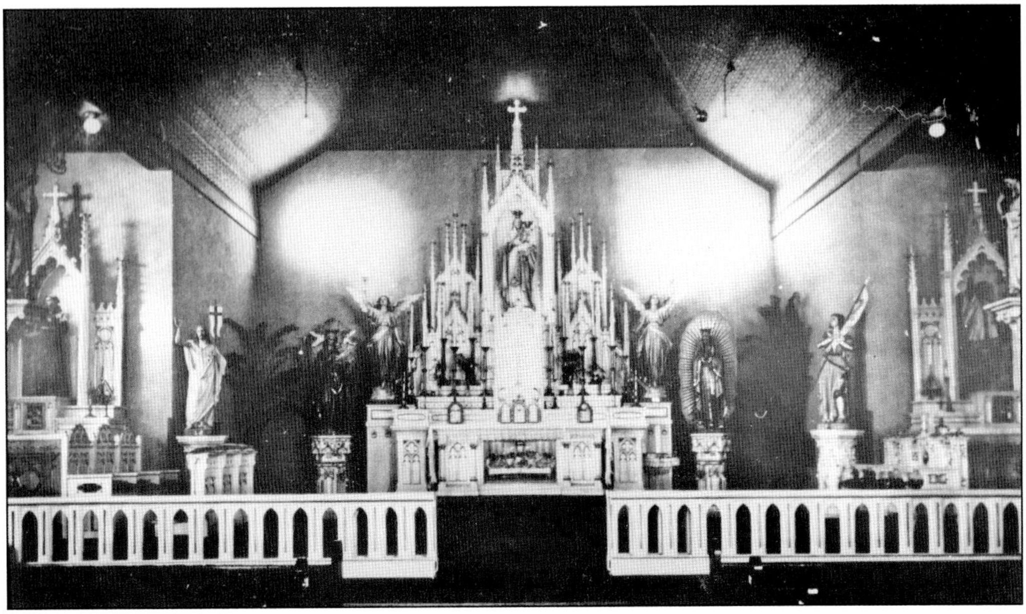

The interior of the second Our Lady of Belen Catholic Church is pictured here in 1918. The church was remodeled in the early part of the 20th century. At that time, the church was enlarged and the altar was modernized. (Courtesy of Valencia County Historical Society.)

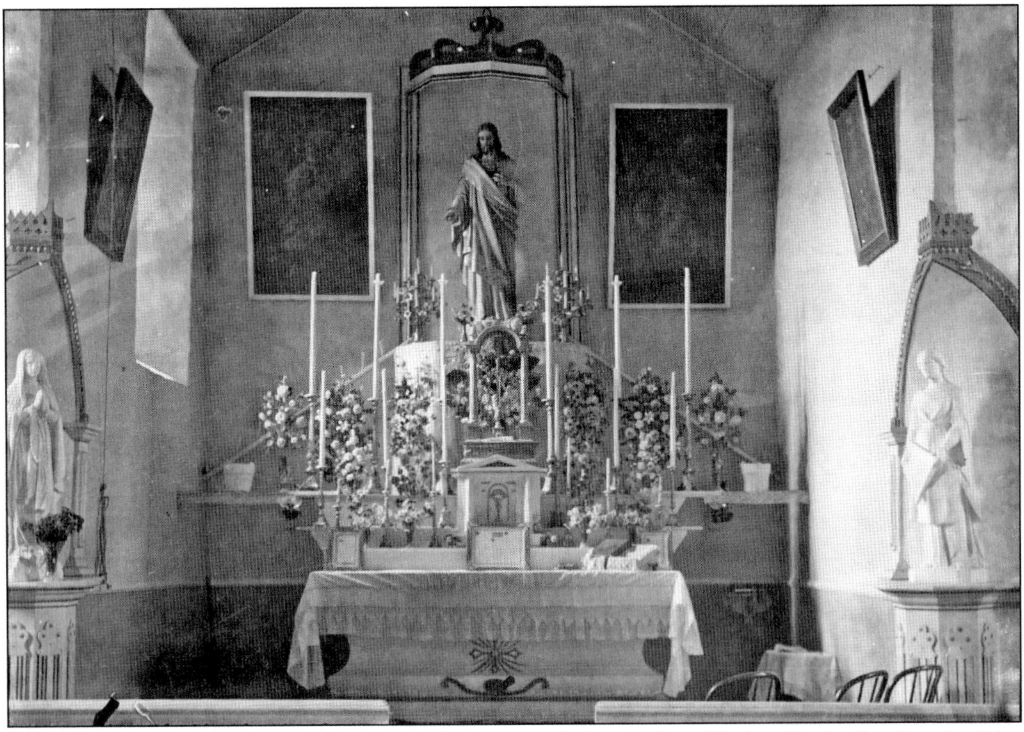

This photograph shows the sanctuary of the second Our Lady of Belen Catholic church. The second church was built in 1860 and served the congregation until 1973, when the building's deteriorating condition required demolition and the construction of a new church. (Courtesy of Valencia County Historical Society.)

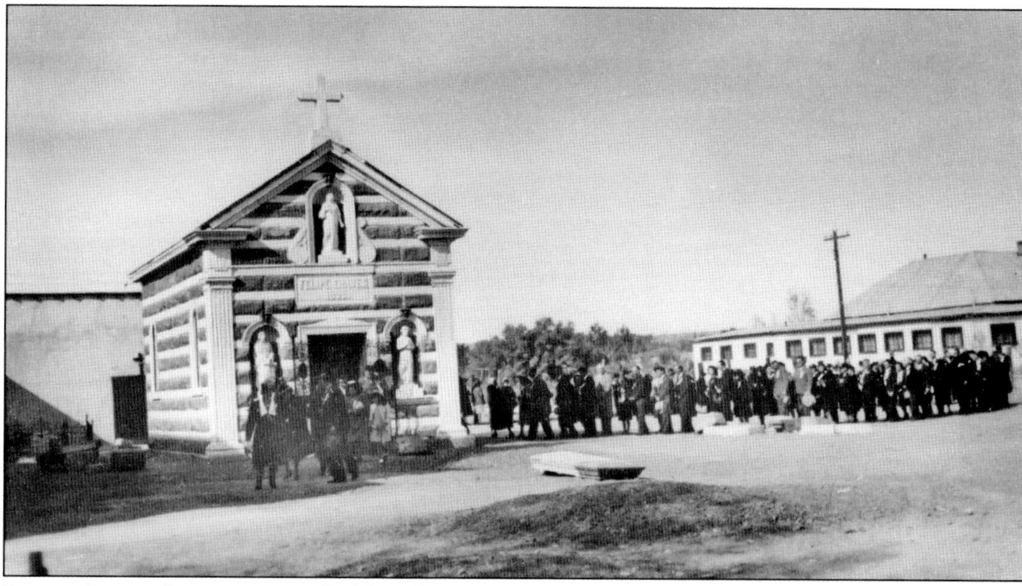

Pictured is a religious service held at the Jose Felipe Chaves mausoleum located at the original *campo santo*, or cemetery, in front of Our Lady of Belen Catholic Church. The mausoleum was so large that certain religious services were held there instead of in the church itself. (Courtesy of Valencia County Historical Society.)

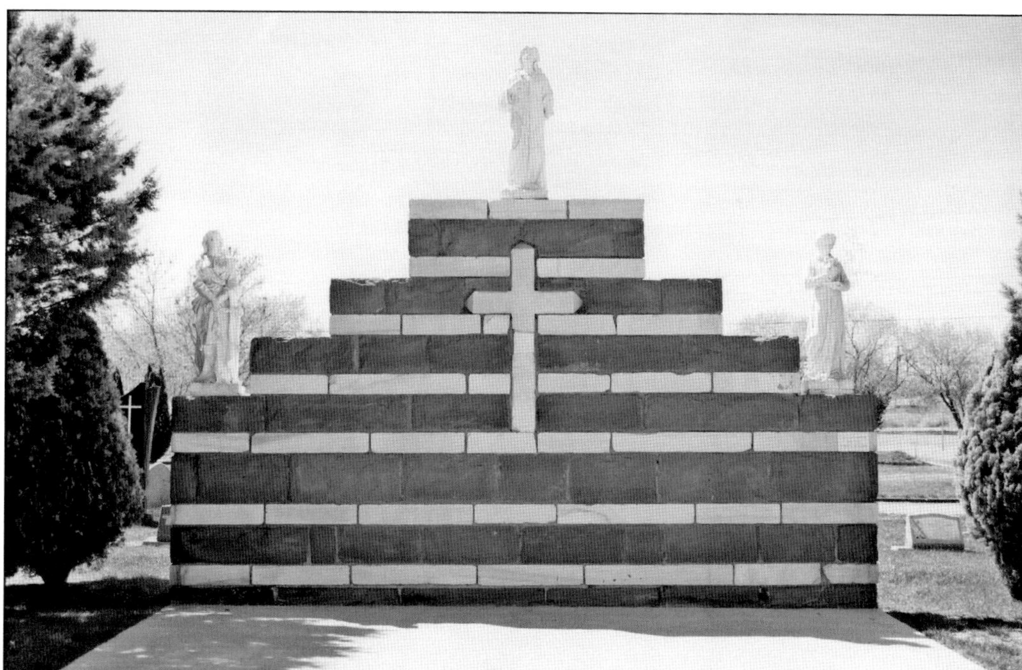

The Jose Felipe Chaves mausoleum was relocated when the campo santo was moved to the rear of the church in 1943 to accommodate a new church entrance. It was dismantled in 1973, and some of the marble and red sandstone was used to erect this memorial wall in the new cemetery. (Author's collection.)

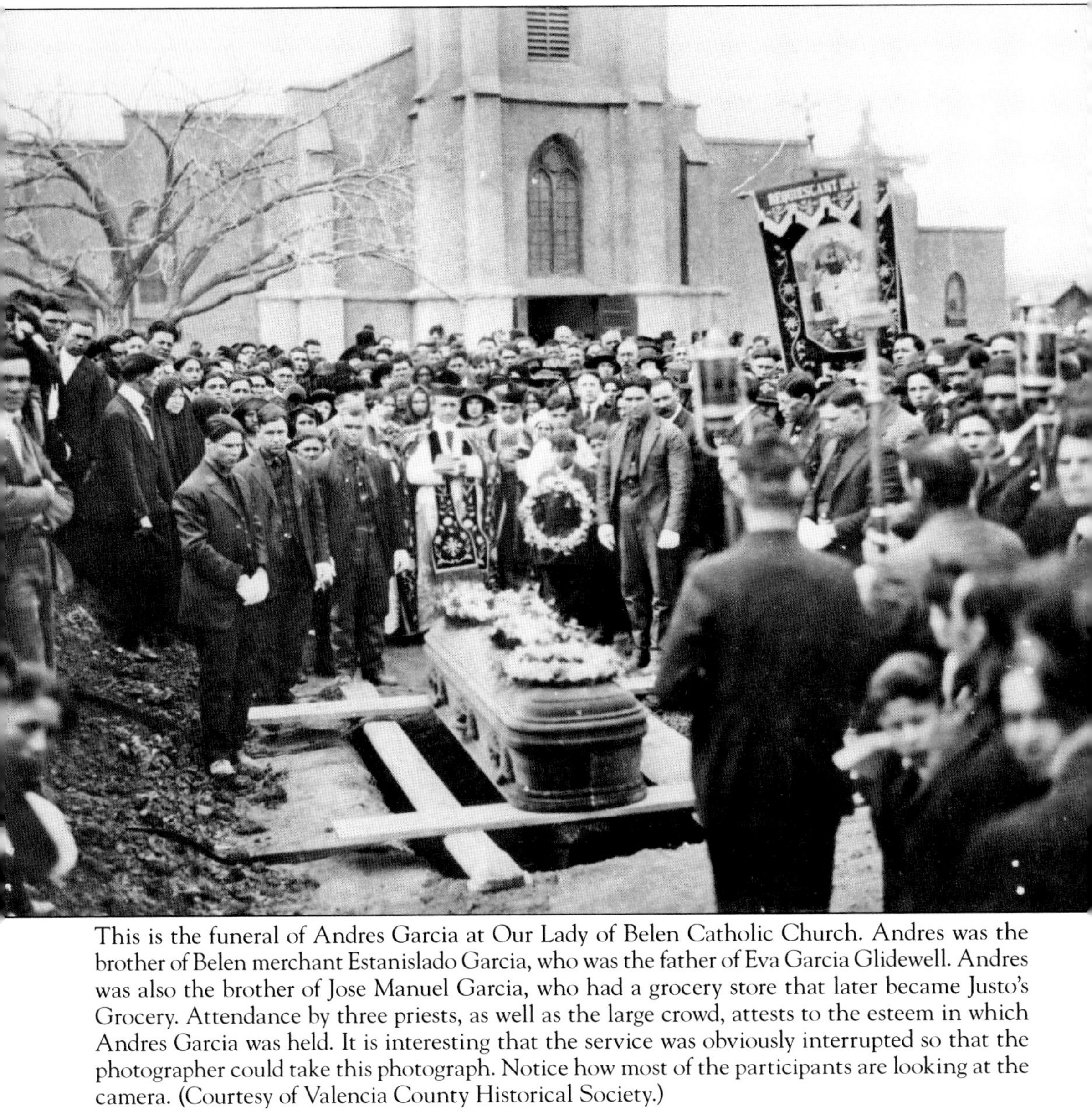

This is the funeral of Andres Garcia at Our Lady of Belen Catholic Church. Andres was the brother of Belen merchant Estanislado Garcia, who was the father of Eva Garcia Glidewell. Andres was also the brother of Jose Manuel Garcia, who had a grocery store that later became Justo's Grocery. Attendance by three priests, as well as the large crowd, attests to the esteem in which Andres Garcia was held. It is interesting that the service was obviously interrupted so that the photographer could take this photograph. Notice how most of the participants are looking at the camera. (Courtesy of Valencia County Historical Society.)

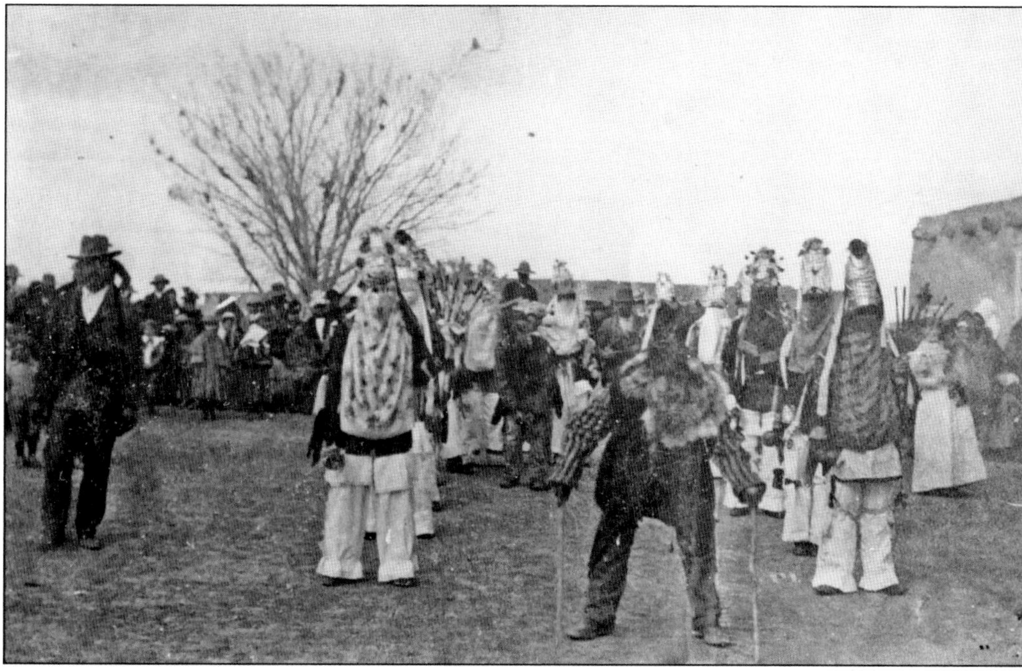

These Matachines dancers at Our Lady of Belen Catholic Church are pictured around 1905. The Matachines is a religious folk dance that originated in Spain and was later incorporated into Aztec dances in Mexico. The Matachines was brought to New Mexico by the first Spanish settlers; the tradition continues to the present day. (Courtesy of Valencia County Historical Society.)

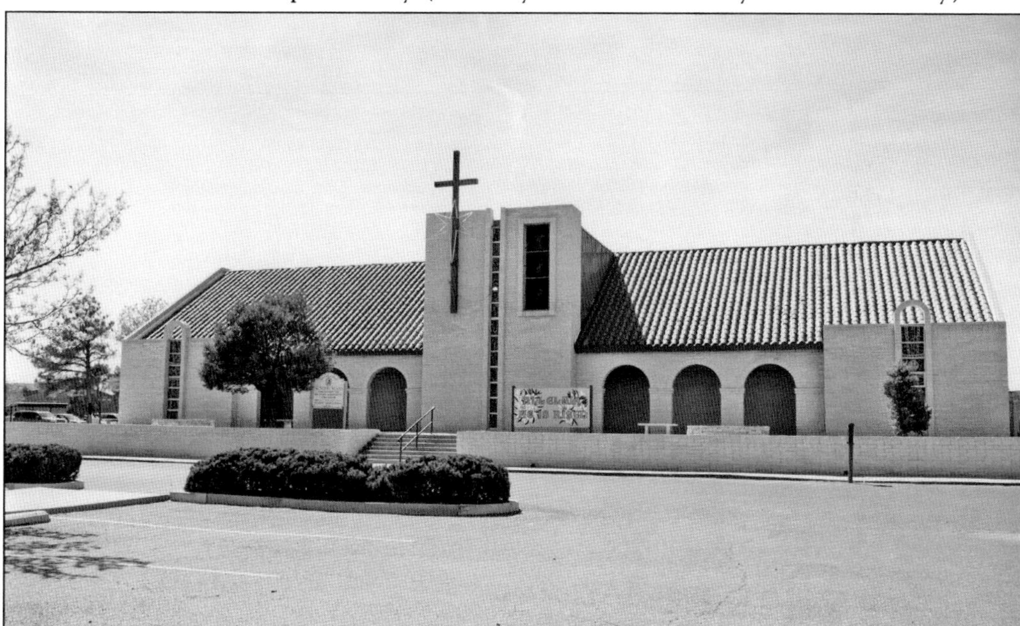

This is the third Our Lady of Belen Catholic Church, constructed in 1973. Contractor Herman Tabet was selected to build the 15,519-square-foot church that when finished would seat 1,066 parishioners. The first Mass was conducted at midnight on December 25, 1973, and formal dedication of the structure was on February 17, 1974. (Author's collection.)

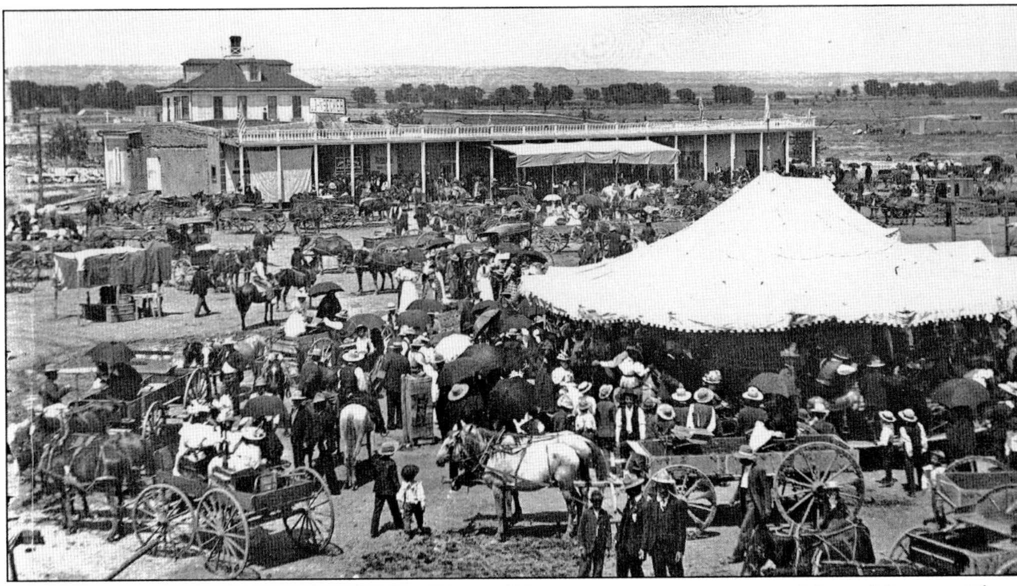

This is a view of the Our Lady of Belen Fiesta. The *carpas*, or tents, are evident. Many residents who had left Belen returned for the fiesta, which was the major social event of the year. The photograph was taken sometime before 1898, when a two-story brick structure was added to the single-story Territorial-style building. (Courtesy of Margaret Espinosa McDonald.)

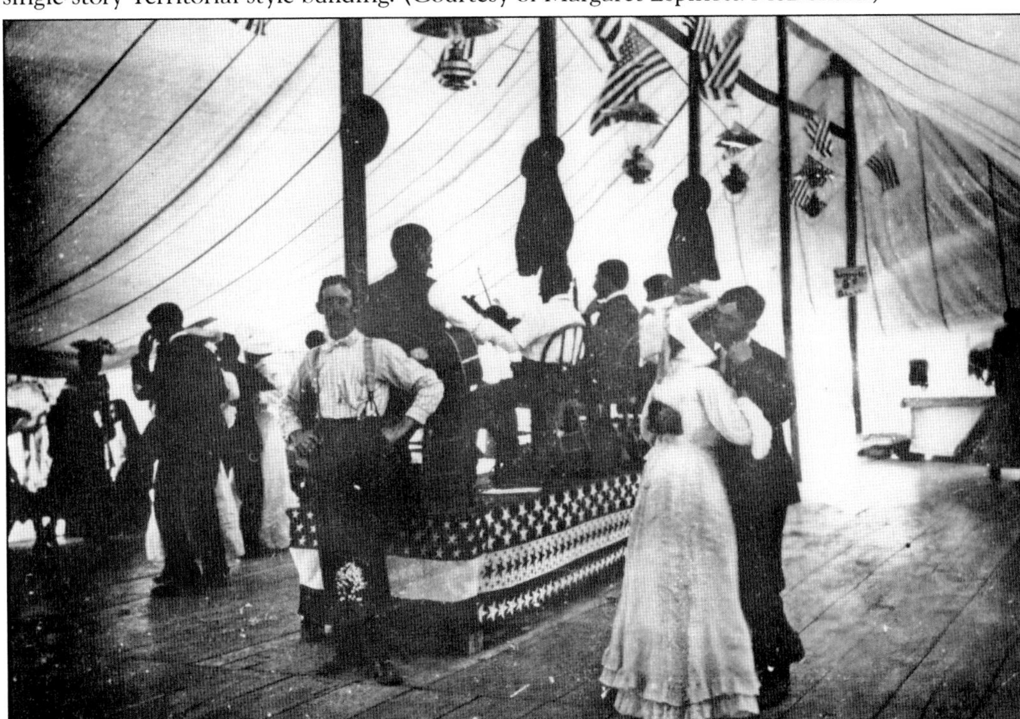

Dances were held in the carpas at the Our Lady of Belen Fiesta. A couple would begin dancing, and after a few minutes a man would come by saying, "Have your dimes ready, boys." The young men would have to pay *un daime* (a dime) to continue dancing. When all of the dimes had been collected, the music would resume. (Courtesy of Valencia County Historical Society.)

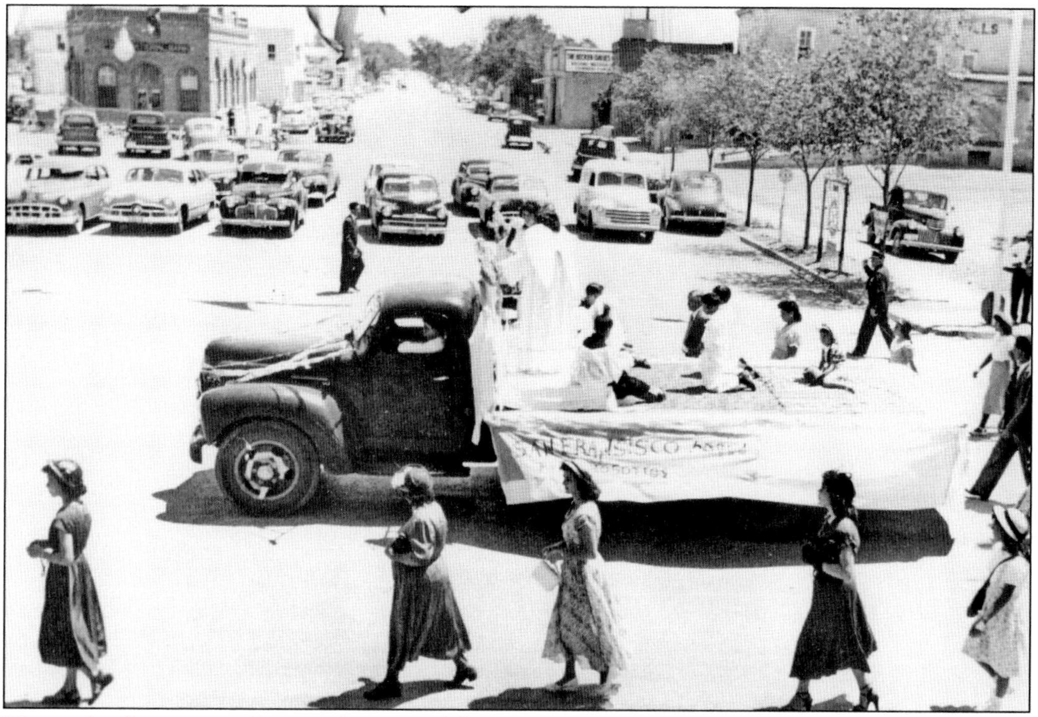

This is the float created by parishioners of the San Francisco Xavier Mission Church in Jarales for the Our Lady of Belen Fiesta in 1947. Each mission church would make a float for the procession. On the left in the background is the First National Bank of Belen, and on the right is the Belen Roller Mill. (Courtesy of Valencia County Historical Society.)

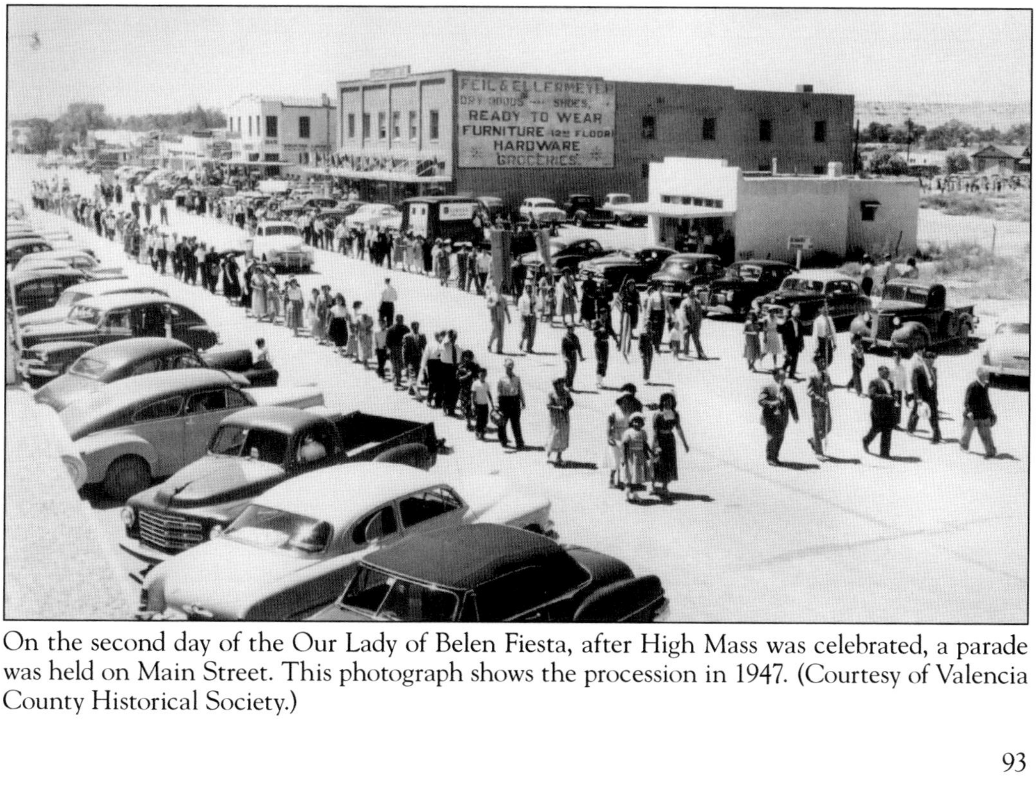

On the second day of the Our Lady of Belen Fiesta, after High Mass was celebrated, a parade was held on Main Street. This photograph shows the procession in 1947. (Courtesy of Valencia County Historical Society.)

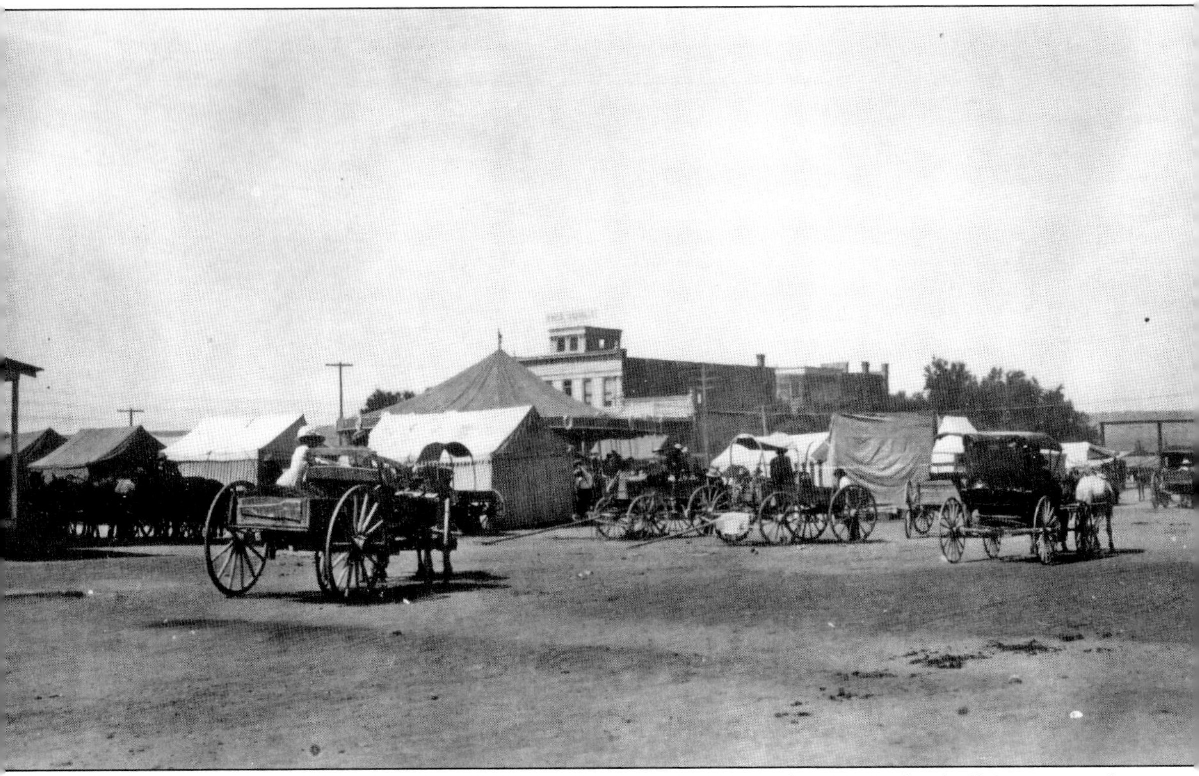

This is another view of the Our Lady of Belen Fiesta, taken around 1900. Fred Scholle's mercantile store can be seen in the background. (Courtesy of Valencia County Historical Society.)

Fr. John Castillo (Order of the Servants of Mary) is seen as a young boy with his mother, father, and sister. John Castillo was born on a farm near Belen, on January 1, 1913, during a thunderstorm that uprooted a cottonwood tree in the family's front yard. His parents were Mauricio Castillo and Francisquita Chavez y Peña, the daughter of Juan Chavez y Peña. (Courtesy of Valencia County Historical Society.)

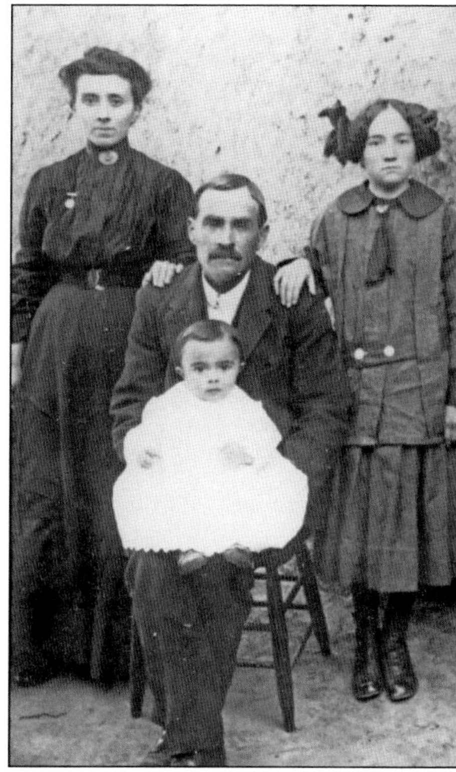

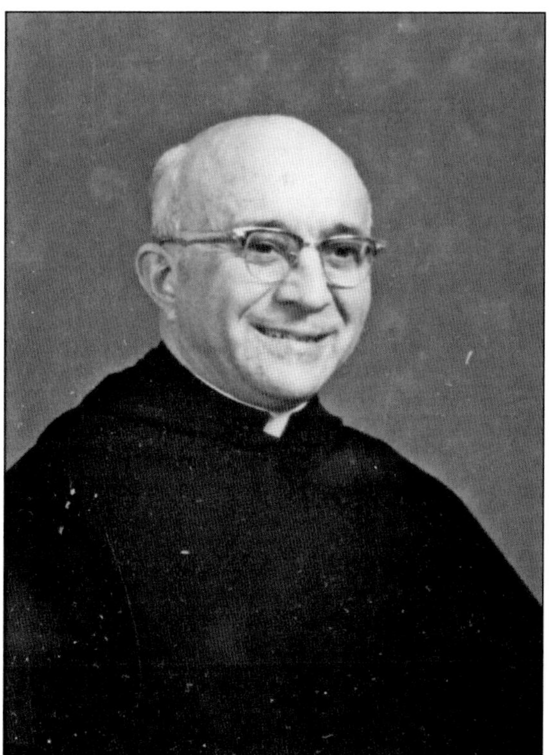

While attending St. Mary's School in Belen, John Castillo decided to become a servite priest. He was ordained at the Chapel of Quigley Seminary in Chicago, Illinois. Once ordained, he was assigned as assistant pastor for nine years in Belen. After service in Detroit, Chicago, and Commerce City, Colorado, he returned to Belen for eight years as a pastor. (Courtesy of Valencia County Historical Society.)

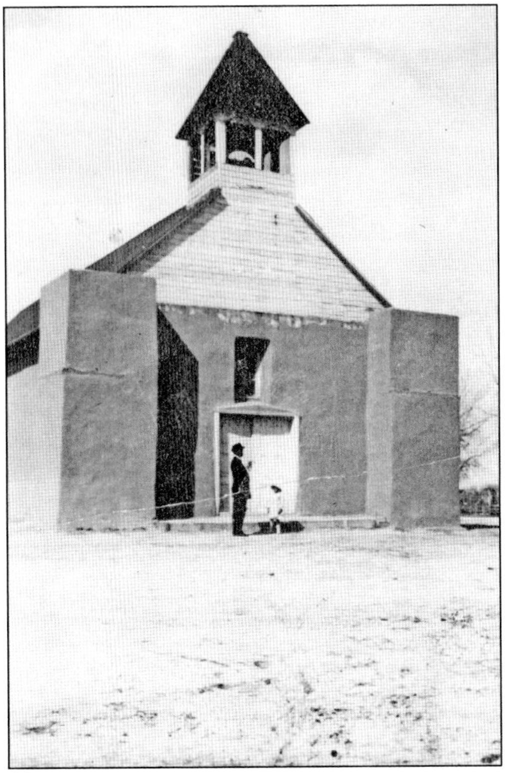

St. Francis Xavier Church, located in Jarales, is one of four mission churches of the Our Lady of Belen Parish. The first St. Francis Xavier Church in Jarales was built in 1876. One of the adobe walls of the church collapsed due to erosion in 1976, and a new church was constructed of modern materials. (Courtesy of Valencia County Historical Society.)

This church, located at the corner of Reinken Avenue and Fourth Street, was dedicated on February 12, 1911, as the Zionist Lutheran Church of Belen. Devout German Lutherans, John Becker and his wife, Anna Vielstich Becker, donated the land and most of the construction costs. In 1922, several Protestant churches in Belen banded together to form the Belen Federated Community Church of Christ in this same building. (Courtesy of Valencia County Historical Society.)

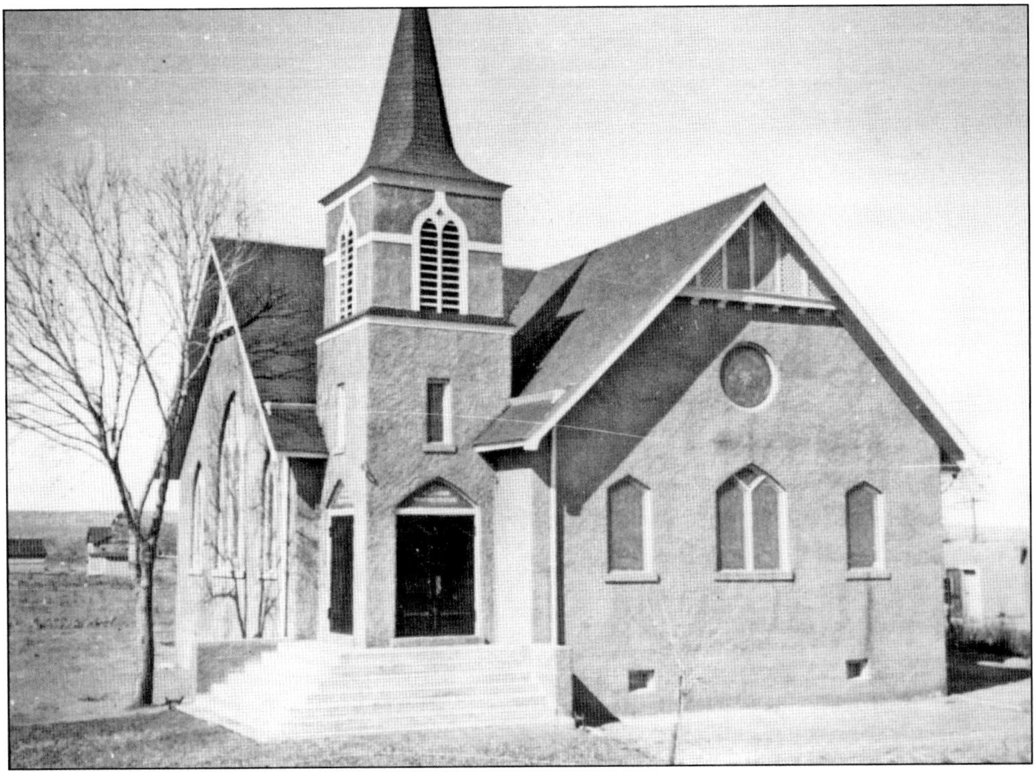

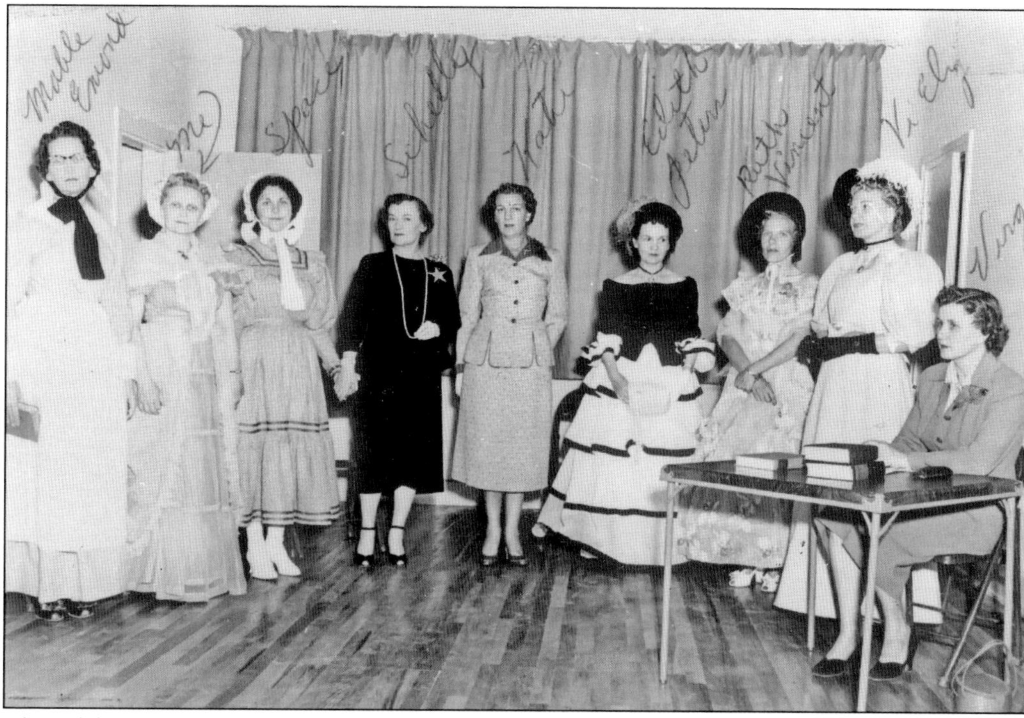

The celebration of Mother's Day at the Federated Church in Belen around 1950 was a costumed affair. Shown from left to right are Mable Emond, Marybelle Keith Jones, Virginia Space, ? Shelly, Kate Calhoun Johnson, Edythe Peter, Ruth Vincent, Vi Ely, and Virginia Seery. Ministers from as many as 19 different denominations preached on different Sundays at the First Federated Community Church of Christ. (Courtesy of Valencia County Historical Society.)

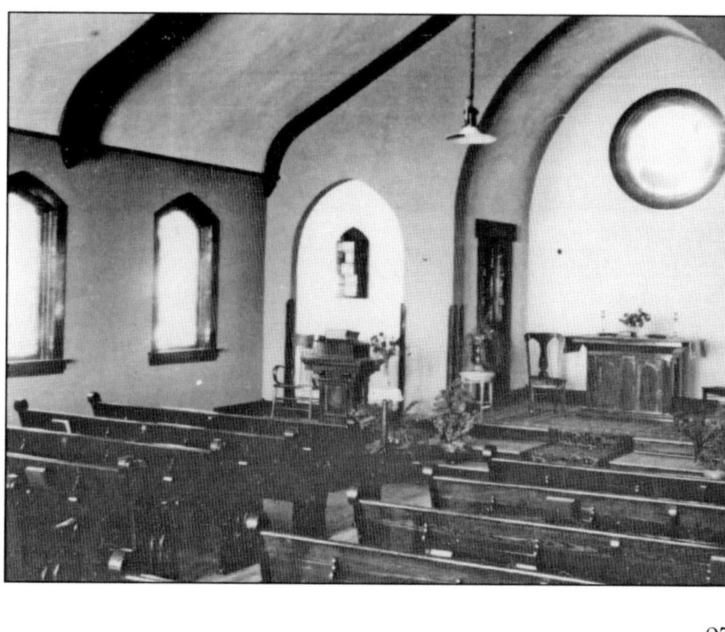

This is the interior of the First United Presbyterian Church in the early 1960s. The church building served three different protestant congregations during its lifetime as a place of worship. When the Presbyterians built a new church in 2000, the building was sold, and became a funeral parlor. (Courtesy of Valencia County Historical Society.)

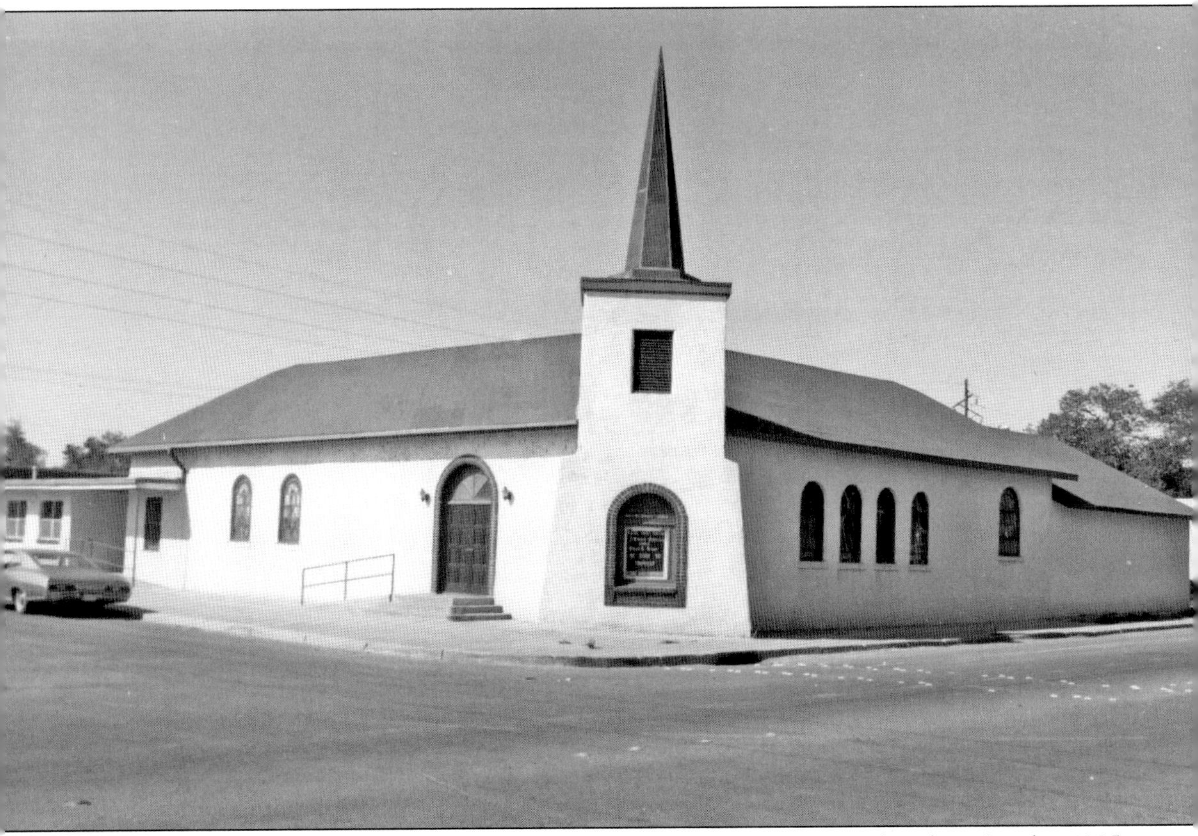

The Belen Methodist Church, pictured here, was established as a mission church in October 1905, with services held once a month. Charter membership day for the new Methodist church was on October 24, 1948, with 84 charter members. A 5,000-square-foot addition was constructed in 1981. (Courtesy of Valencia County Historical Society.)

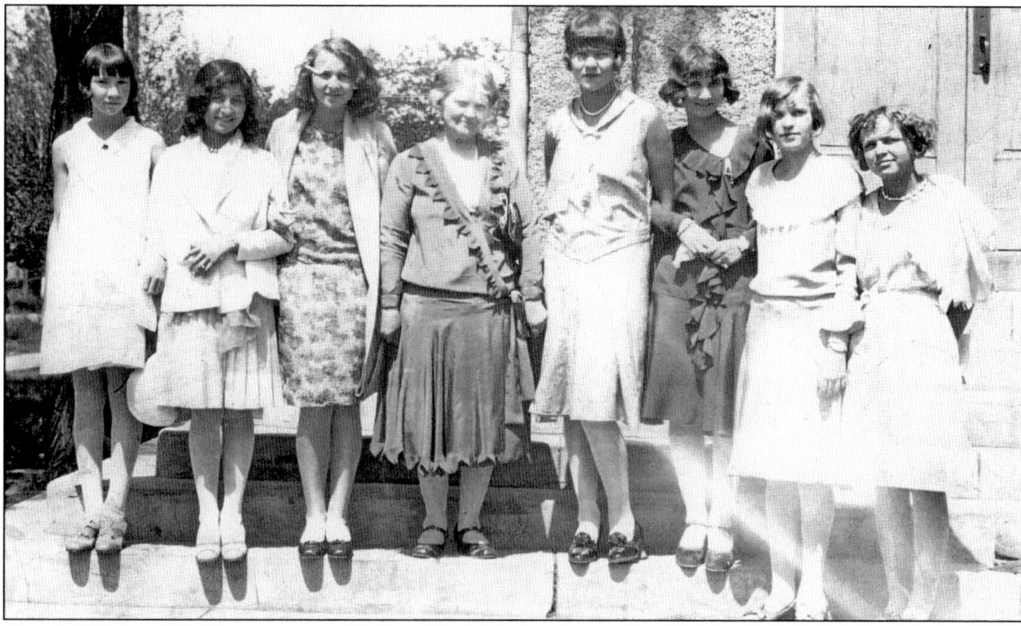

Shown here is Fairy V. Simmons' Sunday school class at the First Methodist Church in 1930. Pictured from left to right are Virginia Space, Elizabeth Enibecker, Martha Wilkinson, Fairy V. Simmons, Helen Rutz Martin, Jessie Sonthem, Irene Wicks, and Ella McCormick. Fairy and her husband, P.P. Simmons, moved to Belen in early 1900 from Missouri. (Courtesy of Belen Harvey House Museum.)

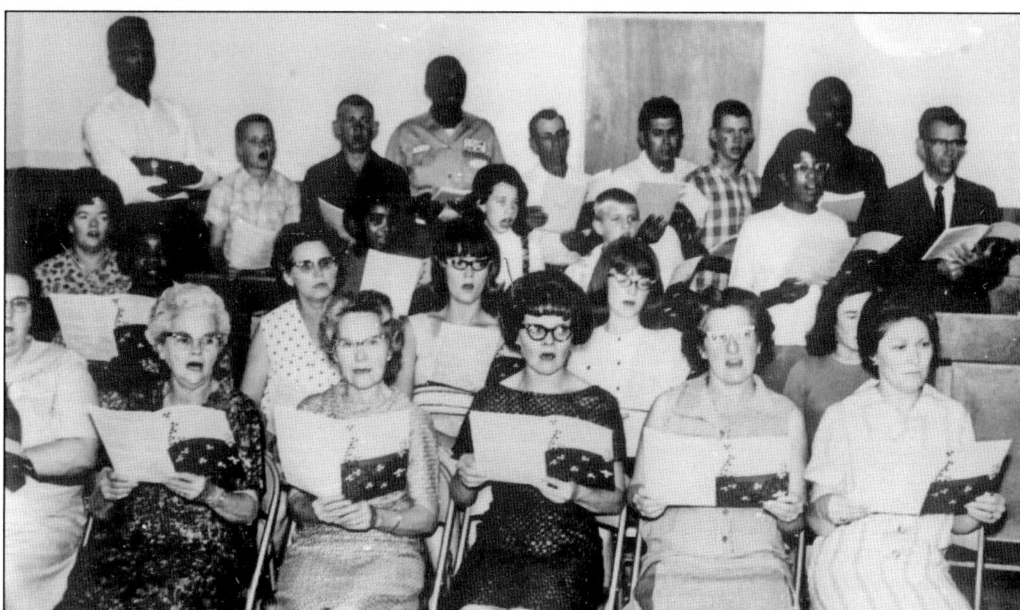

The music study group of the First Baptist Church of Los Chavez is shown here in 1965. A southern Baptist mission was formed in the Los Chavez community, located just north of Belen, in June 1962. Church members remodeled a barracks building, and the first services were held in March 1965. A second building was moved to the property in October 1967. (Courtesy of Valencia County Historical Society.)

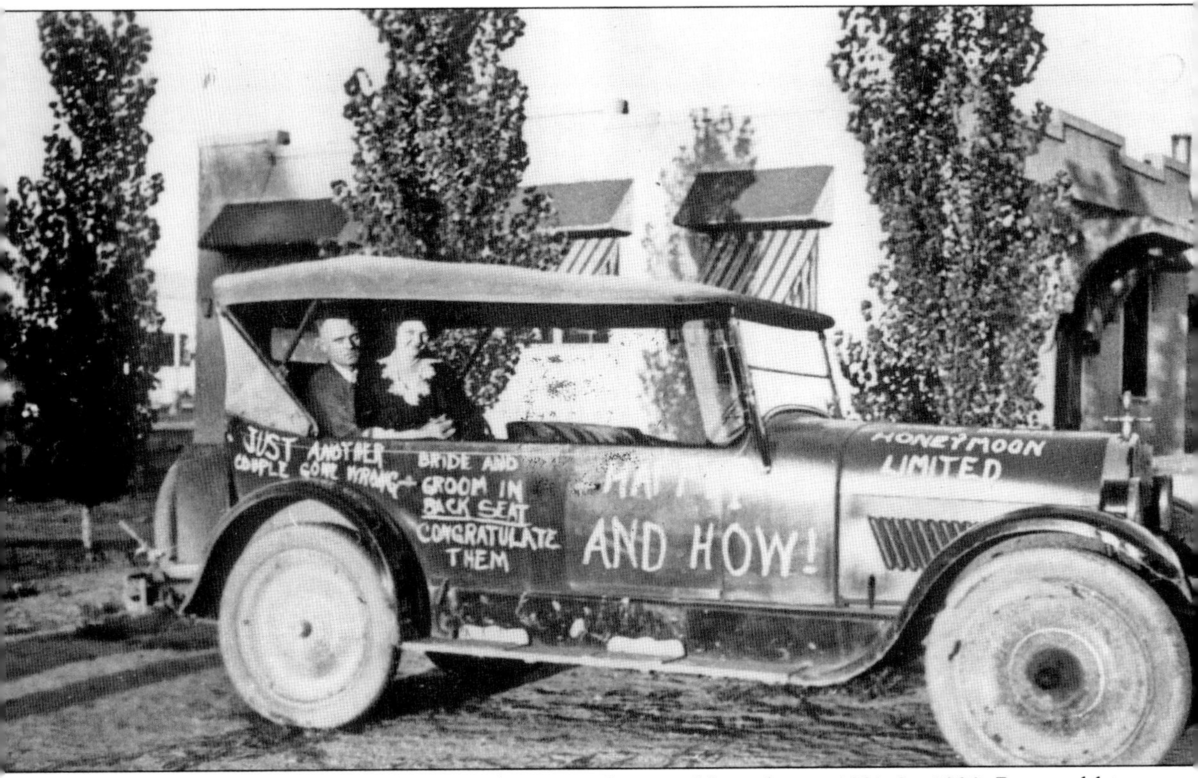

Shown here are Ray and Eleanor Tolman on their wedding day in 1931. In 1920, Ray and his father moved to Belen and opened a shoe-repair business in a tent under a large tree on Becker Avenue. Ray and Eleanor Grapes McLeod met at the home of Frank and Friede Fischer, where religious services were held for Christian Scientists. They were married in September 1931. Ray and Eleanor were among those who founded the Christian Science Society of Belen. (Courtesy of Valencia County Historical Society.)

Seven

Schools, Sports, and Recreation

The first schools in Belen were religious schools. The Sisters of Mercy of Cincinnati, Ohio, opened a Catholic school in Belen in 1888, but it closed due to a lack of funds after only two terms. The Lutheran church opened a school in 1894 to educate the children of the many German immigrant merchants who had settled in Belen. St. Mary's Catholic School was opened in 1927, teaching first through the eighth grades.

In 1907, Belen Central Grade School was opened on Reinken Avenue, and in 1916 a Valencia County High School was built in Belen. The land for the school building, known as the "Red Brick," was donated by John Becker. Students from throughout the county attended high school in Belen until the Solomon Luna Union High School was built in Los Lunas in 1926.

Sports were an important part of school activities; local students were able to participate in football, basketball, and baseball as members of school teams. Community teams also competed, especially in baseball.

Many recreational activities were also available to residents of Belen. Picnics in the bosque were popular, especially on the Fourth of July. Other activities included swimming at the Belen Swimming Pool or at the Belen Beach swimming facility. People also waded and swam in the Rio Grande. Bowling was another popular recreation, and Belen bowlers were winning territorial competitions as early as 1900.

The nearby Manzano Mountains provided many recreational opportunities as well. Hiking, hunting, and camping were popular activities in the Manzanos for many local residents.

Young people enjoyed spending time at local gathering spots like Justo's Grocery Store and, on special occasions, at the Belen Harvey House. There were also many school social functions and private parties. In addition, the Oñate Theater brought major motion pictures to Belen.

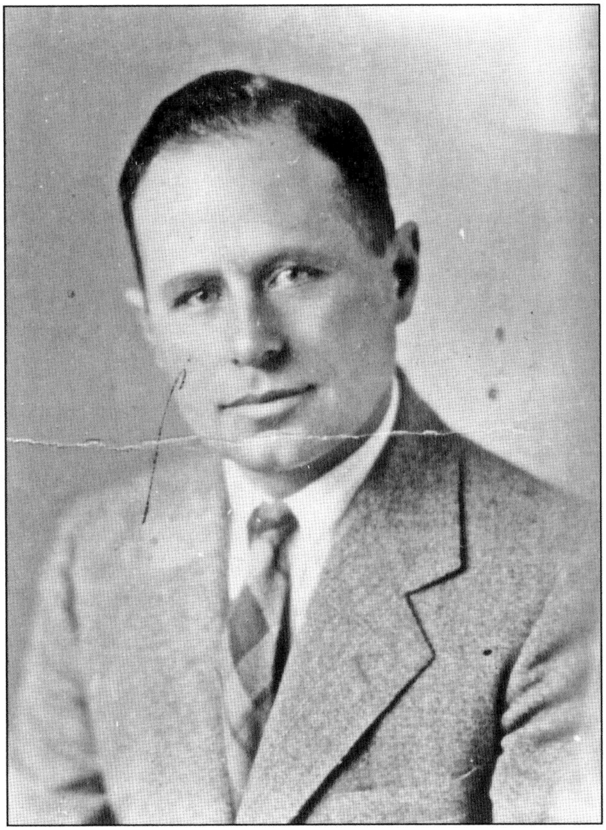

Adelino Sanchez was a leader in the field of education for 45 years, beginning in 1913 and ending in 1958. He was born in Jarales in 1896, the oldest son of Jesus and Beatriz Sanchez. He served as classroom teacher, principal, and superintendent. Adelino Sanchez was one of the founders of the Ranchers State Bank and served as its first president. (Courtesy of Los Lunas Museum of Heritage and Arts.)

These students attended the church school of the First Zionist Lutheran Church around 1900. It was located in the Lutheran church on Main Street before the new church, funded primarily by John and Anna Becker, was constructed at the corner of Reinken Avenue and Fourth Street. All of the students were children of the many local German merchant families who were Lutherans. (Courtesy of Valencia County Historical Society.)

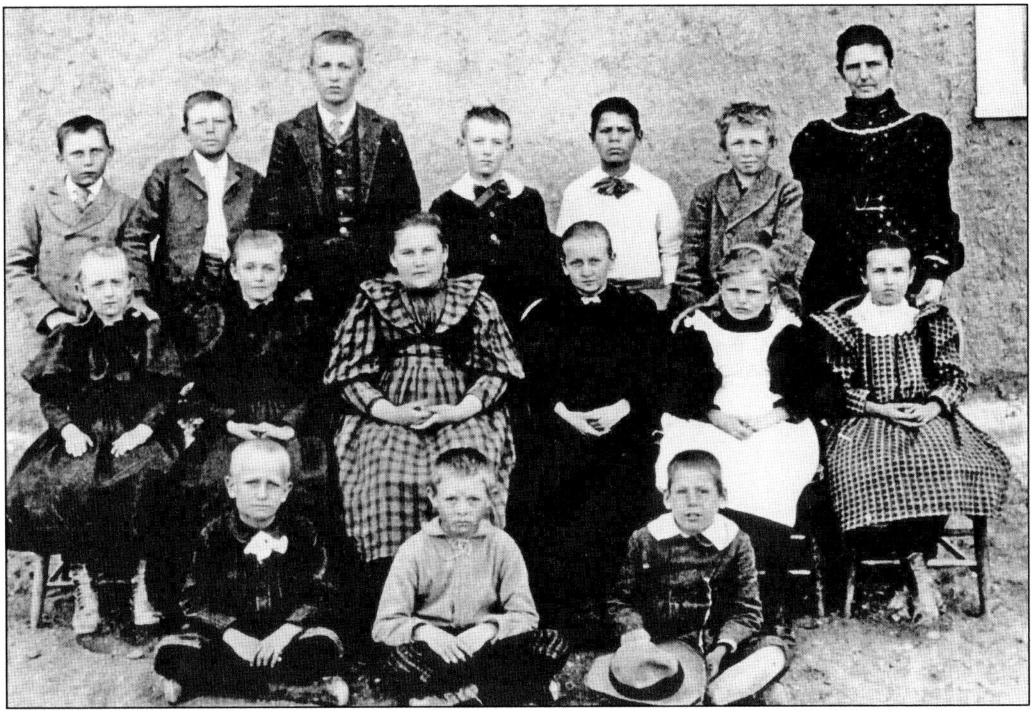

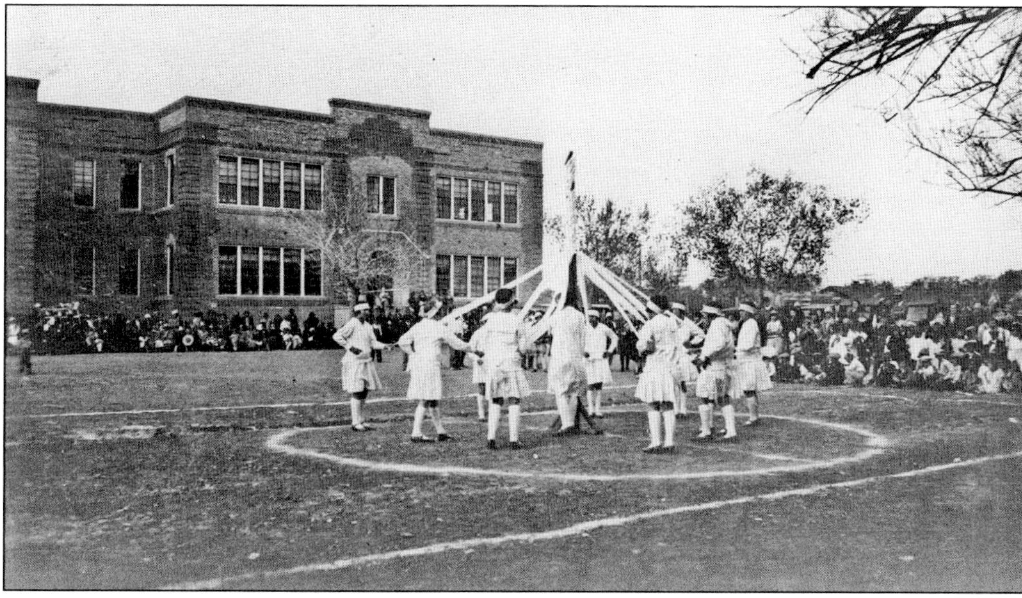

Pictured around 1930 are students participating in May Day festivities, by dancing around a maypole, at Belen High School. A maypole dance was an important component of many high school activities as part of a May Day celebration and signaled the coming of spring. (Courtesy of Valencia County Historical Society.)

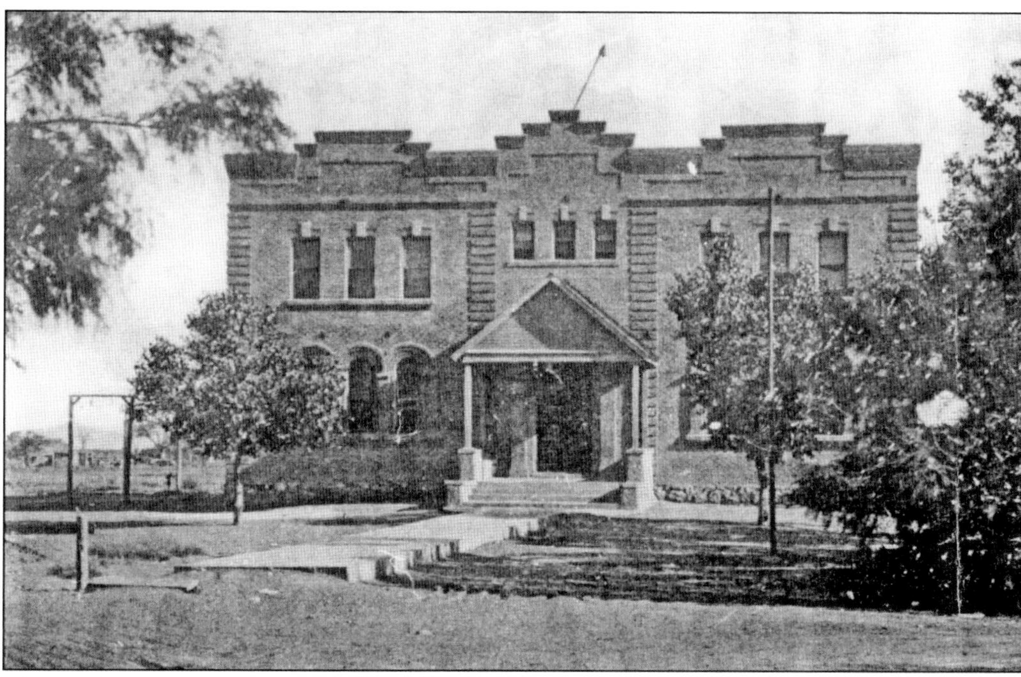

This building, constructed in 1907 and located on Reinken Avenue, was originally intended to serve as a territorial orphanage, but funds for the operation of the orphanage were not allocated by the state legislature; instead, the building became Belen Central Grade School. (Courtesy of Valencia County Historical Society.)

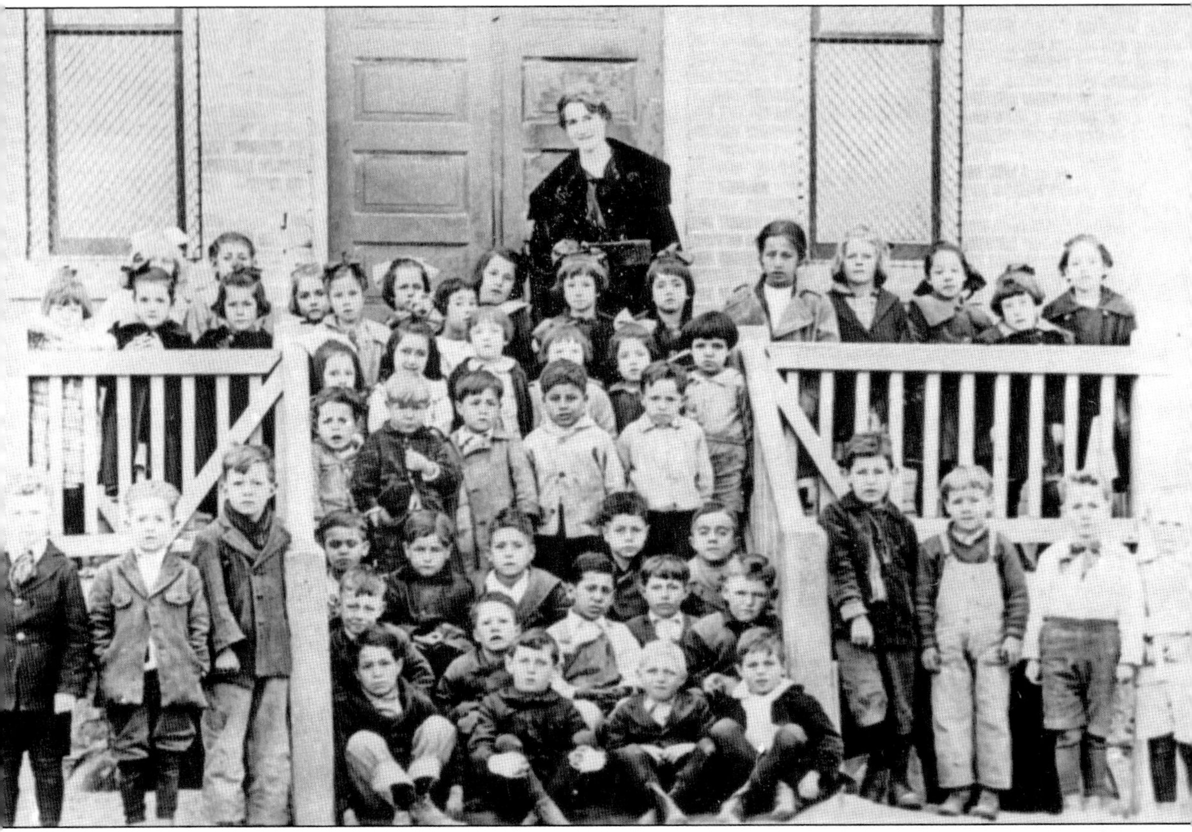

Gertrude Lacey Delgado's large first-grade class at Belen Central Grade School poses for the camera in 1917. Delgado's father was chief of detectives in Chicago for 28 years. Gertrude and her husband, Fidel A. Delgado, came to Belen in 1910. She worked for the John Becker Company until she started teaching school in 1917. (Courtesy of Valencia County Historical Society.)

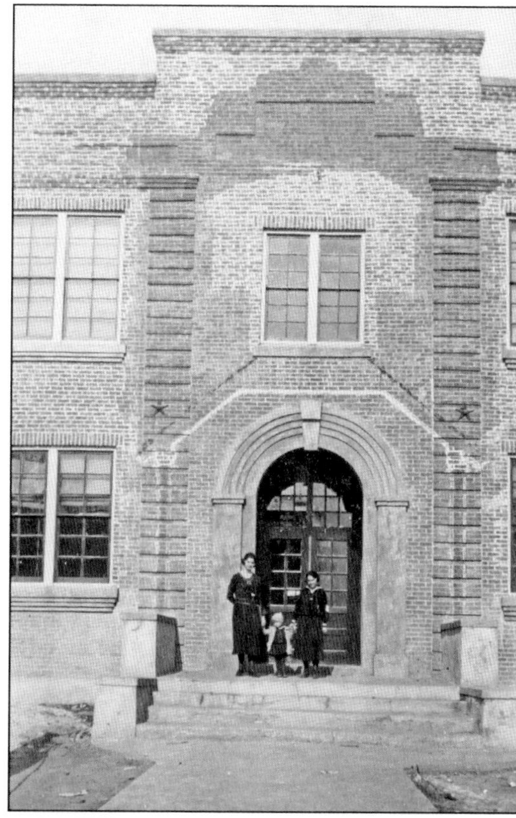

Valencia County High School was built in Belen in 1916 and was designed to serve high school students from throughout the county. Kids from as far away as Los Lunas and Peralta spent hours each day riding in the back of a truck driven by a person contracted to provide transportation. Shown below is the 1933 eighth-grade class at Belen Central School. That grade was an important milestone for some Valencia County students who did not go on to attend high school. (At right, courtesy of Michael Jaramillo; below, Valencia County Historical Society.)

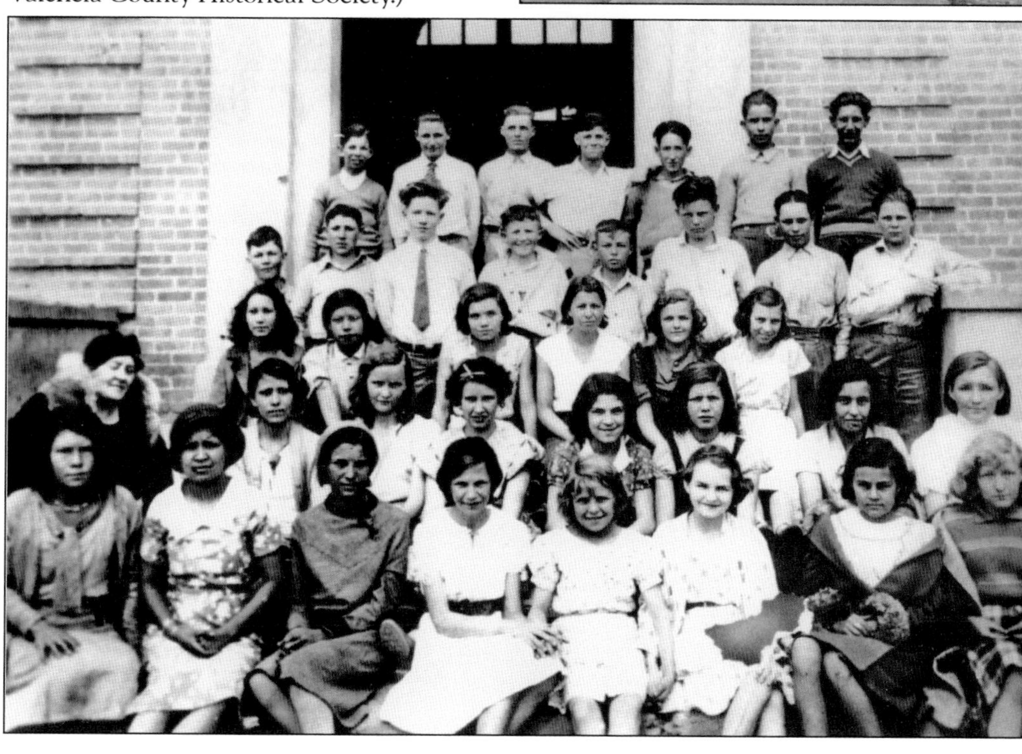

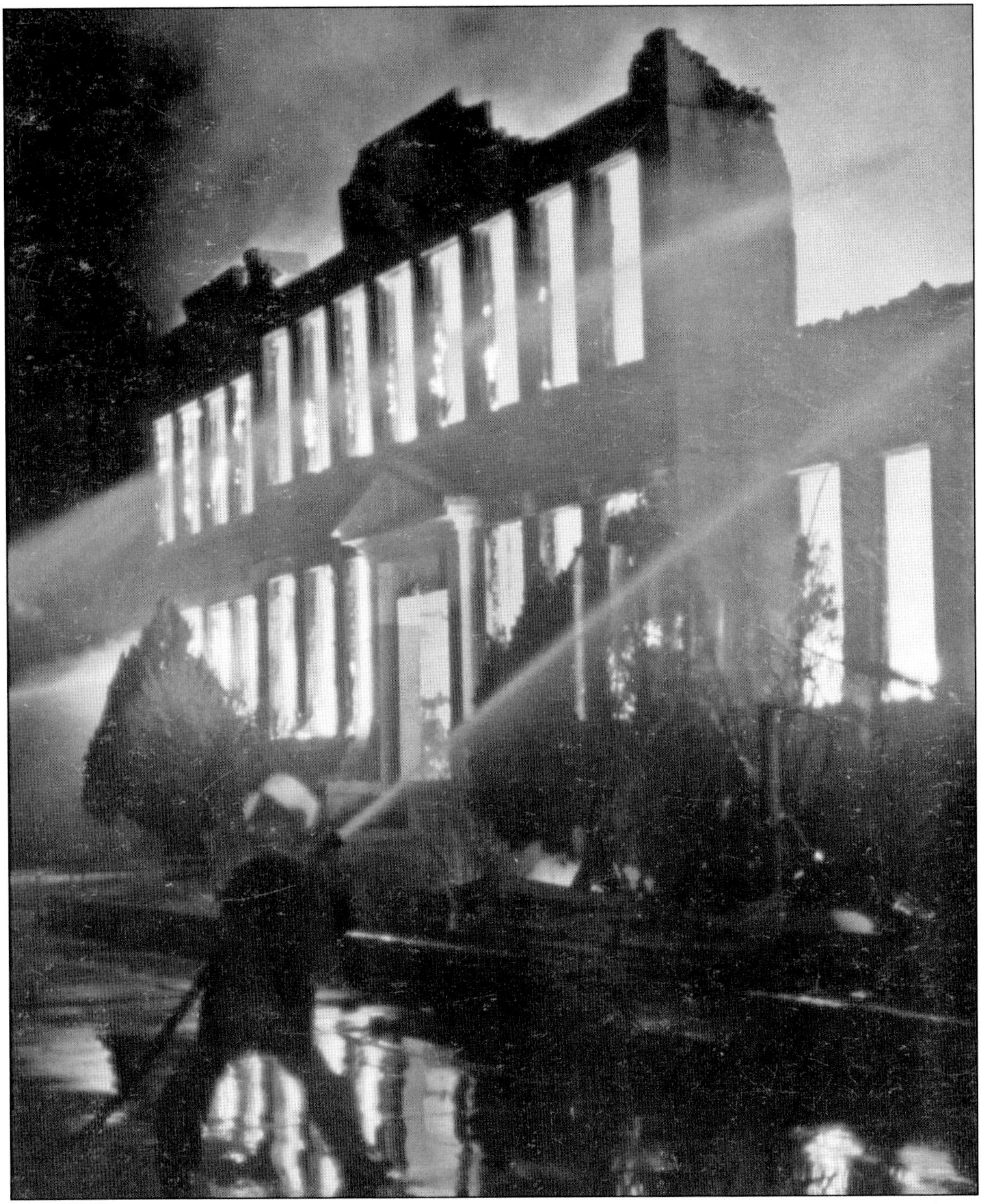

The "Red Brick" school building in Belen was destroyed by fire in 1983. The Vocational Agriculture Building at Belen Junior High School also burned that year. (Courtesy of Valencia County Historical Society.)

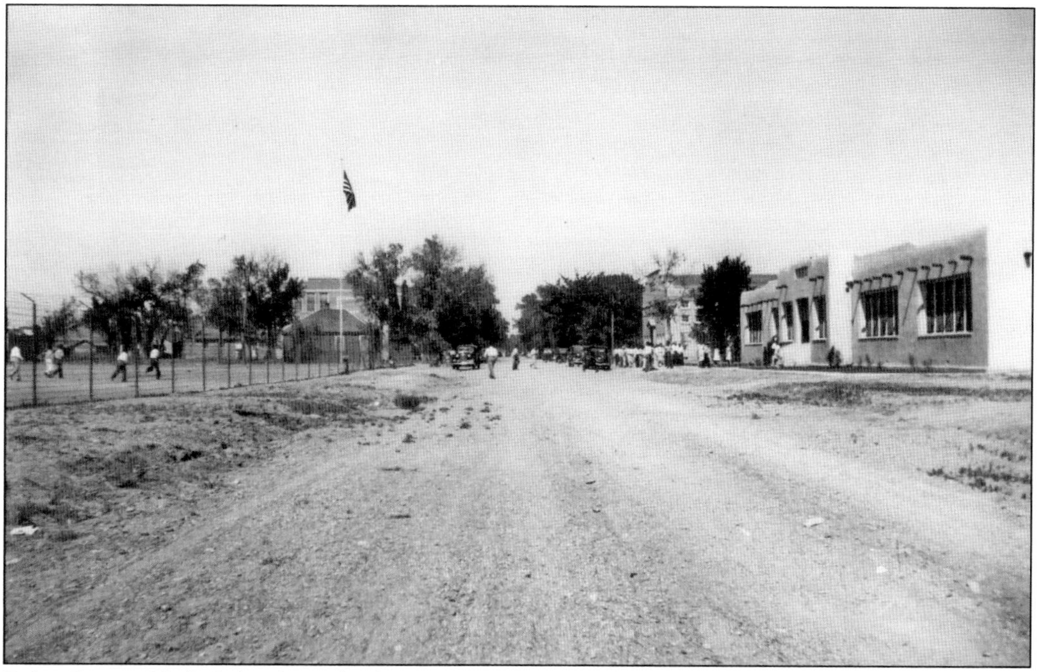

Belen Junior High School was built in 1938, as part of the federal WPA program. At the same time, WPA workers were also constructing Belen City Hall and the Public Welfare Building. New Deal programs provided employment for many unemployed Belen residents during the Great Depression. (Courtesy of Valencia County Historical Society.)

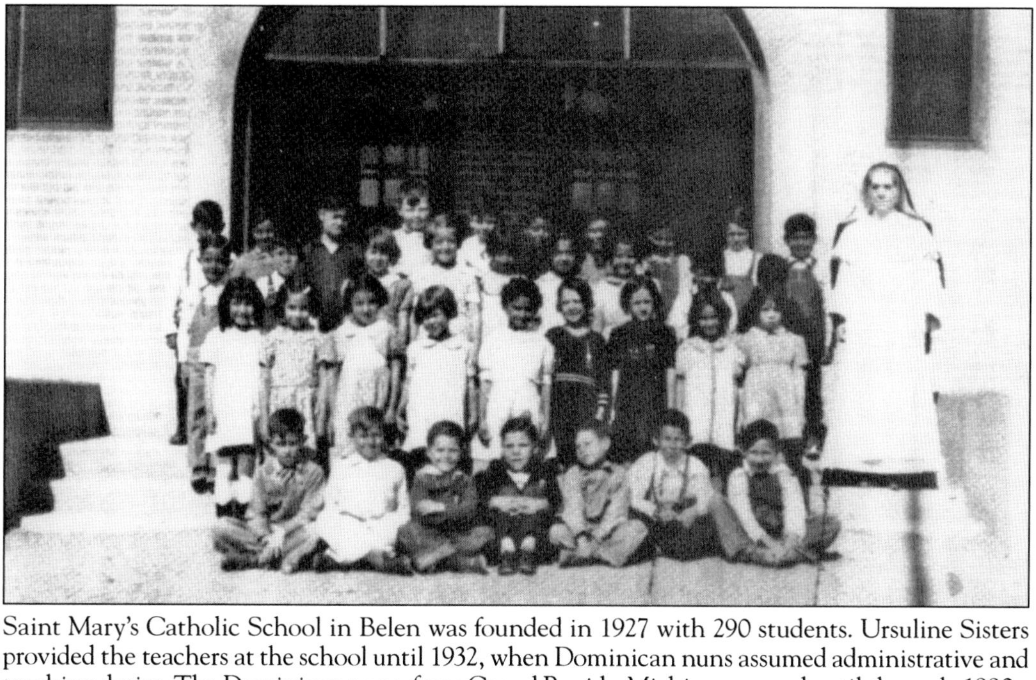

Saint Mary's Catholic School in Belen was founded in 1927 with 290 students. Ursuline Sisters provided the teachers at the school until 1932, when Dominican nuns assumed administrative and teaching duties. The Dominican nuns, from Grand Rapids, Michigan, served until the early 1990s, when lay teachers assumed class instruction. (Courtesy of Valencia County Historical Society.)

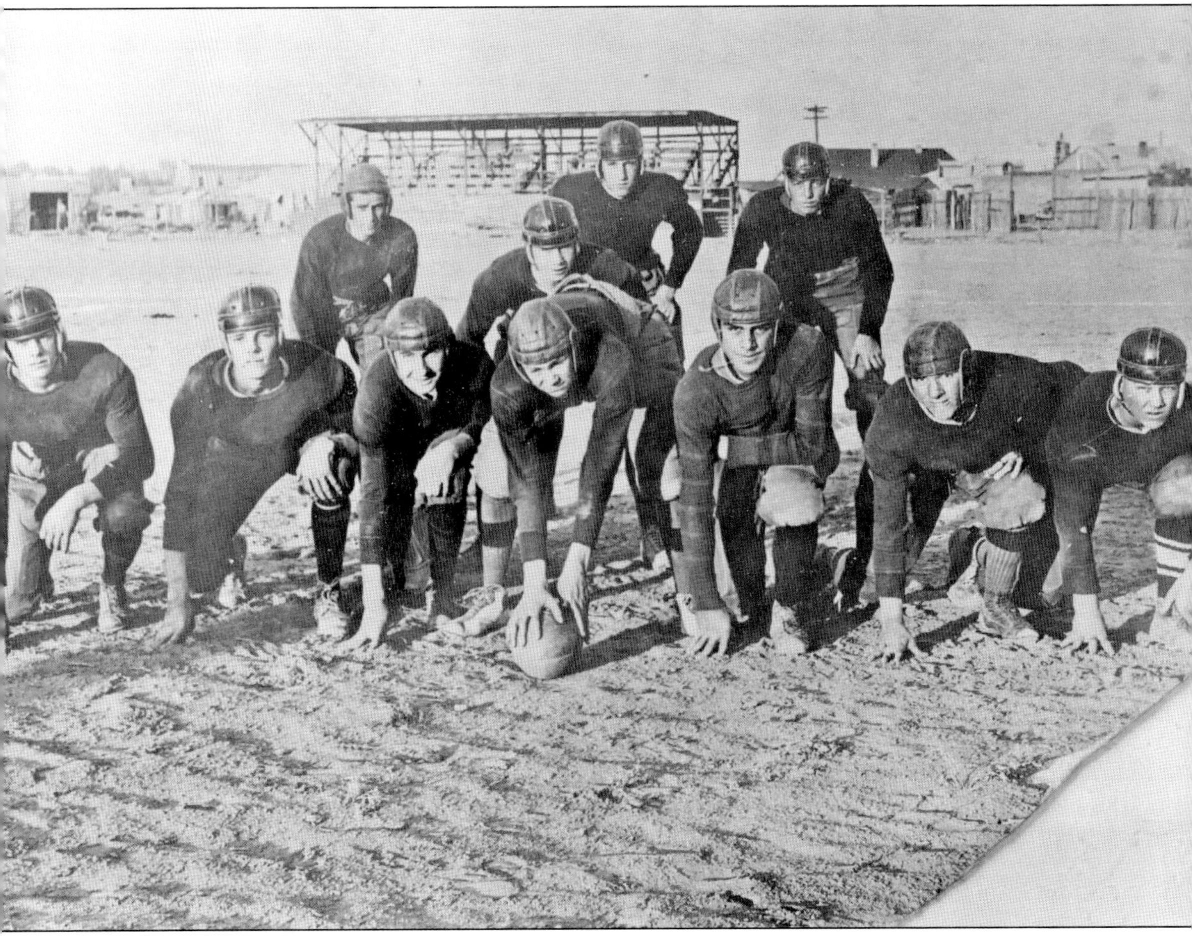

Pictured in 1922 is the first Belen High School football team. The coach was Mr. Ramp. Posing are, from the quarterback's perspective, right end Andre Calhoun, right tackle Merle Ward, right guard Drummond Radcliffe, center Russell Jordan, left guard Jesus Baca, left tackle Tony Sanchez, left end Carl Mayes, quarterback Asher Smith, left halfback Harry Ward, right halfback Alfredo Baca, and fullback Russell Dalies. (Courtesy of Valencia County Historical Society.)

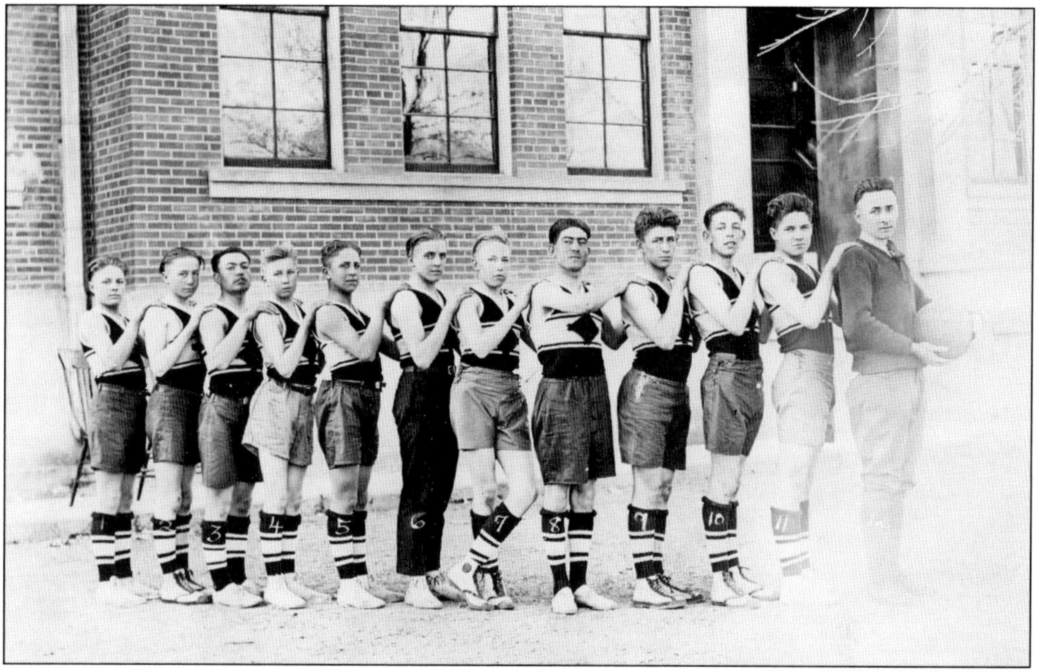

Above is the Belen boys' basketball team from the 1920–1921 season. Shown from left to right are Andrew, Asher, Clarence, Russell, Earl, Ben, Russell, unknown, Ben, Harry, Barton, and coach J.E. Seyfried. Pictured below is the Belen girls' basketball team from the 1920–1921 season. From left to right are (first row) Mary Jane Armstrong and Lois Simmons; (second row) Marcelina Baca, Electa Westfall, Etta Mae Nett, Katherine Seery, Arista Calhoun, and Mary Baca; (third row) Dorie Mae Johnson, coach J.E. Seyfried, Gertrude Becker, and Adella Sanchez. (Both courtesy of Valencia County Historical Society.)

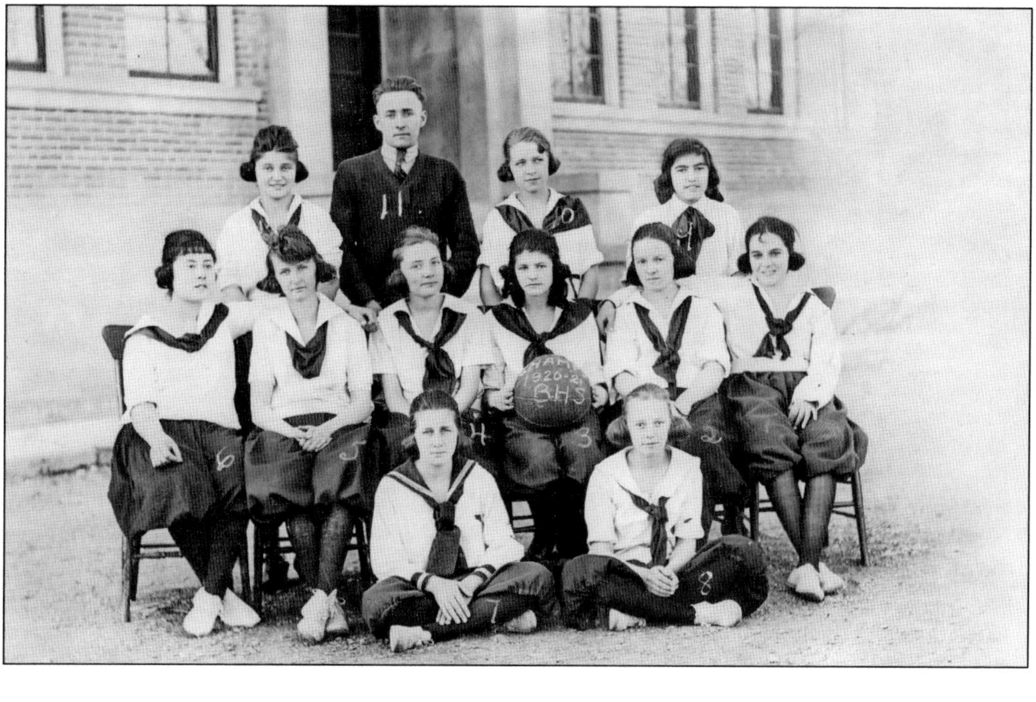

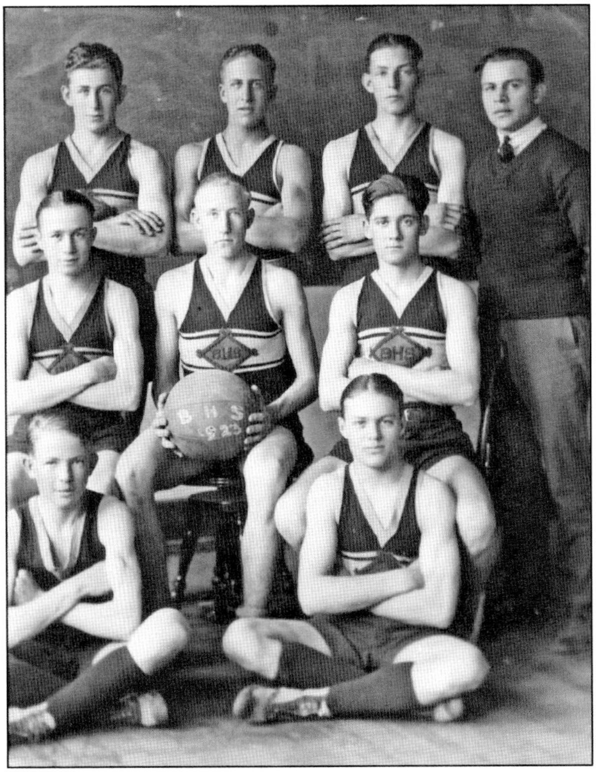

At left is the 1923 Belen High School basketball team. From left to right are (front row) C. Westfall and A. Calhoun; (middle row) C. Smith, R. Dailes, and J. Bryan; (back row) B. Rutz, E. Rutz, H. Ward, and Coach Barnes. Below is the 1937 Valencia County champion basketball team from Belen High School. Shown from left to right are Alfredo Trujillo, Jarano Sanchez, Eloy Garley, coach Joe L. Otero, Frank E. Romero, Nago Jaramillo, Pete Vallez, and Ambrosio Aragon. (At left, photograph by Emgee Studios, both courtesy of Valencia County Historical Society.)

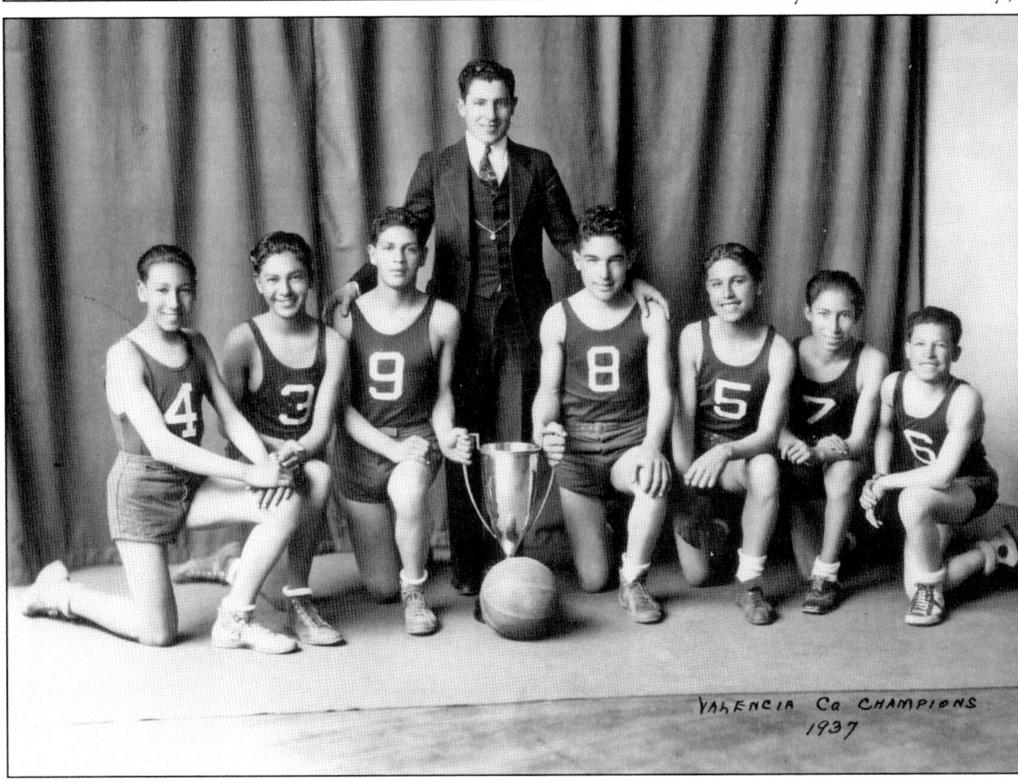

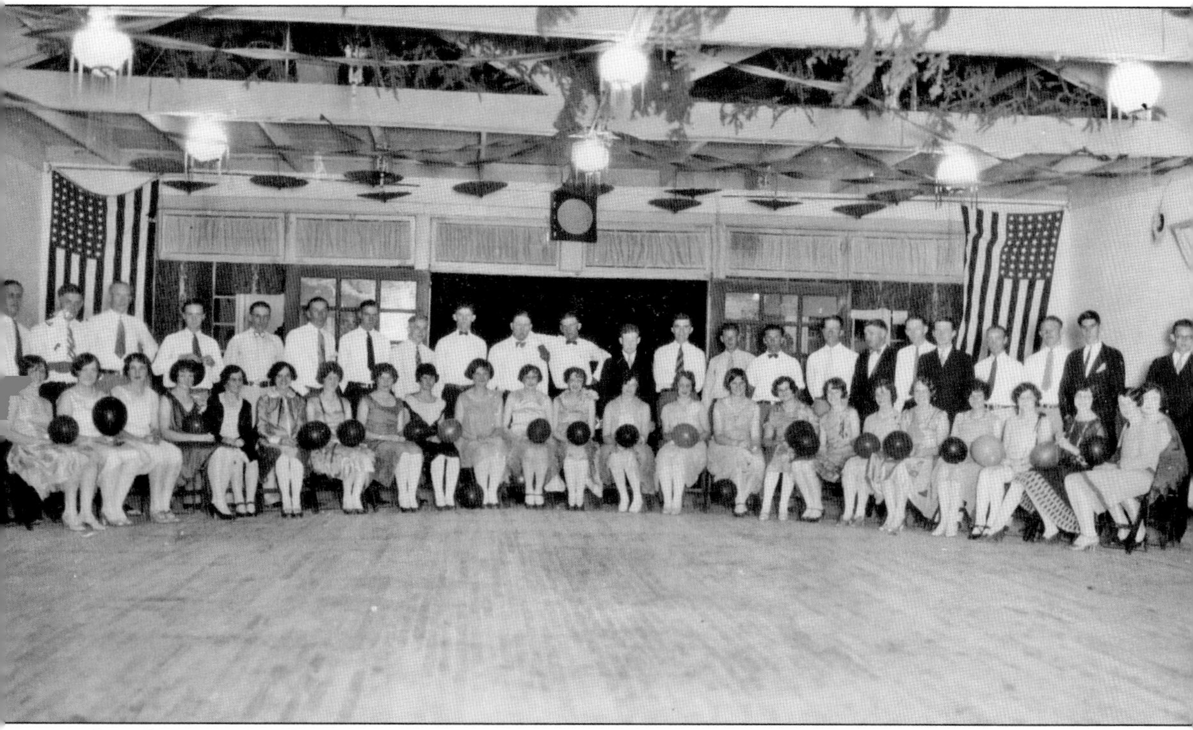

This photograph, taken in 1925 at the VFW hall on Main Street, depicts the birthday party for Dorothy Helen Dalies. Her father was Paul Dalies, a nephew and long-time employee of John Becker, and her mother was Clara Zinth. Dorothy Dalies married Austin Lovett, who also worked for John Becker and was a founding member of the Valencia County Historical Society. The ladies are holding balloons, which were placed between couples as they danced. Someone would go around the dance floor and pop the balloons with a pin, bringing the partners closer together. (Courtesy of Valencia County Historical Society.)

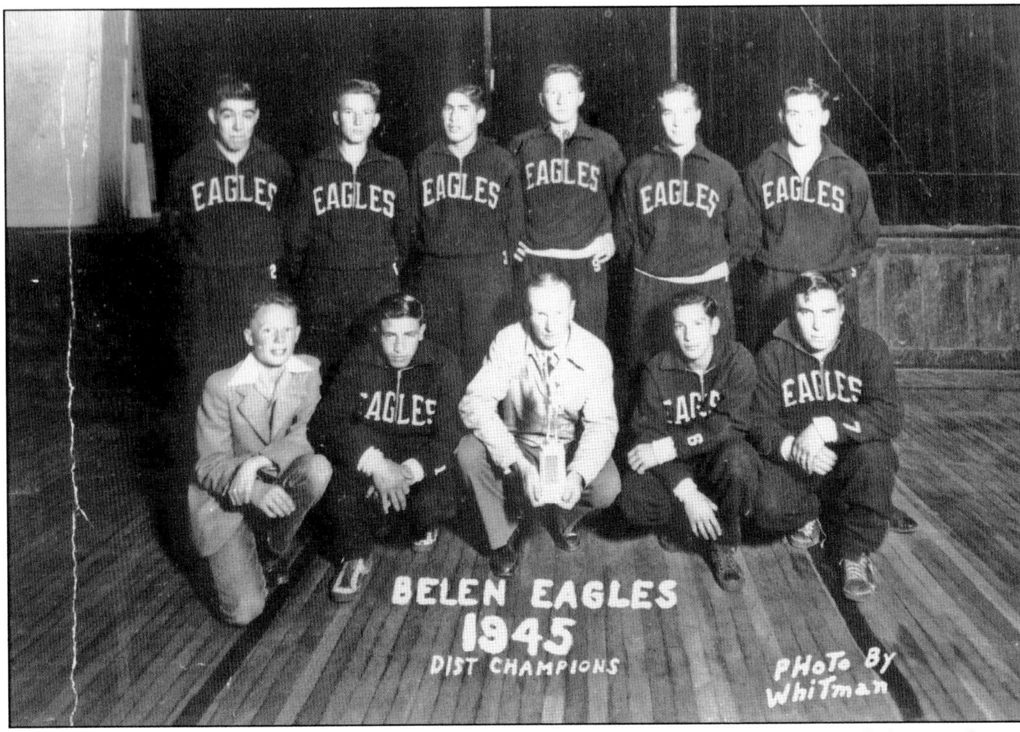

This is the 1945 district champion Belen High School basketball team. From left to right are (first row) Vincent Budenholtzer, Ignacio Sanchez, coach Clifford Keith, Macio Yslas, and Tony Sanchez; (second row) Eddy Quintana, Placido Sanchez, Arnold Romero, John Budenholtzer, Gerald Lovett, and Eloy Sanchez. The team placed fourth at the state championship. (Photograph by Whitman, courtesy of Michael Jaramillo.)

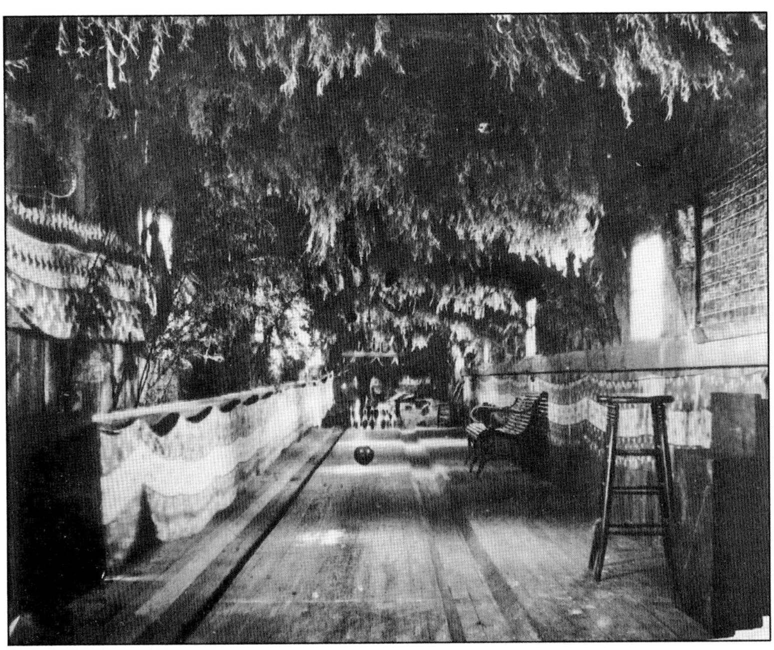

The Commercial Club of Belen, one of the business organizations that eventually became the Belen Chamber of Commerce, constructed a two-story brick building to house a two-lane bowling alley on the first floor. It is not known why Tamarisk plants were hung from the walls and ceiling. This photograph was taken around 1903. (Courtesy of Valencia County Historical Society.)

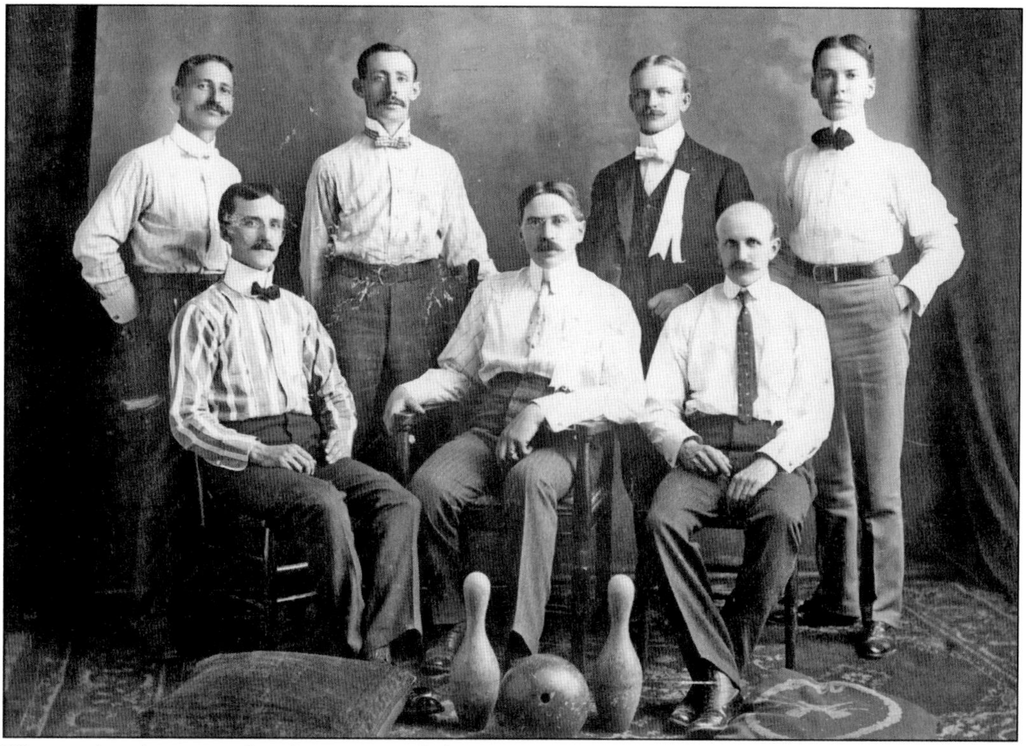

This is the champion bowling team of the New Mexico Territory in 1901. From left to right are (first row) Ernest Zweiger, Charles Reinken, and Paul B. Dalies; (second row) P.P. Simmons, William Le Brun, manager Carl A. Dalies, and H. Emory Davis. (Courtesy of Valencia County Historical Society.)

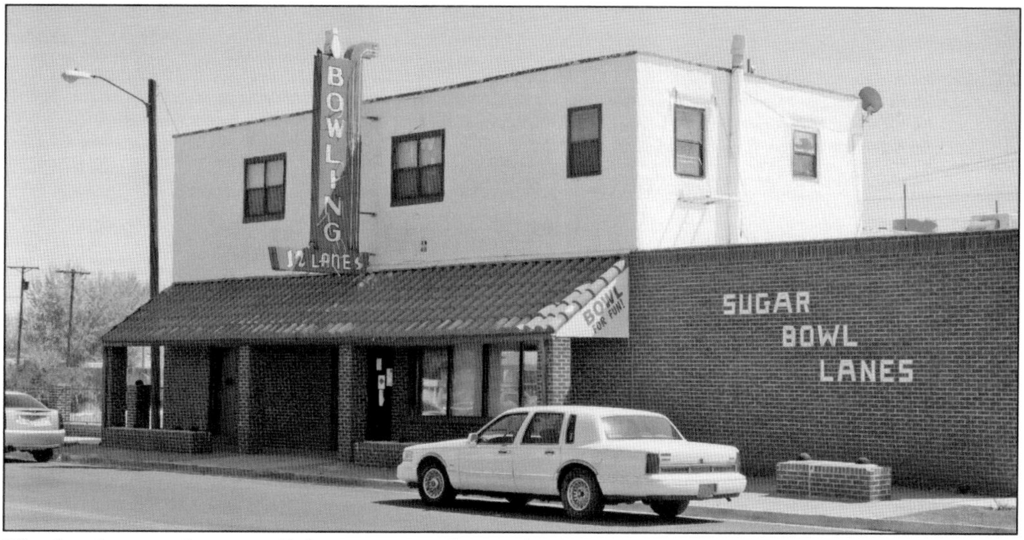

The bowling tradition in Belen continued into the 21st century. Sugar Bowl Lanes was owned and operated by Marvin "Sugar" Glidewell. Marvin was an engineer for the Santa Fe Railway. In 1956, Marvin married Eva Garcia, daughter of Estanislado Garcia. Marvin and Jimmie Jacobs bought the bowling alley from Pat and Ruth Gibson in 1954 and changed the name to Sugar Bowl Lanes. (Author's collection.)

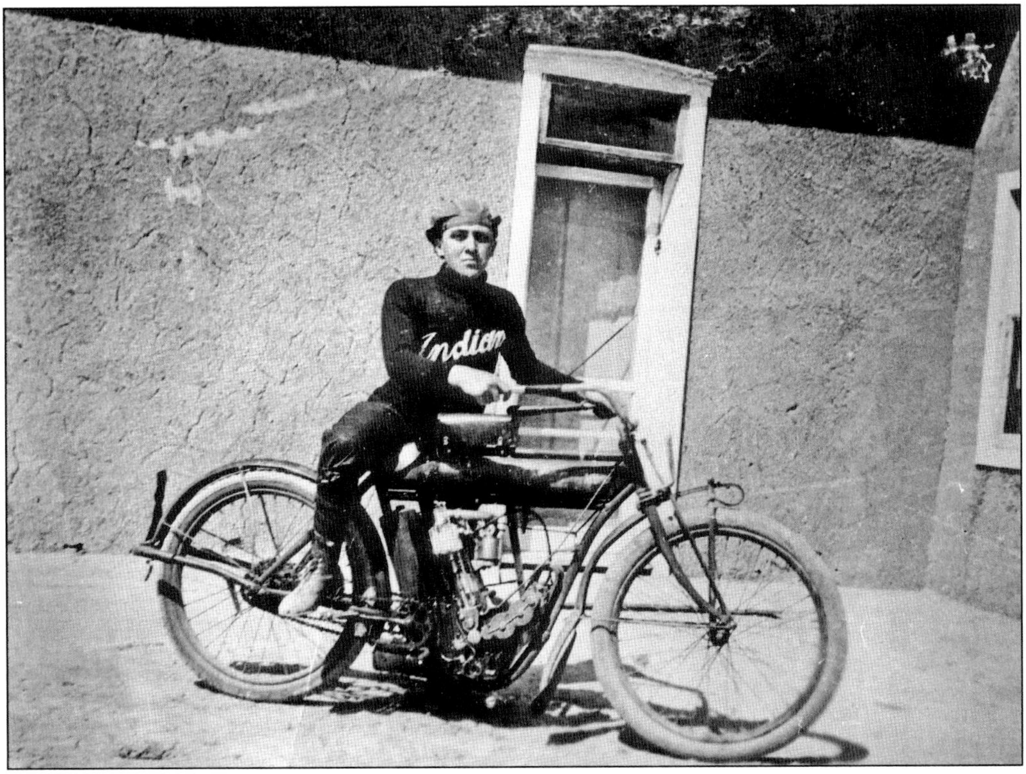

Many modes of transportation were popular in Belen over the years, including this 1911 Indian brand motorcycle. Indian motorcycles were manufactured from 1901 until 1953 by a company located in Springfield, Massachusetts. During the early 1900s, it was the largest motorcycle manufacturer in the world. Due to the poor condition of Valencia County roads, travel by horse, wagon, and even motorcycle was more practical than by automobile. (Courtesy of Valencia County Historical Society.)

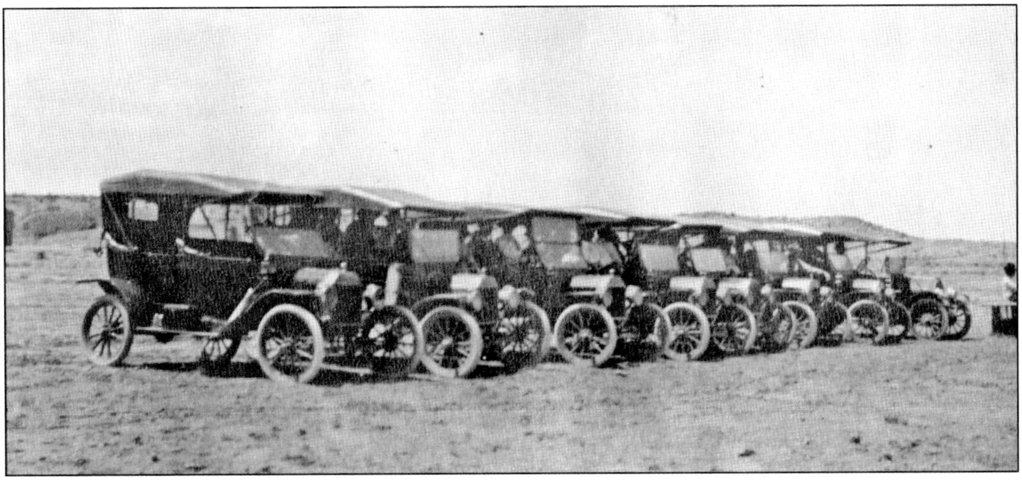

These automobiles are parked at a baseball game in Belen in the early 1920s. The photograph was taken by Edwin Leupold, who owned the Ford dealership in Belen. He commented in a note on the back of the photograph that these automobiles were "all Fords, of course!" (Courtesy of Valencia County Historical Society.)

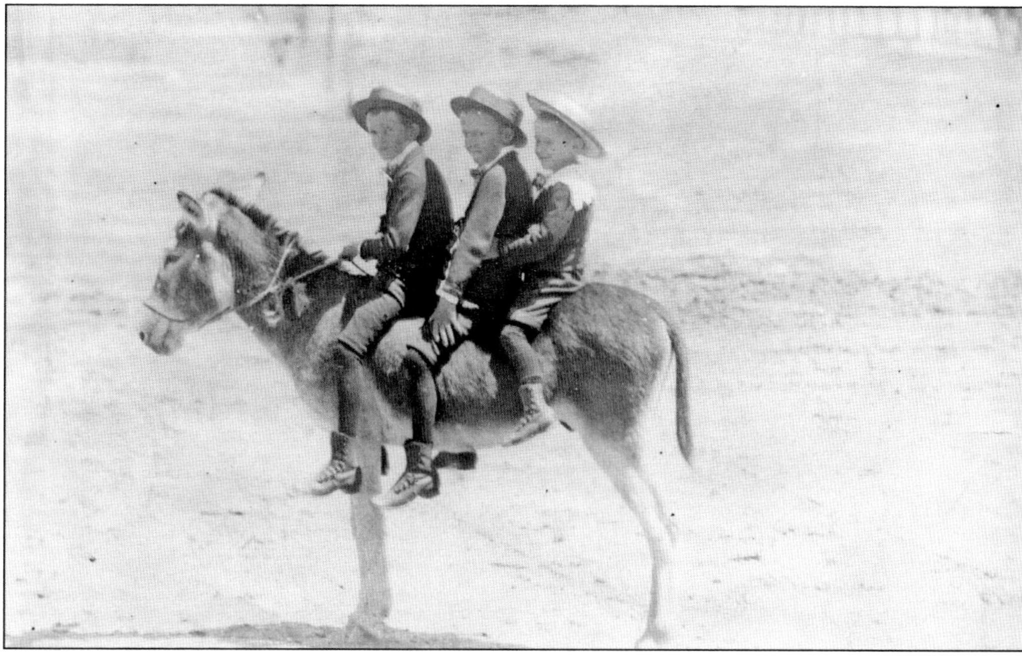

A burro provided both entertainment and transportation for these three boys in Belen. Shown here around 1888 are, from left to right, John and Anna Becker's sons J.H. (Hans), Louis Carl (Dick), and Gustav Becker. Hans joined his father's mercantile business, and Dick went to work for the First National Bank of Belen. (Courtesy of Belen Harvey House Museum.)

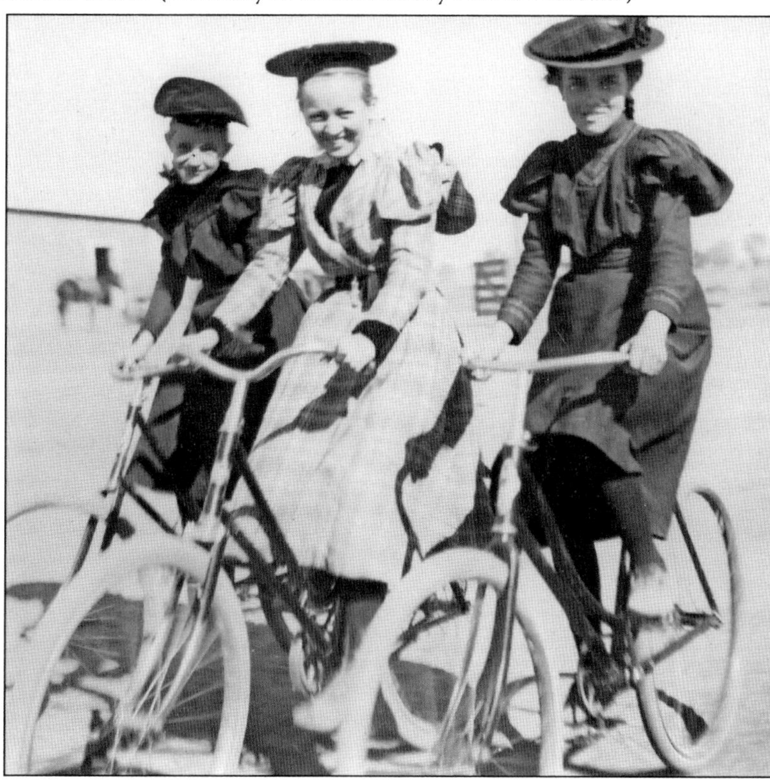

From left to right, Lucie and Anita Becker and a friend are shown bicycling in 1897. The Becker sisters, daughters of Belen merchant John Becker and his wife, Anna, are riding "modern" bicycles. They have inflated rubber tires, which made for a much more comfortable ride, even on Belen's unpaved streets. (Courtesy of Valencia County Historical Society.)

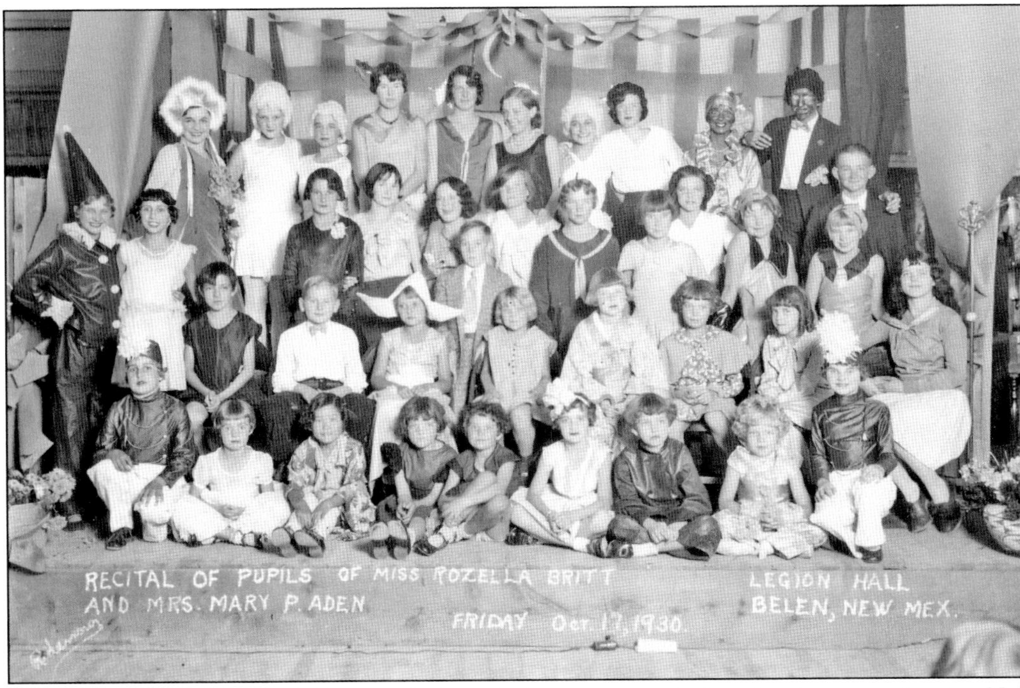

Above, the pupils of Rozella Britt and Mary Arden gave a recital at the American Legion Hall on Friday October 17, 1930. From left to right are (first row) LaVena "Boo" Campbell, Margaret Herlihy, Martha Tuzuki, Helen Louise Waggoner, Bettie Ann Trombley, Lois Campbell, unidentified, June Redenbaugh, and Martha Adair; (second row) Martha Burns, Mary Innebickler, (seated) Marian Barnes, Billy Adair, unidentified, (standing) Bob Perkins, (seated) Mildred Stuver, Mary Eunice Waggoner, Helen Turnley, Lupe Garcia, and unidentified; (third row) unidentified, Louise Space, Deola Robinson, Iris Payne, Edith Hilburn, Sara Minnie Trainer, Burnetta Billington, Jane Wilkinson, and Frank Hilburn; (fourth row) Rozella Britt, Margie Hardy, Mildred Campbell, ? Gilman, Annis Smith, Alma Hughes, Elizabeth Innebickler, Katherine McGrath, Marion Herlihy, and Mary Aden. In the 1930 photograph below, Belen primary school students are in costume for the operetta *Fairies are Really Truly*. (Both courtesy of Belen Harvey House Museum.)

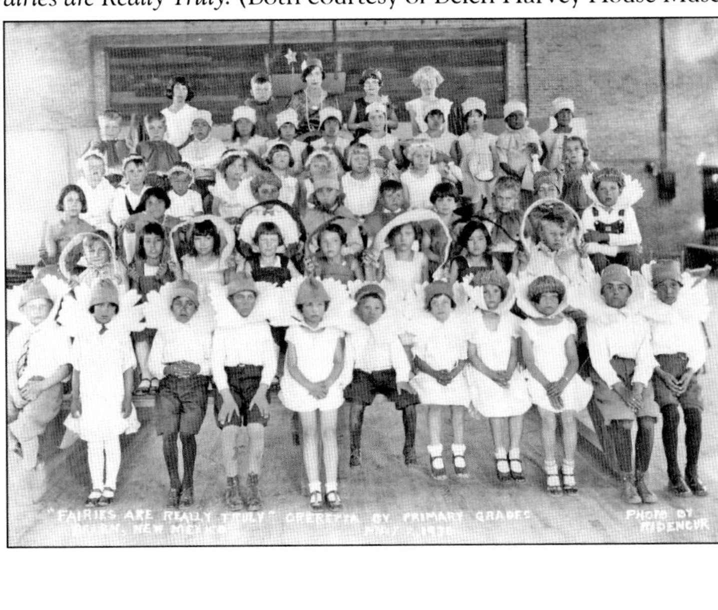

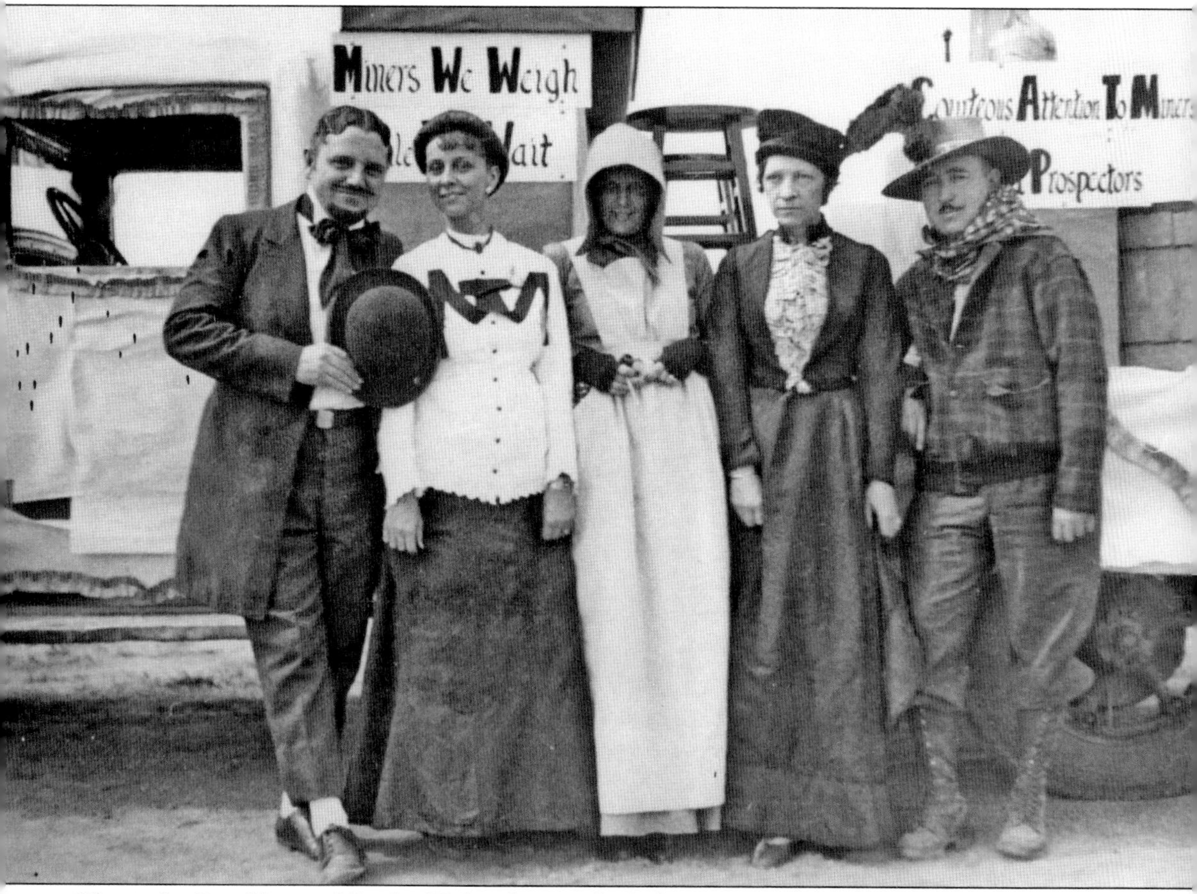

This is the First National Bank of Belen float in the Valencia County Fair parade in 1938. Second from left is Marion Herlihy, a longtime bank employee and a founding member of the Valencia County Historical Society. She was the first woman to hold the position of bank vice president in the state of New Mexico. Marion was also instrumental in efforts to preserve the Belen Harvey House in the 1980s. (Courtesy of Belen Harvey House Museum.)

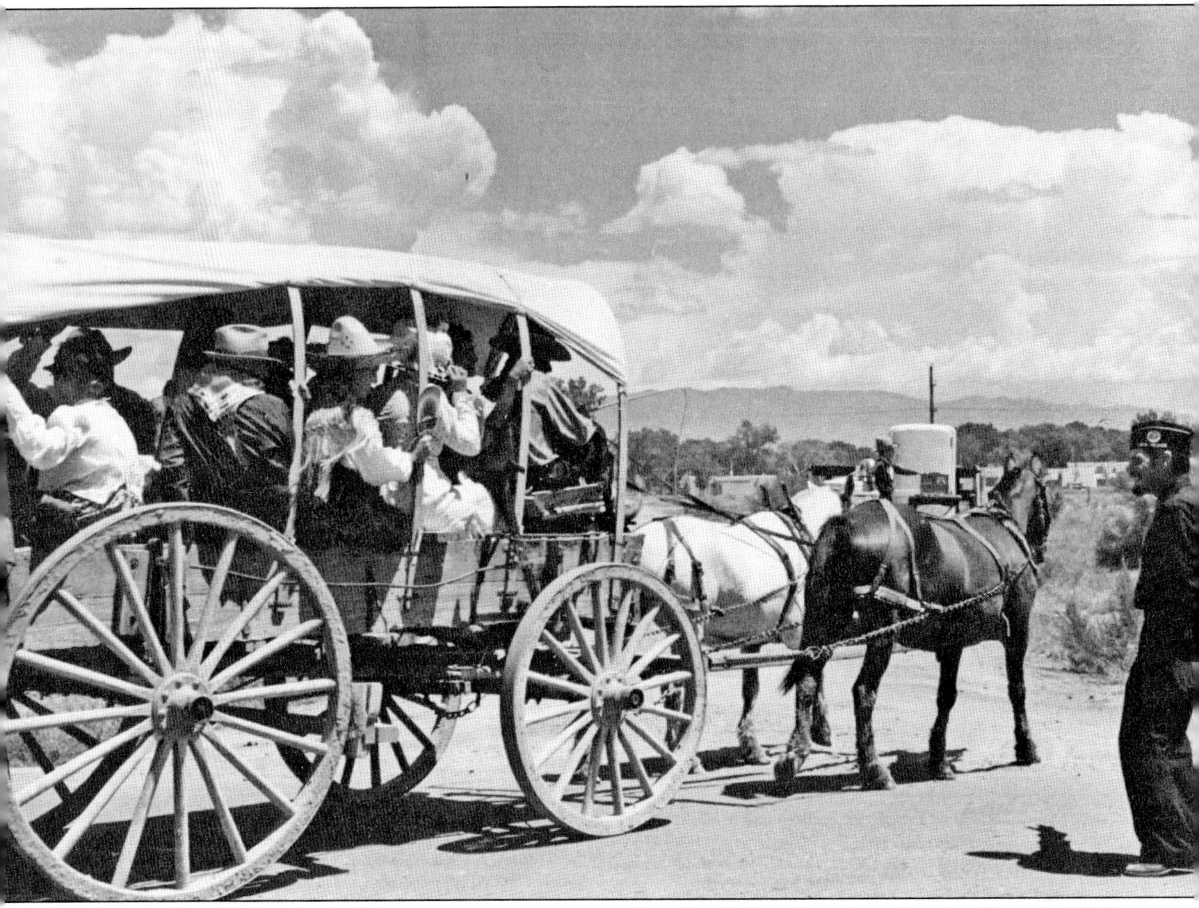

The Belen Days of '49 celebration was inaugurated by the Belen American Legion Post in 1926. Founded in 1919, the post only had three active members until sponsoring the two-day Days of '49 pageant, after which membership increased dramatically. Local businesses, churches, civic organizations, and groups from neighboring communities entered floats in the Days of '49 parade. Shown here is one of the entries in the 1939 parade. Legion member A.S. Torres is on the right greeting parade participants from Mountainair, New Mexico. (Courtesy of Belen Harvey House Museum.)

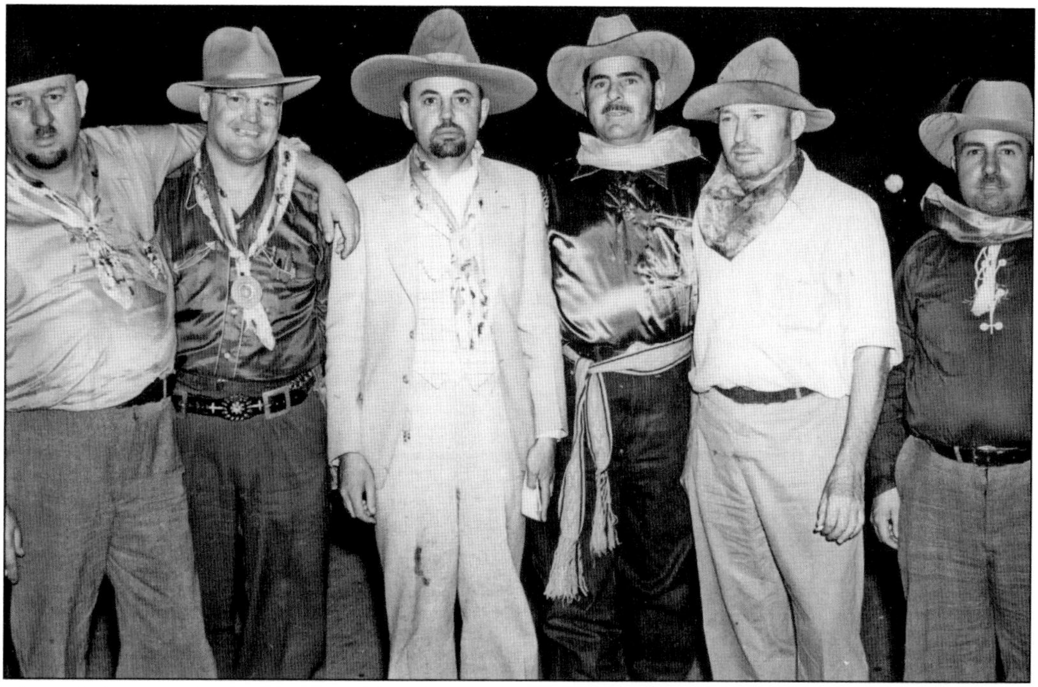

These Belen merchants are dressed up for the Days of '49 celebration in the late 1930s. Pictured from left to right are Don Redenbaugh, Mr. Labbs, Dr. E.G. Brentari, Nick Romero, Hugh Grey, and Henry Sachs. (Courtesy of Valencia County Historical Society.)

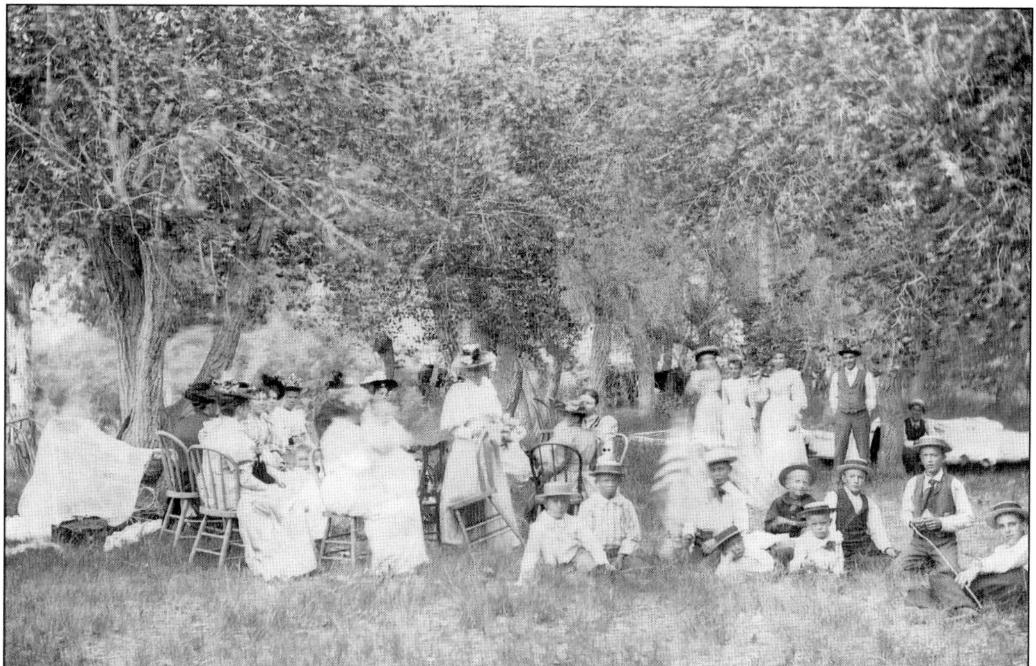

Picnics were a popular pastime for Belen residents, especially during the summer months. Pictured here is a picnic on Old River Road (Gabaldon Road) around 1895. (Courtesy of Valencia County Historical Society.)

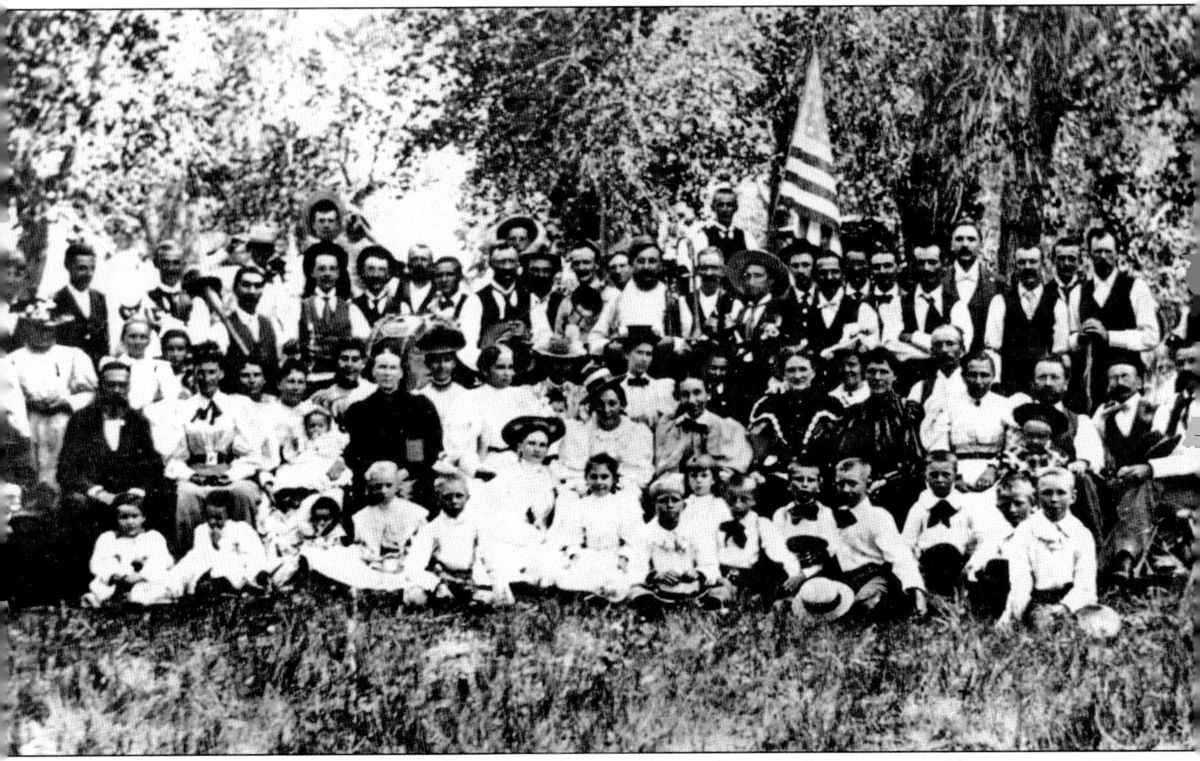

A July 4, 1896, picnic at John Becker's Ranch is seen here. Among those pictured here are a who's who of Belen, including Fred Huning, Carl Muensterman, Louis Huning, Louis Becker, Monte Rigney, Arnold Pohl, Carl Huning, Richard Pohl, Fred Becker, Carl Dalies, Gustav Becker, Arthur Goebel Sr., Jacob Vielstich, Paul Dalies (trombone), P.P. Simmons, Jacob Sichler (trombone), C.W. Uptegrove, L.C. Becker, Fred Scholle (big hat, horn), John Douglas, Louis Vielstich, Leon Herzog, Adam Sichler, Charles Reinken, Bill Spackman, J.H. Becker Jr., Dr. W.D. Radcliffe Sr., Adolph Becker, Anita Becker, Sophia Sichler, Helen Becker, Ida Douglas, Mr. Levi, Mrs. Muensterman, Mrs. Arthur Goebel Sr., Mrs. Arthur Goebel Jr. and baby, Bertha Rutz Daisey, Anna Vielstich Craig, John Becker Sr., Mrs. Geick (mother), Rev. Geick, Mrs. Geick (wife), Mrs. Henry Gleason and son Alvin, Mrs. Jacob Vielstich, Mrs. Levi, Nina Otero, Kate Kroneke, Mrs. Fred Huning Sr., Mrs. Oscar Goebel Sr., Mrs. John Becker Sr., Oscar Goebel, Ben Becker, Carl Muensterman, Martha Geick, Willie Gleason, Lucie Becker, Edgar Goebel, Lolita Huning, Ethel Levi, Carlie Becker, Gotfried Geick, Oscar Goebel Jr., Herbert Goebel, Curt Goebel, and Walter Goebel. (Courtesy of Belen Harvey House Museum.)

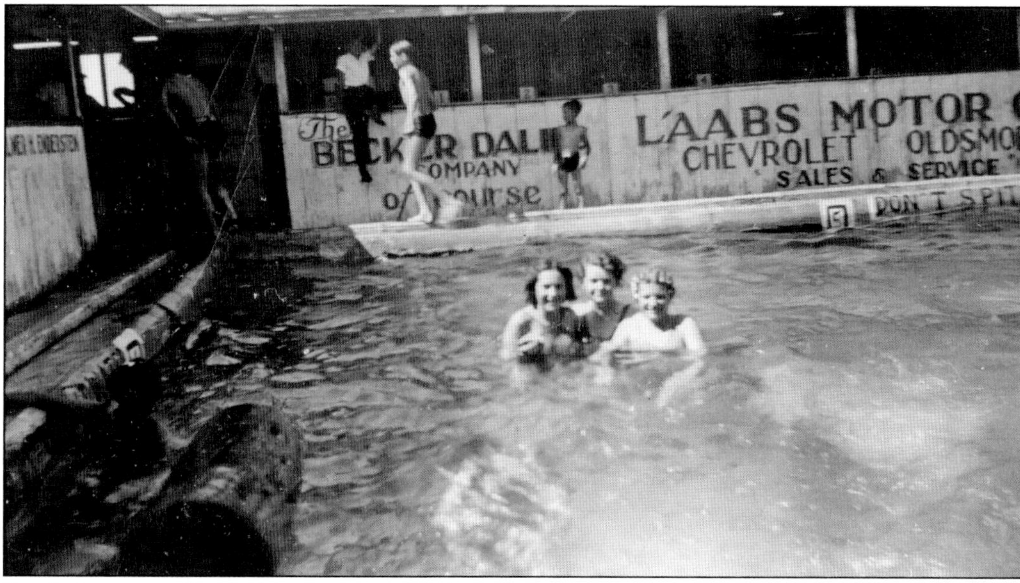

Frank Garcia and Jesus Olguin created Belen's first public swimming pool by digging a hole in the ground and lining it with cement. The pool was opened in 1929, and admission was 10¢. Pictured at the swimming pool in 1939 are, from left to right, Betty Ann Trombley Cline, an unidentified girl, and Faye Le Brun. (Courtesy of Valencia County Historical Society.)

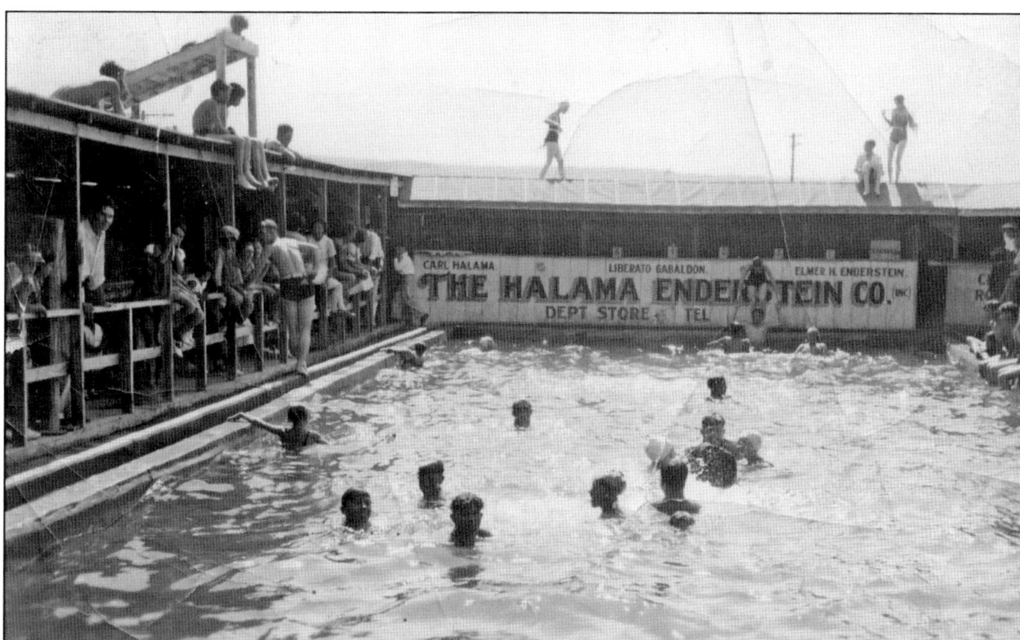

This is another view of the Belen Swimming Pool, taken sometime in the mid-1930s. The public pool provided local residents with a much safer place to swim than the irrigation ditches or the Rio Grande, but, judging by the number of people on the roof, there were still some risks involved. (Courtesy of Michael Jaramillo.)

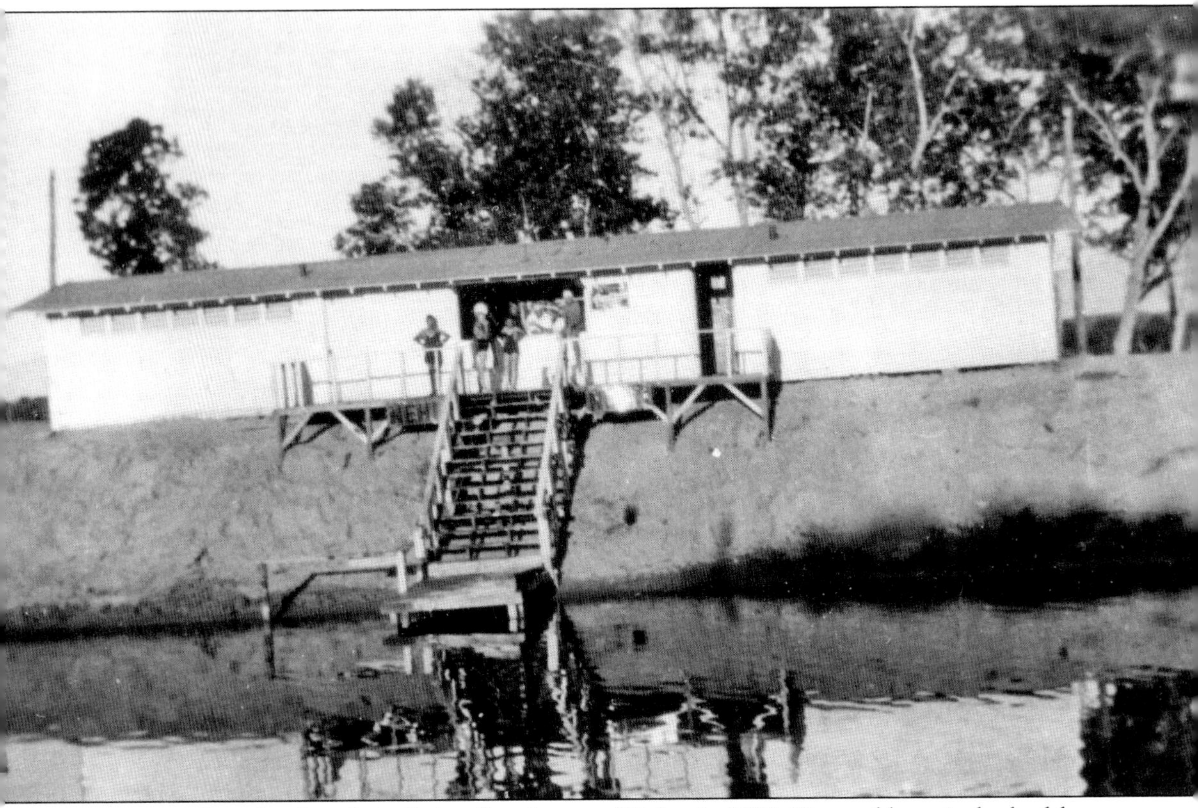

Harry Wilson developed the Belen Beach east of Belen in 1932. Pictured here is the bathhouse and concession stand at the beach. Water was piped from the Rio Grande, and an outlet pipe back to the river kept the water circulating. The pond covered an acre and a half, and there was an island in the center. The bathhouse burned around 1937. (Courtesy of Valencia County Historical Society.)

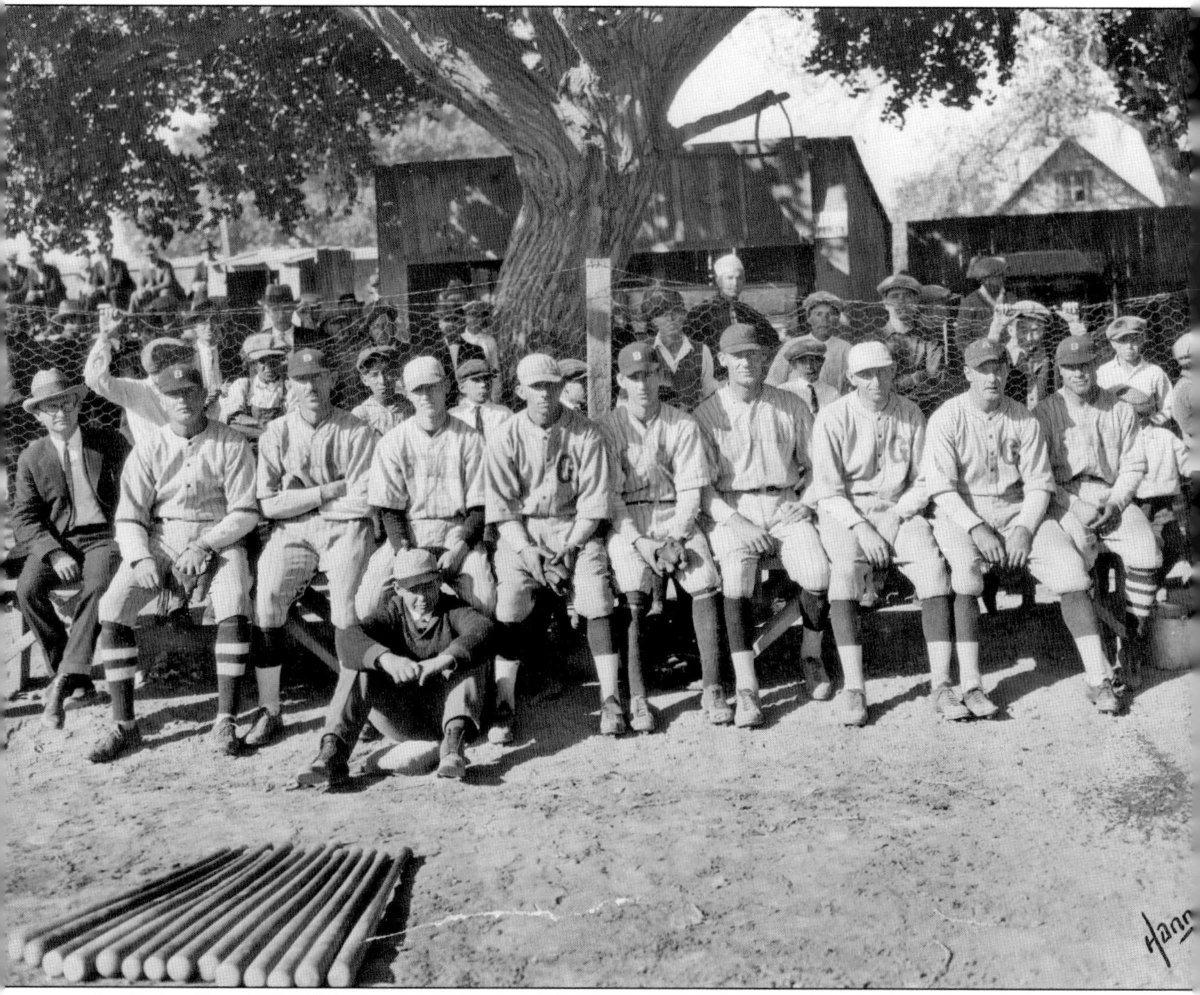

The Belen Baseball Club is pictured in 1925. Players in uniform are, from left to right, Adams, Alford, Alexander, Lefty, Hunter, Collins, Malintenere, Desmond, and Garcia; the batboy sitting in front is Jack Jones. (Photograph by Hanna, courtesy of Valencia County Historical Society.)

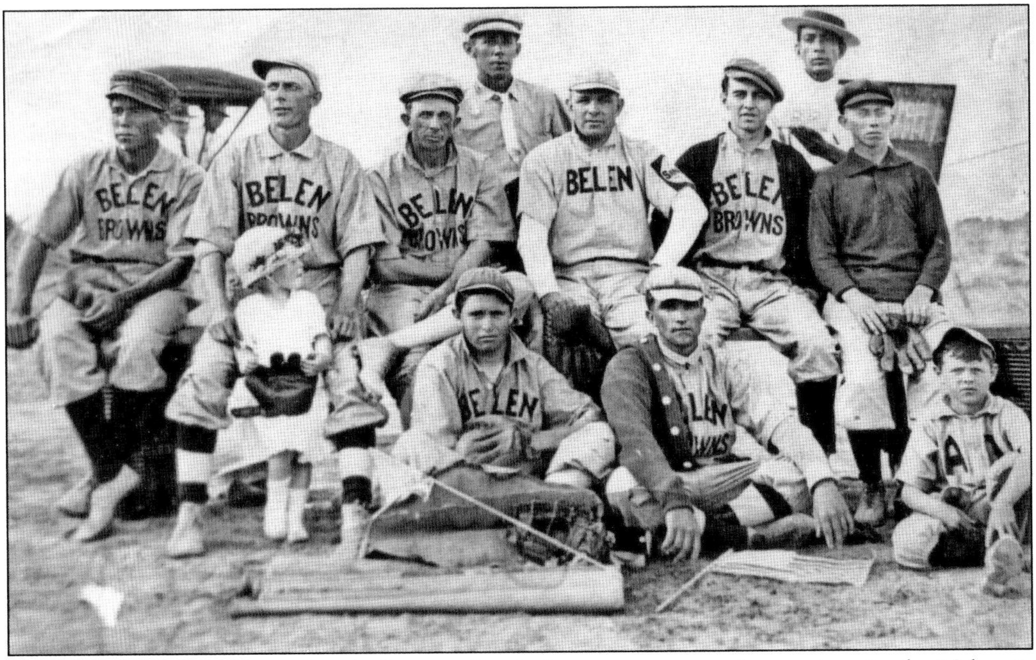

Above is the Belen Browns baseball team. Baseball was a very popular pastime in the Valencia County area, especially from 1910 to the early 1940s. In addition to semi-professional teams like the Belen Browns, each community throughout the area—including Los Lunas, Peralta, Isleta Pueblo, Tome, Jarales, Los Chavez, as well as Belen—had their own baseball team. Team loyalties could be intense. The 1922 photograph below is of the Belen baseball team. (Both courtesy of Valencia County Historical Society.)

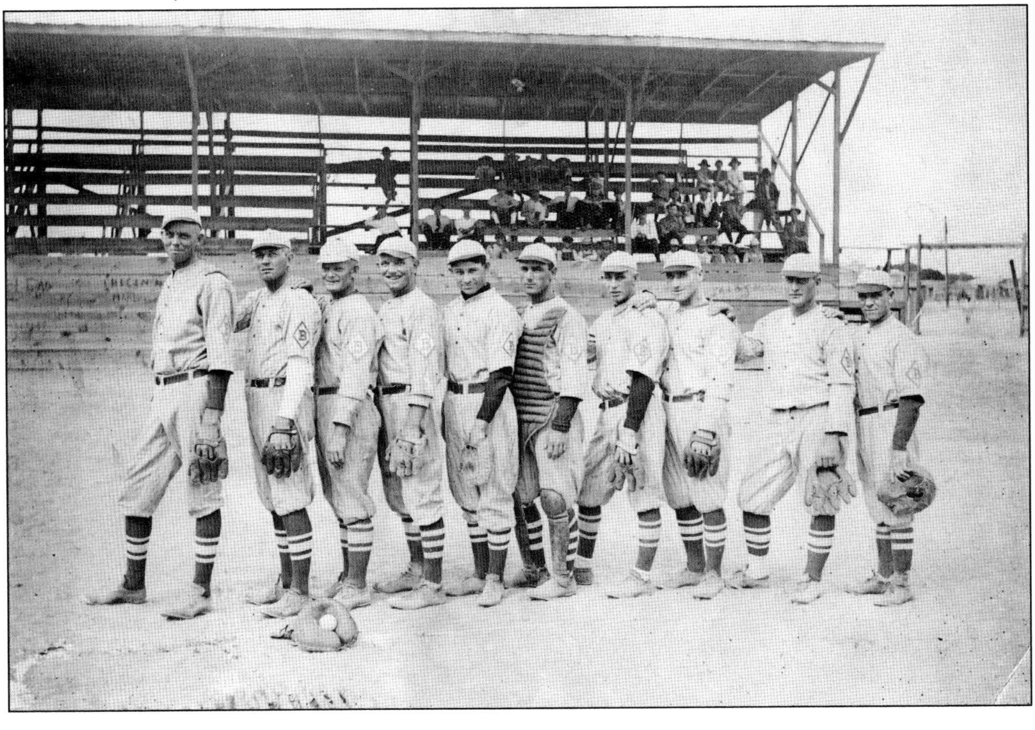

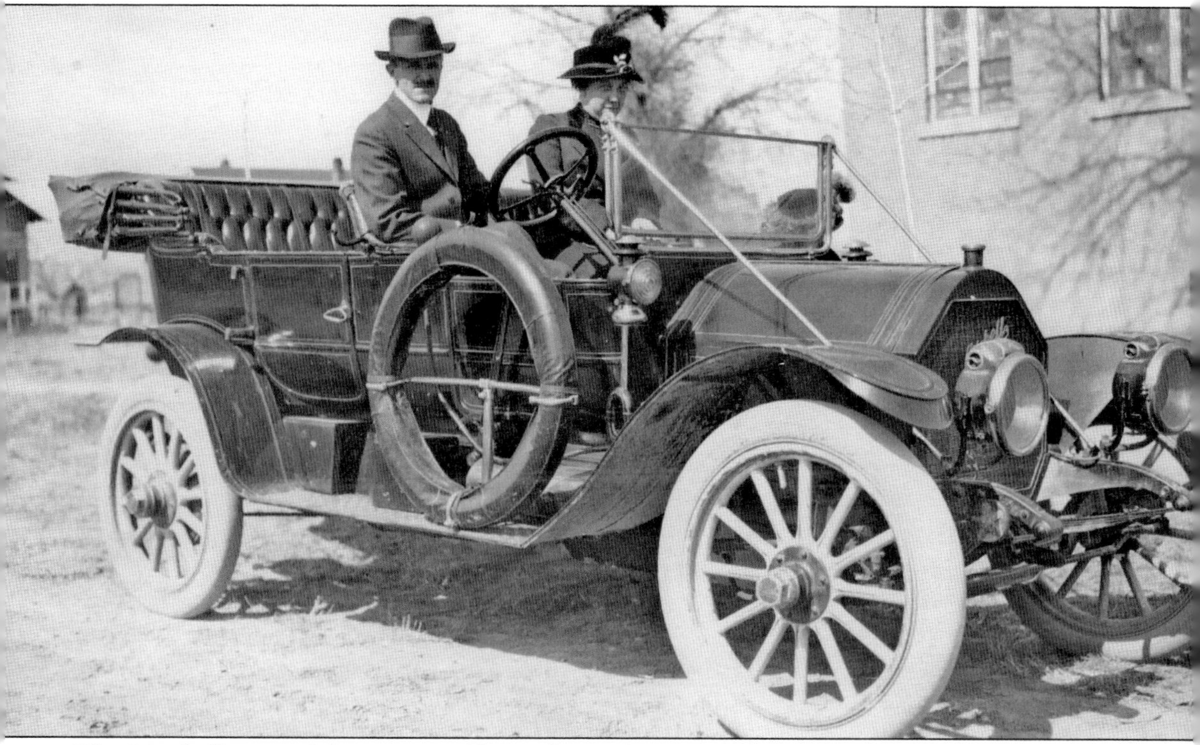

This Mitchell automobile was owned by Paul B. Dalies, seated here next to his wife, Clara Zinth Dalies. Note the steering wheel on the right side. This was the third car in Belen; the other two were owned by John Becker and Fred Scholle. The photograph was taken in 1911 in front of the Lutheran (later Presbyterian) church. (Courtesy of Valencia County Historical Society.)

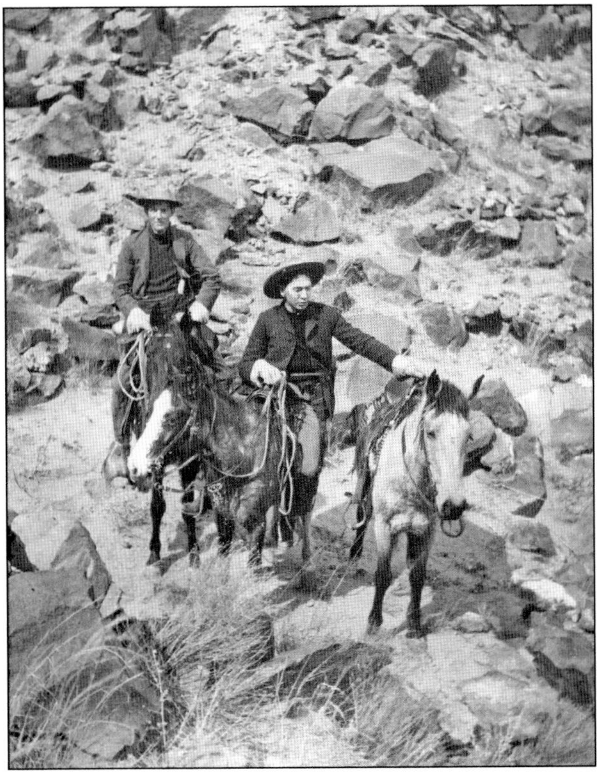

The nearby Manzano Mountains provided many recreational opportunities, including hiking, hunting, and horseback riding. Shown at left are Louis C. Becker (left) and H. Emory Davis. The third horse belongs to an unseen companion, who took the photograph. In the photograph below, Louis C. Becker (right) and H. Emory Davis are seen target shooting in the foothills of the Manzano Mountains. (Both courtesy of Valencia County Historical Society.)

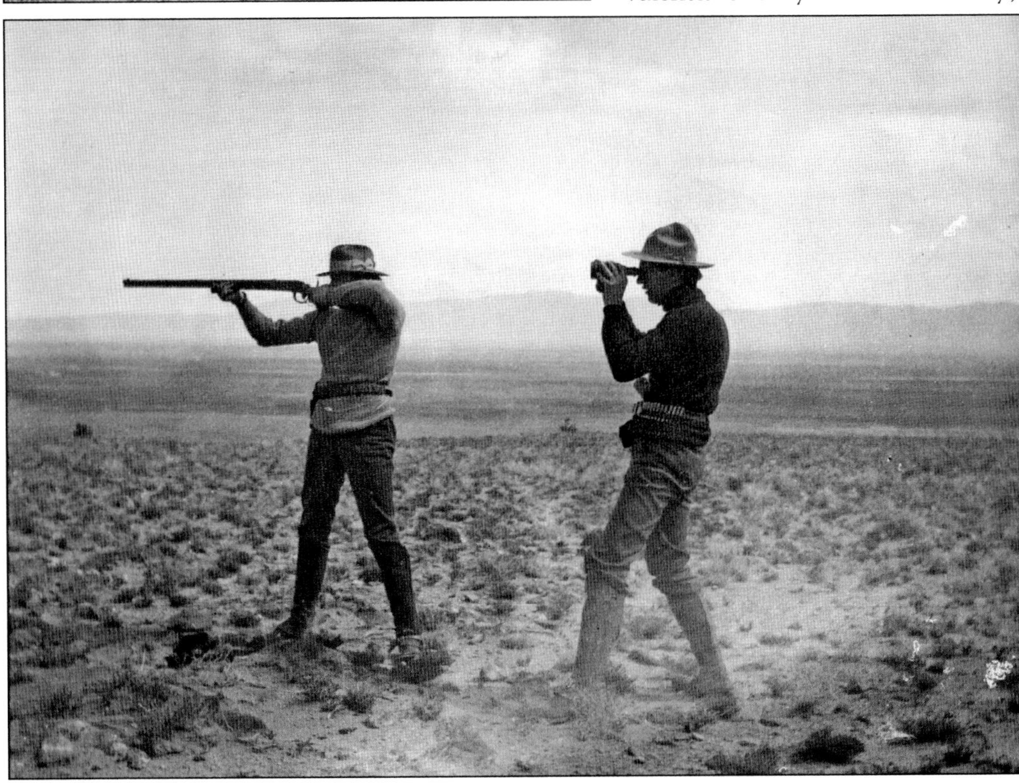

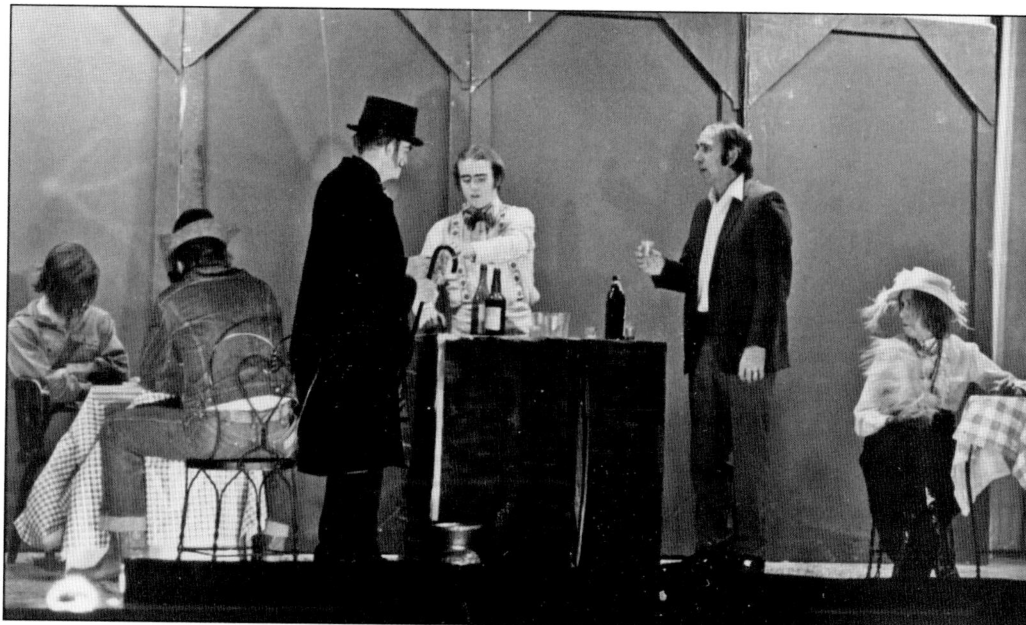

Jack and Charlotte Maguire formed the Firehouse Players theater group in March 1972. The group got its name because the first performance, an adaptation of the melodrama *The Drunkard*, was staged at the Rio Grande Estates Firehouse. By 1981, performances were held at the Tierra del Sol Civic Center. (Courtesy of Valencia County Historical Society.)

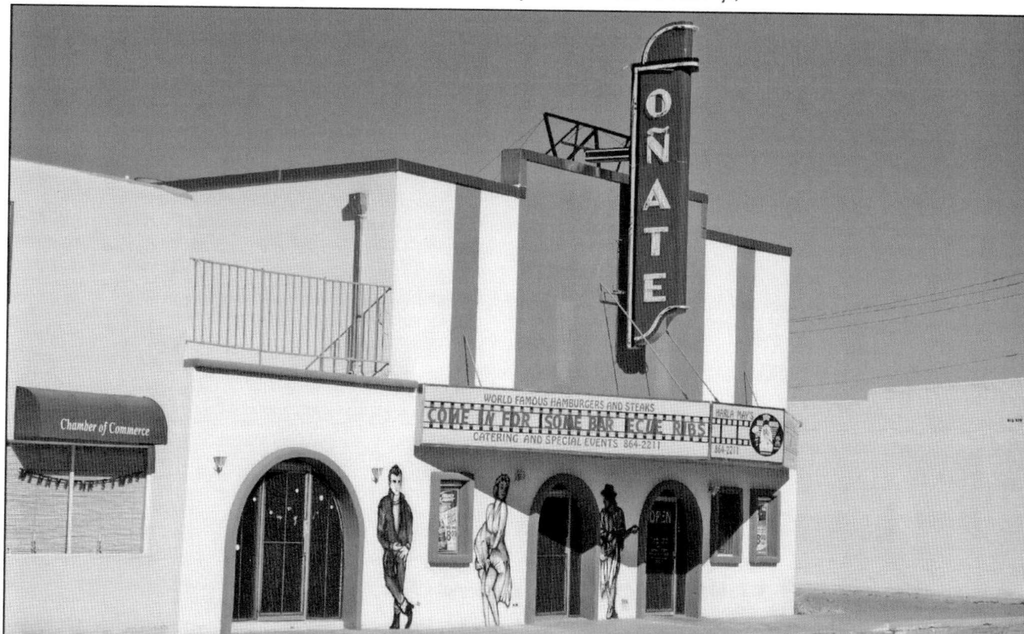

The Oñate Theater served Belen's movie fans for many years. Residents would go to the Belen Harvey House and watch for movie stars who were traveling through town on the train. Several movies have been made in Belen, including *Bunny O'Hare*, starring Bette Davis and Ernest Borgnine, in 1971 and *Swing Vote*, starring Kevin Costner, in 2008. The theater was later converted into a restaurant. (Author's collection.)

Discover Thousands of Local History Books Featuring Millions of Vintage Images

Arcadia Publishing, the leading local history publisher in the United States, is committed to making history accessible and meaningful through publishing books that celebrate and preserve the heritage of America's people and places.

Find more books like this at
www.arcadiapublishing.com

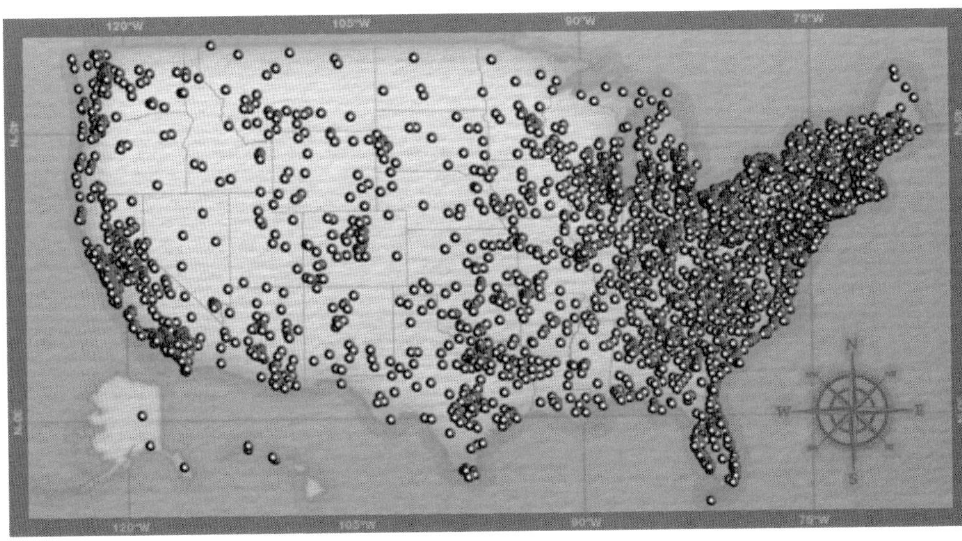

Search for your hometown history, your old stomping grounds, and even your favorite sports team.

Consistent with our mission to preserve history on a local level, this book was printed in South Carolina on American-made paper and manufactured entirely in the United States. Products carrying the accredited Forest Stewardship Council (FSC) label are printed on 100 percent FSC-certified paper.

MADE IN THE USA